Alone in the Wilderness

Mike Tomkies

Whittles Publishing

Typeset by
Whittles Publishing Services

Published by
Whittles Publishing,
Roseleigh House,
Latheronwheel,
Caithness, KW5 6DW,
Scotland, UK

ISBN 1-870325-14-1

Printed by Bell & Bain Ltd., Glasgow

For those who love the last of the wild

Also by Mike Tomkies

Books

Between Earth and Paradise
A Last Wild Place
My Wilderness Wildcats
Liane – A Cat from the Wild
Wildcat Haven
Out of the Wild
Golden Eagle Years
On Wing and Wild Water
Moobli
Last Wild Years
In Spain's Secret Wilderness
Wildcats

Videos

Eagle Mountain Year
At Home with Eagles
Forest Phantoms
My Barn Owl Family
River Dancing Year
Wildest Spain
(see page 168 for further details)

Contents

1 The Immigrant

*P*ausing from my four-mile row, I lay back in the leaky boat and looked over the Pacific Ocean at a wilderness world I could hardly believe was now mine. From the shores of Telnarko Island, the sun bridled a liquid track of gold across the sea like a dazzling path to the heavens. In the distance flowering arbutus trees fringed the lone firs on grey granite islands, while below me in the green waters a school of salmon lazed by. Mesmerized, I watched a rainbow form from a sea mist and touch the nearest island, like a finger from the sky. Drifting gently on the sea, I turned to look at the rocky two acres of my homestead claim in British Columbia. Was it possible this small bay and beach, these trees, this incredible view – the good place for which I'd searched so long – was *really* now my own?

A few months earlier my whole life had hung in tatters. At nearly forty, a thoroughly urbanized man and former journalist whose life in the big cities of Europe had become stale and pointless, I had fled from London and all we loosely call civilization to emigrate to Canada to write in the ancient silence of the wilderness what I hoped would be a successful novel, and start a more meaningful life.

Before my move from Britain, I had found myself becoming bored and depressed. The reasons perhaps reached back to my youth. During early years as a cub reporter in country villages, I had dreamed only of making it to London. The British capital then seemed to me in my painful naïvety a magic journalistic mecca where I'd be accepted into an exciting world of earls, politicians, glamorous women, movie stars, and athletes.

After more than a decade in London, I indeed dallied with the illustrious, the beautiful, and the swift. I was flying between Paris, Rome, Athens, Madrid, Vienna, New York, and Hollywood, mixing drinks, talk, life, love and copy with vaunted famous names whose images I'd once worshipped as a village youth. Meeting whom I chose, writing about whom I liked, my name at the head of columns in widely read magazines, money simply flooding in, I became the complete hedonist. I went through sports cars like a frustrated racing driver and reacted against my shy and awkward country-bred youth by squiring some of the world's most beautiful women.

It was around my thirty-fourth birthday that this fast life and material success began to go sour. Quite suddenly, nothing seemed to lie ahead but boring repetition.

A self contempt grew, fuelled by the advice of two of my close women friends, Ava Gardner and Eva Bartok, both of whom told me I ought to be doing something more intelligent with my life.

Society, too, was changing. The new pop culture where foppishly dressed youth gyrated like battery-reared chickens to the hellish din in discotheques did not attract me. Neither did the hippie drop-out rebellion, the new anarchists from comfortable homes who'd never seen their democracy threatened, nor the students demanding freedom when they'd never known anything else. Britain herself seemed to be degenerating into a land of bingo, brain drain, and backbiting, living on international credit, overworking and underpaying her most essential workforce – doctors, nurses, police, farmworkers – and allowing the unions to hold the rest of society to ransom. It was a disenchantment I shared with many, and most of us failed to appreciate that similar problems were affecting the rest of the developed world as well.

Even my once-beloved London seemed to have become a noisy trap. In the last four years I had changed apartments three times to find a quiet place in which to work. But within a week the workmen would arrive and out would come the noisy drills and up would come the road – the water, gas, and electricity authorities often digging up the same stretch within days of each other.

After a severe illness, my first since childhood, I asked myself, "When were the good times?" Ironically my thoughts returned to the peace and tranquil silences of the wild woods and dappled fields of my childhood. The memories came flooding back – my first holiday in the country as a town-reared boy of twelve: I had walked through forests of waving bluebells and nodding wild narcissus, heard the strident call of the green woodpecker, and from the marshes the plaintive love call of the lapwing. Alone, I was transported into a creation more miraculous than I had ever known could exist. Beautiful jays flashed their rainbow wings and white rumps as they weaved screeching through the still shadows of the pines, purple emperor butterflies sunned the glossy sheen of their wings on old oak stumps, grasshoppers leaped and fiddled in the summer hay, and in the twilight bats flew on skinny wings around the caves of our isolated cottage. I had never been happier in my life. Now I hankered to dwell once again among the scenes of my youth. For a few months I rented a thatched cottage near those old haunts, but I soon found my dream of pastoral bliss there had passed away. The woods were smaller, the rivers muddier, and the fishing lake where the bronze carp had whirled the limpid waters, where coots had bobbed their white pates and the great blue dragonflies had hawked above the reeds like darting wands of fire, was now only a large silted pond surrounded by marsh. The thick hedges that had teemed with wildlife had mostly been dug up. The song of the nightingale came seldom from the thickets, for most of the thickets had gone. I had forgotten my country memories were those of a child, that I had retained only the tiny focus of boyhood. A man can never go back. Yet still I longed to return to more basic values, to live close to nature again.

By now my parents had emigrated to Spain and the only person left of my immediate family was my grandmother. When I drove up to see her in Nottingham, where she lived near her sister and friends, she told me an incredible story; before she had married my father's father, David Tomkies, he had wanted to go to Canada but she had refused to go with him. One night he arrived outside her house and threw gravel at her window. "I'm off to Canada," he told her. After working as a waiter on the Trans-Canadian Express, he had settled down in Calgary, Alberta, as a cowpoke. One day, returning from a beer parlour with friends, he had been ambushed by a group of stone-throwing Indians, his right eye knocked out so that it rested on his cheek. Patched up by local doctors, he was sent to a specialist in Vancouver who told him the best eye surgeon was a Dr. Watts, who lived in Nottingham! Back he had come, had his eye treated, and visited my grandmother again, who this time accepted him. She told me he had been full of stories of how great a land Canada was, of its vast, untouched wild places. As she spoke I remembered with a slight shock that as a child it was a book called *Animal Heroes* by the great Canadian naturalist, Ernest Thompson Seton that had inspired my own first love of nature. As I drove back to London I thought that perhaps my grandfather's desire for the great, free wilderness of Canada had been reborn in me.

A few days later scaffolding shot up around my flat and workmen began drilling into the roof, all without due notice from the landlord. It was the final straw.

I sold my lease, car, and once-precious antiques for less than their real value, settled my debts – for I'd always spent money as fast as it came in – and flew to Canada. Somewhere there, in the harsh, pure wilderness where one faces only the simple physical challenges of the elements, I felt I would be freed, that just by living close to nature away from all I'd known, I might write a fine book and somehow begin my life over again.

British Columbia has a stark grandeur that at first flays the mind of a city-conditioned man. This vast province, almost as large as central Europe, is the last free frontier left in the western world. Here the proud boast "Beautiful B.C." is no defensive pipe dream. Untamed forests clothe colossal mountains in areas half the size of England, some still untouched by man. Bounded in the east by the Rockies and licked and battered in the west by the mighty Pacific, its coastline is an intricate maze of islands and wild rocky inlets, some reaching inland for ninety miles. The sea and rivers abound with five species of salmon, among which a seventy pounder is no rare catch. British Columbia is also a gargantuan, indifferent land with waterfalls higher than Niagara, log jams that can dam up lakes for six miles, cataclysmic forest fires that can clear fifty miles of high timber in a week, and a land in whose great vastness grizzly bears and cougars, the last of the great North American carnivores, find their only real stronghold.

The mountains returned my first looks of awe with contempt, staring down from beneath their skullcaps of snow like great old gods, the custodians of an ancient, primitive treasure. When I first left the ferryboat heading north from Vancouver and made my way up that lonely forest road looking for a cabin, I felt an immediate instinct to rush back to the sheltered life I'd known. I felt utterly alien, scared, sure there could be little compromise for a man living there alone.

To start with I tried hard to fit into the typical work of the coast, first as a logger but, although I'd once toiled at a hand crane and cutting limbs off trees in a Sussex sawmill, I had no experience of carrying twenty-five-pound power saws up giant trees to top them at a hundred feet, or in driving bulldozers or yarding machinery. So I took the lowest job of all – setting choker wires around the huge trees so machines could haul them from the woods. You can't get any lower than that – most of the time I was burrowing like a human mole through mud under felled trunks while a Cat driver with clean hands bawled instructions. For a while I worked as a deckhand on the salmon boats, forking the big salmon into the icy hold of a collector, up to my knees in blood and slime. I even had a job as an assistant blaster – digging holes between root clusters of giant stumps so we could dynamite them for the route of a new road. None of these jobs lasted long.

So I compromised. Donning my creaking journalistic harness, I went to Hollywood to do some writing to restore my finances. But before I left, hearing about a piece of land that might be free for a homestead site, I had rowed down to it, taken a brief walk about it, then had gone to the government agent's office in Vancouver to stake my claim.

The agent had grilled me thoroughly. "Can a child bathe there safely at high tide?"

I said I had no children but I didn't think so. It was an exposed rocky beach. He smiled at my puzzled look.

"We have to be sure anyone who claims land has actually taken the trouble to set foot on it in person," he explained. "Otherwise we'd be full all day with folks who'd done nothing but look at maps. What trees are there on the cliff?"

I frantically tried to recall. "Mostly small fir, pine and a few cedar, alder and arbutus," I said. Then I gave him the number of the marker on the nearest piece of surveyed land that I'd scratched on a scrap of paper.

He went away to check the files. "It *appears* to be free," he said smiling, "though we'll have to check further. If you would just fill out this form …" Under the heading FOR WHAT PURPOSE WILL THE LAND BE USED? I wrote bravely, "To live on. As a permanent dwelling," picturing again the virgin rocky cliff. The agent pointed out there was no water, gas, electricity, telephone line, and no road within a mile of the place.

"I know," I said with a grin. "But the view is unbelievable!" He promised the Lands Branch would let me know in a few months.

That day I bought an old milk truck for $300 in whose cavernous metal-barred interior – it looked like a jail cell on wheels – I built a caravan home, complete with clothes locker, bookcase, folding bed, water tank, and white-gas cooker. Then I set off on the 1,672-mile trip to Hollywood. There I turned myself into a workhorse to earn enough money to begin my wilderness life. And when my mail brought a British Columbia Lands Branch letter saying that for $110 a year I could have the two wild acres, I packed my belongings and drove the truck north. I rented again the cabin and boat I'd used on my first visit to the coast and rowed down to my new land.

So here I was once more. "Well," I thought, "before I take a really good look at the place, I'd better see how the fishing is in my bay!" I let down a handline and within moments hauled up a great gaudy rock cod, looking like a strange Oriental ornament of bronze, orange, and green as it swirled up through the crystal waters. As I sat there in the sun watching an otter ribboning over the rocks on my beach, I felt I was adrift in an enchanted world, sitting upon a painted ocean created by Turner.

But now there was work to do. I had less than a month to erect a shelter on my land before I had to leave the rented cabin. I rowed to my beach and unloaded the initial equipment I'd bought – a four-foot bucksaw, an axe, a sledgehammer, and two alloy tree wedges.

I was strapping the saw to my belt so I'd have two hands free to climb up when I heard a shrieking commotion far away to the left. Over the northern land spit of the next-door bay two bald eagles had been wheeling in circles. Now, as one broke away and soared in my direction, two gulls launched themselves from a cliff where they had their eggs. Calling loudly, they banked, turned, and dived at the huge bird that, unperturbed by the clamour, merely sideslipped now and again before landing on a lone spar. But the gulls kept up the attack, screaming and diving and just shearing away at the last moment.

I couldn't quite see how it happened, but the eagle leaped violently, there was an explosion of white feathers, and then it came beating toward my beach, the gull held lightly in one huge talon. The sea bird looked puny in death, its head dangling from a broken neck and bright blood seeping from its side. As the great eagle passed above, its white-feathered head turned momentarily, its baleful yellow eye glaring down at me.

Chastened, I climbed the cliff. The land went upward at forty degrees in a hill of large rocks and gullies. There was no level spot on which to build. The agent had been right. No water, power, gas, phone line, road, or track – and the only way to transport materials was by sea. Apart from the superb view, there was little but rocky ground covered with wiry salal brush, shore pines, alder, a few cedars and some firs. Building a home here now appeared a daunting if not crazy prospect for a man alone.

Clearly my biggest problem would be how to get the heavy logs from the beach up to the site. The cliff was over twenty feet high but there was already one large tree trunk forming a bridge between the top of it and the beach. Twenty-five yards up my hill, but leaning too far to the south, stood a seventy-foot fir some two feet thick. It was my only hope. Somehow I had to fell that tree and manoeuvre it so it dropped side by side with the tree already there. I could then cut steps across both trunks to make a log staircase.

The tree was an awkward bender, first growing out toward the sea, then doubling back slightly at the top. I axed away at the thick bark, then sawed in the wedgelike undercut facing the way I wanted the tree to fall. With frequent rests, for it was hard work, I cut into the back of the tree until the saw nearly met the undercut, but still the tree gave no sign of which way it would go. Drawing from my short logging experience, I drove in the wedges with the sledge-hammer, so the tree would go the way I wanted, but there was still too much wood holding for the wedges to tip it over. I knocked them out and immediately the tree shuddered as if it would fall too far to the left. I then cut away from the left side, leaving the right edge holding strongest, then drove a wedge back into the left side to tip it.

Suddenly it started to go. I leaped back behind another tree in case my amateur calculations had been wrong. The fir went down, fibres tearing with pistol-like cracks, straight toward the side of the fallen tree, hit the cliff top, bounced up, tipped over, then slid with a tearing noise and an earth-shaking thump right next to the tree already there.

I now had two trees going down the cliff exactly side by side, not more than three inches apart all the way down. Most incredible of all was that their bottoms were dead in line. I stared in total disbelief. Surely some unknown power or mighty beginner's luck had come to my aid. That log staircase would cut my labours by half and it seemed a fine omen for the future.

Rowing back to my rented cabin in the dying sunlight, I had covered only half a mile when I noticed a man on the shore. He was old, grey-haired, and deeply tanned, and he was sawing a large drift log with a bucksaw. I felt unreasonably annoyed. What on earth was he doing here, so far from civilization? He worked with an easy, rhythmic power, clad in a white sleeveless vest and a pair of baggy linen trousers.

When he'd cut through the log he tapped it with his axe, as if to double check its soundness. Then he heaved it upright, knelt down, and let it fall across his shoulder, and set off with short determined steps down to the water where he had a rowing boat even smaller than mine. The log must have weighed over two hundred pounds. As I went past him he hitched the log to another he had in the water, then he too rowed out, rowing the logs behind him. It looked like hard, slow work.

Back in the cabin, I lit the black iron stove and, as the fir logs whined and spat and their heat slowly filled the room, large spiders emerged from crevices and sat on the rough wooden walls, their rows of eyes glowing red in the lamp light. With my stew bubbling merrily away, I sat down before the stove's open door feeling happily self-satisfied. It had been an extraordinary day. I had seen an eagle kill a tormenting gull – an almost unique experience, for in the wild a bird under attack seldom turns on its pursuers – and I had felled a large tree with pinpoint accuracy by hand in the old-fashioned way. In such a blissful mood, like some middle-aged boy scout, it was impossible not to reflect on my former life.

Certainly my past seemed distinguished by a singular lack of achievement. At the six schools I attended I was a nervous brat, not bright, who spent most of his time catching up. I was never popular, for all team and ball sports bored me, and while I could run like the wind and leap like a deer, I could never sleep the night before a sports event and thus would fade the next day, letting down the great expectations of my House. I also developed a ferocious facial twitch that seemed to fulfil a need but didn't help make friends. My one great joy was to escape into the wild woods and fields of Sussex. Every bird or butterfly seemed a magical creature and I studied, collected, painted and wrote about them until I reached adolescence and discovered the local ice rink. There an ambition to be a top speed skater vied with an equally powerful ambition to actually date a pretty and leggy girl skater.

My first paid job at seventeen was as a trainee auctioneer in an animal market and, from sticking the ears of squealing pigs with branding clippers to holding rabbits and chickens aloft near the rostrum, I dreaded every moment. Indeed, the auctioneer wrote to my father, "Your son shows no initiative whatever." Feeling I might relieve my shattered parents by running away to join the Foreign Legion, I compromised. I ran off and joined the Coldstream Guards, which, I was told, would make me a man. But guard duty outside Buckingham Palace plus several years in the immediate postwar deserts of Palestine, then Egypt, Malta and Libya, only taught me that obeisance to a discipline imposed from without is a poor substitute for a discipline imposed from within. "Join the Navy and see the world," went the saying of the time. I joined the Guards and nearly polished it. It hadn't helped, either, when I was stuck as a duty clerk in Tripoli to have the brigade major come weaving in from the officers' club and find me devouring Karl Marx's *Das Kapital*. At the time I'd applied for a transfer to the Education Corps, so I was horrified to read on his report "Not recommended. I fear this soldier's political beliefs will conflict with his loyalty to King and Country ...". I'd been given no chance to explain I was merely *reading* the book, that even at nineteen I found communism to be a conspiracy against true individuality. The injustice, the blank wall against my protests, infuriated me. I saved up for six months and finally bought myself out of the army.

Back on civvy street I was convinced my destiny was to be a great writer. But my piles of stories and essays were soon matched by equally high piles of rejection slips. I managed only to win a precarious foothold in country journalism at thirty shillings a week. For four years as I biked between small towns and a score of villages taking the names of mourners at gravesides, racing to fires, plane and train crashes, city courts and meetings of town councils, I had little to show but two-finger typing and highly developed leg muscles.

One day after being hailed by a labouring cyclist whom I had outdistanced on the road, I joined the local cycling club, and astonished myself by winning my first race and my third, and even more so when I started winning medals on the sprint track at Portsmouth. That was it – I was going to be a great cyclist! That ambition ended the next time I went on the track for a major event. Somehow the rear wheel of the star rider hit my front wheel. Up I went – and down. Crash. I got up, wheeled my bike from the stadium, then remember nothing until I found myself standing on the wrong ferry going in the wrong direction. I must have boarded it while under the effects of a slight concussion. My club colleagues had all gone home by train. I had a thirty mile ride home alone, and that was the last sports club I ever joined.

Jumping in and out of almost everything, I worked in a sawmill, as a reporter on four more papers, trained as a singer, hired myself out as a male secretary, then in 1952 boarded an eighty-foot ketch along with a few other foolhardy characters in an attempt to sail around the world. But a sudden storm and near-shipwreck as we headed for Tangier in winter without an engine – we'd sold it at sea to some smugglers –

soon scotched the adventure and resulted in an arduous walking trip from Lisbon to Madrid. My few funds got me home with six shillings in my pocket. Then from provincial journalism at the seaside resort of Brighton, I finally made it to London, my base for the big city years that I had now abandoned to find a new life in the wilderness.

It was only later, as I ate my stew in the flickering candlelight, that I felt a twinge of fear. All my London friends had told me I was crazy to live out this primitive dream at my age – and maybe they were right. The realization that I was now completely alone in the wilds was swiftly killing the optimism I had felt when driving back from Hollywood. I knew little of the sea that would now have to be my main source of food as well as transport, had no experience running my own boat, and both bear and cougar were said to inhabit the mountainous terrain behind my land. All my roots had now been severed.

Sleep came hard that night, and as the logs spat, the cabin filled with the perfume of burning resin, mosquitoes whined, and mice charged about the floor. But at least I had my schedule planned: I'd rise at dawn, write for a few hours, then go down the coast to work on my new home site for the rest of each day. Thus, as in the ancient myth of Athenian man, mind and body would be exercised in harmony together, the beauties of the wilderness acting naturally as a spur to both.

This naïve idea soon went awry. Next morning as I shuffled through my notes, a most almighty hammering broke out from above the cabin. I rushed out, climbed the log steps, and there, before a tiny, dilapidated cabin I'd been told would be empty, was the old man I'd seen on the beach. He was levelling a log with an axe. I felt unreasonable resentment – as the noise rang starkly against the silent trees, it seemed worse than being back in a city.

"Well, hello there! So you har my new neighbour!" he said heartily, oddly putting h's before some of his vowels. "Come hup, come hup. Hi hope my noise doesn't bother you!" And he stared at me quizzically, his blue eyes ringed with the grey of age, piercing and dark like a falcon's. He was a square, chunky man of average height, his body old but tanned and honed to fitness by hard work. His name was Ed Louette and he was a retired log carpenter from the northern interior. It was impossible to remain annoyed before that cheerful face, and after the introductions I told him my problem.

"So, you build with words and hi build with logs! Hi've never met a writer before," he continued. "Well, we must let you write. Hi was due to leave here last week but two days ago hi wrote to the landlord hi'd stay and rebuild this old cabin. Well, hi've nothing better to do! But your work his important, so hi won't start hammering until one o'clock, how's that?"

After such hearty *bonhomie*, I said that was fine. Ed then tapped a thick log he'd carried up the previous day.

"That's yellow cedar. Nothing like it for cabin walls, y'know. Hit's hard as iron - and warm. A man should halways live in a wooden house because wood *breathes*."

I laughed and stared at the big log. "Ho, they're not too heavy," he said. "Hi only bring three up a day. If hi was a young man hi'd carry them hall day, but now I'm sixty-seven and have a weak heart so hi take life easy!" I bent down and, staggering, managed to get the log onto my shoulder. It was as heavy as boxwood. Yet this old man was towing them several miles in a rowing boat, then carrying them up the steep cliff path and a hundred yards along the road! I could feel my spine creaking. I dropped the log, staring at Ed Louette in amazement. Sixty-seven and a weak heart?

"Ho, you see? Not too heavy!" said Ed, dismissing the subject. "Now look at these rotten foundation sills – hemlock. Who could have built this cabin, do you think! Hit's turrible work, turrible. Hi'll have to pull all those old sills out first."

Feeling guilty that I'd silenced Ed, I tried fitfully to start work on my book, but I couldn't concentrate – the land down the coast was calling. I gave up and, snatching my tools, went to my "property". Until now I'd only seen the place from the beach. This time I had to find it through a maze of old logging tracks that had not been used since the start of the century. With an old map, I drove up and down the forest road, made three wrong sorties down overgrown tracks before finally locating the right one. It turned off at a sharp angle on a blind corner, dipped down a steep incline and, after an alarming S-shaped curve lined with saplings that ripped at the truck, ran on for another quarter-mile. Then it petered out completely above a drop into a dense tangle of young alder trees.

Leaving the truck at the top of the hill, I threaded my way down through the alders. After two hundred yards of blundering progress, I found a deer trail leading off to the left through a dark wood of fir and cedar. After nearly a quarter-mile the trail led into an open clearing. I climbed up a high mossy escarpment and tried to see the shore. Surprisingly, it was still far below and there was no track or even hint of a trail through the trees and thick salal brush.

It took half an hour to find a way through, but finally I stood again on the rocky cliff above the beach of my little half-moon bay. Standing there panting, I felt like a poor man's version of the Lewis and Clark expedition. Yet again I had the feeling I must be mad. When I'd applied for the land, the lack of every modern convenience had seemed a small problem when weighed against the idyllic surroundings. Now I found myself wishing I were ten years younger. It would be as much as I could do in the month for which I'd rented the cabin to build a log *platform* on which I could put a tent, never mind a whole cabin.

For the next few hours, until it was almost dark, I cleared thick, tangled brush from the area. Then I climbed back up to where I'd left the truck. As I backed out, one of the young alders broke off my only wing mirror, but I resisted the vengeful urge to hack it down. It had been my fault.

That night as supper simmered on the spitting stove, I sat down by candlelight and made a list of the essential tools I would need to build with logs and cut a trail through fallen trees:

> Power saw (for cutting out the trail and shaping logs for the cabin)
> Machete (for cutting out the trail)

Pickaxe (for digging out rocks)

Five-foot crowbar (for digging out rocks)

Oilskins

Nylon rope (for holding logs upright when plumbed and fitted)

Two two-gallon water containers

Three bags cement

Twelve-foot tape measure

Building tools (planes, claw hammer, pliers, screwdrivers, chisels, screws
     and nails)

Gumboots, spade, and shovel

One-inch rope (for hauling logs up cliff)

2 Building a Wilderness Home

*A*t dawn next day I was awakened by a loud crash. Ed Louette had dumped a sackful of oysters on my veranda. "There you har, neighbour!" he cried. "Some fine hoysters from the hisland for you!" It was his peace offering and was both the first and last easy food I was to receive in the Canadian wilderness.

"Hoysters are good for you," he said emphatically. "All that phosphorus! Do you know what I eat? Hoysters, heggs, and honions! "

"Oysters, eggs, and onions?" I muttered, bleary-eyed and incredulous, wishing he'd just let me sleep.

"Yessir, hoysters, heggs, and honions! They're full of vital sea minerals. Ho, if you only had a young lady with you!"

Ed never ate raw oysters but had his own recipes. And he breathlessly gave them to me right then. I could dip them in egg white, roll them in breadcrumbs dried in the sun, and fry them lightly in butter. I could make oyster stew by mixing them with fried onions, rice, peas, and a tin of mushroom soup. Or, his favourite way, I could fry them in bacon fat and eat them with oat or wheat cakes. There were enough oysters in his sack to have stacked a city oyster bar for a week. And all free. Touched in spite of the rude awakening, I thanked him and told him not to worry about his hammering. I had more important things to do than to write.

That morning I drove to the small town some twenty miles south and bought the items on my list. The bill came to $472 – little enough for the tools for a new home; most of my building materials would come from the beach.

For the next few days I cut a trail through the thick brush and alder to the rear of my two acres. As I'd have to carry things on my back, I wanted to make the route as easy as possible, yet not make it obvious to any occasional passer-by. So I left the first twenty-five yards of alder wood almost as it was. After that the rocks had to be dug out by crowbar. It was hard work, as the salal was thick and its roots were embedded around the rocks. Frequently I would cut through several three-foot thick fallen trees with the power saw only to end on a small rocky escarpment.

I started the saw respectfully by standing on its handle on a flat stump with its twenty-one-inch blade projecting. Trying to emulate the fallers I'd known, I got it buzzing strongly, then directed it head-on into a fallen hemlock. Immediately it shot up into the air and narrowly missed cleaving my head in two. I tried again, but holding it slightly downward; it again leaped back at me. And when I tried to cut the willowy alders on the upper track they were so whippy they fell at all angles, twisting so the saw became stuck. Eventually, though, I got the hang of it.

It soon became clear that with the underbrush so rank and thick with salal, salmonberry, wild thimbleberry bushes, and fast-growing alder keeping the trail clear alone would be a twice-yearly job. After an hour of machete swinging, blisters made the work even harder because the pain forced the hands to relax, and if one wasn't careful – goodbye foot.

On the third day it began to rain. I'd never seen rain to equal the torrential downpours on the British Columbian coast. As I worked it seemed to have a vengeful malice of its own. It beat into my eyes, sneaked down my back, and even crept through the ventilation holes of my rain jacket and trickled down my armpits.

After six days I had a passable trail, though I had to manoeuvre sideways through clumps of trees when my hands were full. The next two weeks were spent assaulting the rocky site on which I was to build. I dug out the loose rocks with pick and crowbar and rolled them over the cliff. This had a treble effect: it made the forty-degree slope level, raised the height of the beach below, and trimmed a good deal of useless fat from my waist. Once the site was ready, I dug holes through thick fir roots down to bedrock to anchor the two front log pillars of the platform. But how long would these logs need to be so the platform would be level! I had forgotten an essential item – a spirit level. Faced with that forty-mile journey, I improvised. Using a flat bottle of suntan lotion left over from Hollywood and a weighted tape measure dangling from a straight cedar pole held level in one hand, I found the logs would need to be nearly eight feet long.

At the back of the site I hacked holes in the exposed bedrock into which I could hook and cement the rear foundation logs so the cabin wouldn't fall into the sea. As I hacked away at the granite with a rapidly blunting pick and crowbar, a chip flew out and embedded itself half an inch below my right eye. I was lucky not to have lost the eye, but from then on I wore an old pair of plastic swimming goggles for that work. At first I'd been loath to use the boat to carry materials. I wanted to conserve energy, and rowing to the site, working there all day, and then having to row the four miles back, often against heavy winds, seemed like unnecessarily hard work. But faced with having to carry heavy joists and fourteen-foot boards down the long trail, I was forced to use the boat more.

When I first arrived with the laden rowing boat the tide was half out, and in that exposed rocky place I couldn't land. The rest of that day was spent cutting out a rounded boom log, fixing a spike and pulley to it, and attaching it to an anchor to make a mooring buoy.

One day I took an afternoon off and stayed in the rented cabin to write. As I worked, I saw half a tree float past the window. Ed Louette was beneath it, his head twisted with the weight, shuffling along quietly with little stumping steps. Later I heard him row off in his little boat. He always rowed with short, jerky strokes and on windless days I'd hear the quick, rhythmic *clunka clunka clunka* of his oars banging in their locks. Then I'd look out and see him rowing away like a little clockwork man on his eternal search for cabin logs from the island beaches. I thought I'd try and help him.

Down on the beach lay a yellow cedar he had already cut into eight-foot lengths. I lowered one onto my shoulder and shakily set off over the rocks. I wobbled and wavered, and halfway up the stony cliff path a whitish mist swam before my eyes and I had to drop the log on one end and pause to ease my pounding heart. I couldn't get that log up to my cabin, let alone Ed's, without stopping twice. I had yet to learn fully the lesson one learns many times in that land – what a city man deems fitness counts for nothing there. Years of hard work in those great forests creates a thickness of tendon, bone, and ligament alignments against which artificially trained muscle means little.

After the pauses and a further hour's writing, I went down and repeated the process with another log. Twilight had fallen before I heard him rowing back, towing more logs behind him. I snuffed out the candles and stood in the dark so he couldn't see me as he walked up the cliff path. For a few seconds he looked at the two logs I'd brought up, then went on his way. Several days went by but Ed never said a word about them until one morning I met him on the path and told him I'd brought them up.

"Ho, did you," he said, removing his checked cap and scratching his grey hair in what I thought was embarrassment. "Hi wondered about that. Hi couldn't recall bringing them up myself. Well, well! " And he went on up to his cabin.

I felt slightly miffed he hadn't even thanked me. A few more days went by, then one evening I found Ed sawing the logs into short lengths. "Hello there," he said. "Hi just thought you may not have a saw" (I kept it at the site) "so I'm cutting them up for you!"

Embarrassed, I explained I'd only carried them up for *him*, to save him the bother. "Ho, well, I misunderstood you." He laughed. "Hi thought … well, thank you, professor, thank you. But hi've started now so we'll put these on your fire!" And he went on cutting them up.

To show gratitude I took my axe and started chopping the chunks of yellow cedar into quarters. Ed watched me silently. It was hard wood and my axe got stuck in it. "No, no, that's not the way," he cried suddenly. "You'll not get hanywhere haxing them like that, you have to twist-chop. You halways hold the hax at an angle," he said. "You point the blade out to the left but you bring it down straight." With that he halved the block with one blow. Kicking one half aside, he raised the axe and with swift blows reduced the block to a neat pile of two-inch-thick dominoes. It was like watching a machine. I never did achieve old Ed's proficiency.

Back on my land the next day, I searched my beach for stout yellow cedar logs for the cabin's foundations. The beach was stacked high with drift logs of all kinds – fir, hemlock, spruce, with a few yellow and valuable red cedar spars here and there. I cut the first two thick eight-footers from a straight yellow cedar, drove nails into their tops and with quadrupled nylon rope around the nails, painfully dragged them over the rocks.

Several times as I rested the logs on each step of the staircase after an almighty heave, they nearly rolled off – and me with them. But finally I had the logs in place as the front pillars. There were no others straight enough for the rest of my foundation on my beach so I rowed half a mile to another, where I found two the right thickness. By the time I'd cut them up, dragged them to the water line, and then towed them back, the tide was well out.

I realized then I wasn't being too intelligent. Rather than drag or carry heavy logs over two hundred yards of rocky beach, why not use the tides to float them in! If I worked *with* the high tides, I could stack all usable drift logs and lumber just above high-tide level on various beaches, then fetch them later with the boat. The sea's broad breast would do most of the work. The only problem now was that the next high tide wasn't until four in the morning. I dared not leave the fourteen-footers to drift, even on a line, in that exposed spot. It took me the rest of the afternoon to drag them to the foot of the cliff, but they were too heavy for me to haul up the staircase.

It was time for more hard thinking, for many problems were looming. I sat on a mossy boulder watching some cream-pated wigeon drakes crowding around two dowdier grey-brown ducks, and made a mental note that I needed four of these fourteen-footers for the cabin base, eight more for the rafters, four logs for the corner posts. To haul them up the cliff I'd need a gin pole and a block and tackle with a ratio of at least four to one. I could also use this to haul up the floor joists, side studs, boards, the cedar shakes for the roof and, later, for hauling my boat onto a log wharf I intended to make. In a few days I would have to leave the rented cabin and its little boat, so I needed a boat of my own. And while I liked rowing, I wasn't sure I wanted to tow the basics of an entire cabin with a mere pair of oars when the only place I could put loads into the water was a dilapidated government wharf some four miles away. So I'd hire an outboard engine for a few days. Above all, I needed a good strong tent in which to live for the rest of the summer.

Next day I hired an old 5½-horsepower outboard, then drove on down south and caught the ferry to Vancouver. There I scanned the boats sections of the papers and found a secondhand ten-foot plywood dinghy for $56. In one of the stores I bought a heavy nine-foot-square tent and an elegant throne of a plastic toilet. I bought the block, tackle, and rope at a pawnbrokers' shop. The place was full of logging bric-a-brac at bargain prices, and I picked up old axe heads, cold chisels, and other tools. All had been made by real craftsmen in the days when iron and steel didn't splinter with the first hard use.

Too late to catch the return ferry north, I spent the night in the truck by the waterfalls of Furry Creek some twenty miles out of town. After a sizzling breakfast of fried trout, caught with feathers as a bait, I picked up the boat, crammed it into the milk truck – breaking my wooden bed in the process – and caught the ferry back to the wild coast. Rising early next day to catch the high tide, I launched the new boat at the dilapidated old wharf. The hired outboard coughed and spluttered but a new plug solved the problem. Then with all my purchases aboard, I happily puttered the four miles to my site.

Over the next few days I set up the gin pole, tying its support ropes to various trees, hauled up the big logs for the cabin foundations, curve-notched and nailed them into place, and cut in the slots for the floor joists. As I came back to the rented cabin one evening, Ed was waiting.

"Ho, so you have a new boat," he said heartily. "I saw you go past this morning. Hi thought you were hup to something! Are you staying here now?"

I couldn't hide it from him any longer. I told him about my land and the platform I was building for a tent. He laughed, surprised. "Well, good for you, professor, good for you! Hi wondered what you were doing, leaving early hevery morning."

He looked into my boat and noticed I still had the oars from the rented cabin. "Ho, you'll need some hoars. Hi'll make some for you." He turned suddenly and picked up a piece of springy spruce he'd found on the beach that day. "They made hairplane wings from worse spruce than this during the war!" he said, fondling the wood lovingly.

Two days later he handed me two perfect oars, copperbound at the ends, that he'd carved from the spruce. And he refused to take any payment for them. I had cause to thank him that very day. It was windy, and when a mile had been covered in choppy seas, the engine broke down. As I'd forgotten the pliers for removing the fouled sparkplug, I couldn't restart it. With the boat and joists drifting toward some jagged rocks, I had no alternative but to row the rest of the way – awkward when towing a load of heavy joists as the jerky action of the rowing caused the joists to bang against the stern of the boat.

Transporting thick plywood for the floor and to box in the pie-shaped kitchen and toilet between the cabin floor and the sloping bedrock of the cliff proved less tedious but on one afternoon dangerous.

I loaded the boat with some sea-sodden drift timbers, tied five sheets of plywood across the top to keep them dry, and set off. But the wind sprang up, the sea became rougher, the waves began hitting against the plywood and splashing into the boat. Suddenly I was in six inches of water, which started to lurch ponderously about inside the dinghy, which then became uncontrollable. Throttling the engine up to top speed, I tried to use its powerful thrust to keep the bow up long enough to hit land.

We didn't quite make it. Some forty yards offshore the plywood slipped slowly from its fastenings. The front and left side of the boat, went under with it, forming a graceful downward arc under the extra weight of the sodden lumber in its well, and the flooded engine chugged to a stop. Then the stern of the boat, under the weight of the heavy, old-fashioned engine came to a stop, the engine prop clanking against the rocky sea bed in ten or twelve feet of water. I realized with horror the engine's safety rope had tangled itself round my left boot. I frantically kicked and wrenched off my boot, then managed to swim to the beach. Luckily the tide and wind were coming in, and freed of my weight the boat rose slowly again until the bow quarter broke surface, then drifted toward me until I was able to reach it and haul it onto the beach. I had learned my lesson and I never again tried to keep any wood dry on top of the boat.

Such accidents weren't rare and one quickly learned to respect the sea and take nothing for granted.

My most immediate problem concerned my inadequate mooring. Sometimes when I was working, a high wind would cause the mooring line to chafe through at the pulley setting the boat free, unnoticed, to crash on the rocks. The steam-tarred nylon and smooth pulleys I needed lay in piles in Vancouver chandleries, more forgotten items. In choppy seas, too, it was hard to leave the boat near a rocky beach while levering logs into the water for towing. It was some time before I learned to use a stern anchor. In the process my gumboots and legs were soaked nearly every day. I lost two watches through seawater immersions and, as I watched the last one twinkling down to vanish into the kelp on the seabed, it seemed a symbolic, last farewell to my civilized life. I had no appointments to keep now.

On the last day in the rented cabin I ferried out all my belongings – a mahogany filing cabinet with four long drawers with a score of books to maintain my "education" in the wilds, a tape recorder, fishing gear, bedding, ornaments, a gilt mirror, two more cardboard packages of books and notes for my novel, shoes, four suits (which were never used again) and other clothes, boxes of personal documents, photos and classical records. Also, there was the two-burner camp cooker, fuel, kitchen implements, a laundry basket, and a couple of antique lamps. And there was a nine-foot-square blue carpet that had landed with a thud at my feet as I once walked past a Hollywood apartment house. The workmen who'd dropped it from a window had shouted that it belonged to a well-known actor who'd bought another. Finally there was a slimline TV set I'd bought to help out a friend in Hollywood who'd been in need of quick cash.

As I was loading this paraphernalia into my boat, Ed came down the cliff path and offered me his. It was a calm day and by towing his boat astern of mine, I took everything at once. I set up the cooker in the pie-shaped kitchen and hung the pans from nails in the floor joists above. While I had cursed when making this basement to find the bedrock ended in a jagged series of shelves, I now had cause to be thankful. I stowed all the unwanted relics of my life in civilization on these rough stone tiers, placing the gilt mirror in such a way that when I sat down to eat meals from a small driftwood table (which saved me carrying my food up to the tent above) the mirror reflected the superb view over the islands, an idyllic scene of which I was now sure I would never tire.

On my fortieth birthday, I took up residence. It was a proud moment. The piping *whee-oos* of the male wigeon came up now from the placid gold and blue waters of my bay, and I looked down possessively from the sun-drenched platform at a small courting party. A grey-brown female was swimming around in apparently aimless circles, closely followed by three urgent drakes. What superb creations they were, for their finery would have graced any admiral of the fleet. Their creamy head-crests that give them their nickname Baldpate shaded abruptly into the green eye-stripe and speckled chestnut of their heads, and their pinky-brown flanks changed suddenly into dazzling white underparts. Their greyish backs, finely pencilled with black, were broken by broad wing patches of startling white, and their secondary wing feathers overlay their primaries like black epaulettes.

As they crowded around the lady, they raised their head-crests slightly and sometimes lifted their wings. Not for them the squawking, squabbly notes one usually associates with ducks, for their soothing *whee-oos* sounded so plaintive and sweet they seemed the very embodiment of peace on that late spring evening. Occasionally they jostled each other to get nearer to her, like men at a bar when a beautiful girl comes in alone, but there was no fighting. She plodded solemnly along, making an odd purring note, but her bright eyes betrayed her air of studied unawareness. She seemed to be sizing them up, for after a few minutes she quietly moved away, followed by only one drake. The other two stared mournfully but, accepting the situation like gentlemen, they paddled slowly toward the rest of the flock, now diving for eel grass and weed titbits near a small island away to the south.

Relaxing sleepily on my platform as the sun winked and dipped with golden flashes between the firs on the islands, I opened the bottle of cheap pink champagne I had bought for the occasion. It tasted like nectar.

3 The Sea Provides

*E*ach morning dawned in a silent primrose sky, the early light filtering through the firs and pines, etching the tangled, twisted shapes of the arbutus trees against the canvas above my head, turning the tent into a warm cauldron of green. Rising early, I'd see a salmon swirl against the placid water as it headed down the coast, scenting for the creek or river from which it came and where it was now returning to spawn. Or I'd see one of the lordly eagles passing by in lazy flight, though its glassy marigold eye missed no likely prey.

At first, I'd begin to work on the novel after only a hasty breakfast. Guilt was as much a spur as any desire to write. Only hard work makes an honest man, my generation had been taught. Yet such work can really only be measured against the efforts of others. And here there was no one; my only neighbours were the deer, mink, eagles, raccoons, skunks, gulls, ducks, mice, pack rats, the free-running salmon, and the occasional cougar or black bear. For weeks I suffered an obscure pressure, the guilt that I was not shaping up to "responsibility," that I was too old for hippiedom.

Nature solved the problem, for along with the fine, dazzling days came rainy ones. I learned these could be used for writing, while on the others I could work on my shelter, explore, or merely relax. There was no real hurry. I had no deadlines to meet.

Fishing daily from the tiny rowing boat with Ed's home-made oars became more than a hunt for food or even a day's sport – it became my way of life. To be able to haul the boat down the ladder of cedar poles Ed had shown me how to make, and to row out into the superb tree-fringed bays and sit fishing in the sun seemed the finest freedom I had ever known.

I learned to live almost entirely from the sea. Apart from the oysters that lay two feet deep in a bay on one of the islands, I found clams and I fished for red snappers, rock, and ling cod, as well as occasional coho salmon. On windy days when rowing would have been a chore, I tied a cut-off trouser leg onto my belt and swam out to the nearest island, filled it with mussels, and swam back – dinner secured. I also felt much better than after merely lining up at the corner fish store! Many were the devious recipes cooked on the little stove. And occasionally I bought meat at the distant store for a special treat. With care I could live easily on five dollars a week.

At first for bait I bought packets of frozen herring strip from the store or rowed to a tiny marina six miles up the coast that sold live herrings. Then I rowed out to a natural gulley between two islands, estimated where the big holes lay, then baited up my two treble hooks as if for river pike and cast them out with a four-ounce weight. Instantly the rod would be almost jerked from my hand and I'd start hauling up the rock cod. Once I was pulling away when my rod bent almost double. I felt a great surging run, the reel spun on its check, and I felt sure this must be my first salmon. Feeling naïvely that the few skills I'd learned when sea fishing off Littlehampton, England, were still there, I played the big fish. Keep the line at seventy degrees, don't point the rod at the fish, let it run but keep the line taut ... gradually I worked it up to the boat until in the green misty depths I saw not a salmon but what looked like a small shark. It was a dogfish and I stunned it with an oar and gaffed it into the boat.

Rowing back, I almost banged into Ed, who was returning from a trip behind Oyster Island. "Ho there, professor! What have you there?" Proudly I showed him my catch as we pulled ashore. His face dropped. "Rock cod and a dogfish. What are you going to do with *them*?"

"Eat them, of course."

"Heat them?" He stared at me in disbelief. "You can't heat fish like that. Well, rock cod are hall right if you've nothing else, but a dogfish! Dogfish are vermin ..."

"Well, we eat them in England," I said defensively. "We call them rock salmon, eat them with chips."

"Vermin!" he repeated. "Scavengers! They heat the young salmon and they wreck the nets. Just bang them on the head and throw them back, that's what we do with dogfish!" He turned back the wet sacking in his boat to reveal two five-pound ling cod and a fat vermilion fish with bulging golden eyes. "Those are the best eating fish here," he said. "The ling cod and the red snapper, next best to salmon. Here!" He stuck a finger in the red snapper's gill and flicked the nine-pound fish into my boat. "Try that. Fry it in bread-crumbs and corn hoil and when you eat it, dip it in malt vinegar!"

He stared with good-humoured contempt at the broken herrings about my boat. "Were you fishing for salmon?"

"No, just rock cod."

"Good God," he snorted. "You don't need herring for cod. You pay ninety cents for twelve herring and all you end up with is cod? You could buy two cans of salmon for that!"

He showed me his own fishing rig. He used hand lines and never bothered with costly rods and reels. His lines ended in a rough, metal bar with wires from each end, carrying large treble hooks. On them he had impaled pieces of red and white rubber that he had scissored into little grass skirts. To catch the big red snappers Ed would row out a mile or more, then heave the metal contraption overboard and let it down into a large hole. Once there he'd jig about till the fish struck, then hand over hand it up again, often with a six-pound red snapper on each hook. Ed had no time for "those finicky sports fishermen." He was fishing for his food.

I learned from him that the way to catch bait herring along that coast was to tie two dozen hooks to a weighted line and jig the line up and down through a shoal. Some always became impaled. I tried it, and stared dismally as my hooks shot up and down and the herring dodged with irritating ease. Finally, taking another cue from Ed I made a paternoster from which I dangled *two* weighted lines of hooks, rowed to the small harbour mouth five miles north, where the herring shoals were more constricted, then jigged it with a zigzag movement. This new method worked and I caught all the bait I wanted.

Ed also taught me the best way to catch ling, the huge, green, snakelike Pacific cod that looked like the river pike of my English boyhood. "Ling cod har always in holes," he said. "They can't see down, only hup as their eyes are on top of their heads, so you must come at them from above." The idea was to find an underwater slope, then to row away from it, or let the wind drift you, and bounce your bait downward over the rocks. The ling would see it coming and would surge out of their holes and grab it. You could use a tiny crab for bait, a mussel (half-cooked to hold it firm), or just a chromium cod jigger, a strip of light rubber or tin. I soon found out why Ed did not waste his pension on real herring. The bays were so full of fish and since there was barely enough food to go around, they attacked anything bright before any other fish competitor could reach it.

Watching Ed gut a fish was an entertainment. He'd take them to a drift log, pick up his hand axe and, while discoursing about some natural marvel like how young geese rejoin their parents thousands of miles away in South America each winter, he'd go chop and off would come the head. *Chop,* that was the tail. *Chop, chop* and open the stomach; a quick pinch like milking a cow's udder and away would go the insides. Two quick slashes down the back and he'd rip out the spiky dorsal fins as if they were on a zipper fastener. The whole operation took a few seconds and he never missed a word of his conversation.

In truth, however, I usually saw little of Ed, and it was three weeks after that excellent fishing lesson before I met him again. I had mislaid an axe head and was sure I'd left it under the rented cabin. I drove back along the forest road in the truck and just as I found the axe head, Ed's chunky figure blocked out the light. He held a bottle of rye in his hand.

"Hello, neighbour! Hi thought that axe head was yours, so I sharpened it up but put it back there." He had, too. "Well, hi'll be leaving here soon, so would you care for a drink?" It was the first time I'd ever been invited to his cabin and as I stepped inside the whole place smelled of linseed oil. His floor was covered with wood shavings and his tools, fashioned by craftsmen at the turn of the century, lay everywhere, the symbols of his passion for creating in wood. He walked over to a kitchen corner, dipped his hand in a large bucket and pulled out two red snapper fillets, rubbed them in his sun-dried breadcrumbs, and popped them into sizzling oil in a skillet on his wood stove. I asked him what the bucket was for.

"That's my refrigerator," he said. "A bucket of brine! Best thing for keeping fish fresh, y'know. Vinegar's good too - if you can afford it!"

As we ate the crisp fish in the flickering candlelight, mere hors d'oeuvres Ed explained as he heaved a vast pot of oyster stew onto the stove, we started on the rye. I noticed there were small spiders' webs in some of the cabin's window frames and high log corners.

"Hi always leave spiders alone," he told me. "They are good friends of man, y'know. They kill mosquitoes and hall the flies that get on the food. No, I never harm the spiders. They're more than welcome!" I felt guilty. I had hated spiders since childhood and always whacked them to death when I saw them. From that evening on, like Ed, I left them alone.

Shyly at first and then with growing confidence as the rye warmed him, Ed showed me some of his work – the new A-frames of small squared logs to support his roof, an elegant serpentine-fronted garden seat with hand-axed slats of red and yellow cedar, the gables outside his front door made from natural cedar crooks found in the forest above his cabin. Most impressive were the natural "art works" that he'd discovered hidden in the roots of old trees – a giraffe's head from a burl of fir, a chunk of hemlock that looked like a seaman's head complete with cap and beard, and a fir root carved into an abstract running rooster. His gnarled hands fondled the objects lovingly. He had only carved them enough to bring out their natural lines, then to preserve them he had dipped them into boiling linseed oil. He thrust the rooster into my hands, waved away my protests, and insisted I keep it. It is my talisman to this day.

Ed was a gifted creator. He had no artistic pretension and sought no recognition. As a youth, just after the era of the bullock and horse teams, he had toiled in Canada's great forests as a logger. Approaching forty, knowing he would soon be too old to climb and top the big trees, Ed had turned to carpentry and cabin and bunk-house building. As his skill had grown, so had his reputation, and the province governments across Canada had employed him as a working foreman. And now I saw in the faded, yellowing pictures he held out that all over Manitoba, Saskatchewan, and northern British Columbia there were great log ranchhouses, beloved by today's tourists, standing as mute testimony to the life of this man, one of the last of the North American log craftsmen.

We put the world to rights that night. He demanded to know about my life and told me some of his. He listened gravely, never interrupting. Then he talked and I listened. In the wilds any talk was rare, and good talk a luxury, to be respected and enjoyed. Two men meeting over a bottle of rye or a few pipes of tobacco was an occasion, and just to hear the softly expressed feelings of another filled one with well-being.

Ed loved the wild and free creatures with a passion that matched mine, and he kept many wildlife books on his shelves, checking the birds he saw each day with the pages at night. He dropped a hint once about a wild grizzly bear trek he had made when younger, but withstood my queries with, "Well, professor, I may tell you about that one day when you've been here a bit longer. But hi'll be leaving here tomorrow."

He was going to Lasqueti, one of the southern gulf islands, for the rest of the summer.

"Shall we write?"

"Well, I'm not much of a letter writer," he replied, but he told me the post office where he would be checking his mail. And that he would be back on the coast around September.

When I left Ed in the early hours, I felt presumptuously foolish for once having resented his presence. He was a part of that harsh land, and I knew I would miss his company.

As I left he asked, "Have you a a lamp?" "No, but I'll manage."

He smiled. Suddenly he got up and, picking out a large silvery can from his garbage container, banged a hole in its side, thrust in a candle, and held it out to me, using the candle end as a handle. "Light that when you get onto your trail," he said. "Good as any battery lamp you ever had."

I thanked him. But after I left the truck and faced the pitch-black forest I cursed to realize I had run out of matches. I learned that night that alcohol and the wilderness were a poor mix. I could only find the trail by feeling for the spaces I'd cut between the brush and the trees. I fell into every dark hole and hearing occasional scuffles nearby thought "Bears!" I desperately sang and talked to myself, trying to keep my spirits up and to frighten any bear or cougar that might be around. By the time I finally found my cliff top, in the faint glow that came off the Pacific, my imagination had every bear and cougar in British Columbia coming after me. Hardier spirits than mine quailed before spending nights out alone in such wild forests, and I swore I'd never again leave day or night without some means of ignition.

In my kitchen I lit Ed's candle lamp. It threw out a faint beam like a searchlight, and the sides of the tin helped throw the beam forward and protect the flame from wind. I hoped Ed would be back in September. I did not intend to face winter in that exposed place in a tent, and if any man could teach me how to build a good cabin it would be Ed Louette.

I woke before dawn with a raging thirst and as I climbed down the rocks from the tent platform to my kitchen, holding the gin-pole rope for support, I heard a thumping, scraping sound. I shone my torch and there on the log rafters sat a huge pack rat as big as a beaver, with a long bushy tail and eyes glowing red in the sudden beam. I shouted and followed its flight down the rocks, its plop on the toilet floor, and its hurried exit over my feet with hefty swipes from my broom, I didn't relish the thought of a rat that size rummaging around my tent as I lay sleeping.

Next morning dawned bright and clear and I rowed three miles out to the reefs where the homing coho and big spring salmon fed, gathering their strength and awaiting the rain freshets for their spawning migrations up the rivers. When you're far from land in a small rowing boat, the sea at first seems more dangerous than it is. Nothing between you and a watery death but half-inch plywood, so that fishing for supper was spiced with a touch of adventure too, as I hauled out like some amateur Viking for unknown lands.

For weeks salmon eluded me completely. I saw the pleasure boats come up from Vancouver and the fishermen aboard pull out the fighting, silvery form of salmon. As I wended among them in my dilapidated rowing boat I felt like a pauper. City men or not, these B.C. Canadians knew more about salmon fishing than I did. I did everything by the book. To attract the fish I towed bait behind my boat by trolling with lead weights, and flashed dodgers and strips, spoons and plugs at the end of my traces. I varied the lengths of the traces to change the action of the lures behind the dodger. I trolled near the surface, at mid-depth, and almost bouncing along the bottom. I tried drifting slowly over the reefs and letting down herring slabs and strips, retrieving them jerkily in the true "mooching" method. Nothing. Once, emulating my days on the professional trolling boats, I tied four traces onto my line weighted with a three-pound lead ball, tied on four different lures, then lost the lot when the ball wedged tightly between rocks. That was a loss of some six dollars on one snag, so I didn't try that again. I caught rock cod, which I now dropped back in disgust, and ling cod, some of which also broke my tackle, for a twenty-five-pound or bigger ling often will suddenly barrel straight down and snap even a twenty-five-pound breaking-strain line, especially when you're trying to stop it from reaching the rocks where it could cut the line.

One morning, I had been sitting for an hour over a ledge and was about to give up, when the water surface broke a few yards away and out came a bowler hat with two nostrils. It turned toward me, and I saw two huge dewy eyes regarding me with interest. It was a small hair seal, its furry body marbled with dark brown, olive, and white, and as I turned, it slid silently below water again, then rolled forward and down, like a slow porpoise, and swam under the boat. All around me now seal heads were popping up, looking, and quietly diving again. It didn't seem much use fishing for salmon if a herd of seals was there, and I was about to pull up my line when I felt a tug. Immediately I started hauling in. The tug was heavier than a rock cod but unlike the twisting of dogfish or the violent jerks of a ling. As I reeled upward, wondering what it was – surely not a salmon – the line stopped dead as if it had hit a rock. I waited, let it go, pulled again, then there was a vast slow heave down, as if I'd hooked into a submarine. I resisted as hard as I dared without breaking the line, then suddenly it went free. I hauled it up with just a few minor wriggles and straight into the boat. There at my feet lay the ugliest, oddest-looking creature I'd ever seen. It had a boxlike head, long snout, bulbous eyes, spiky fins, and a long skinny body – skinny for the simple reason that a long nine-inch curve of it had been cleanly bitten out. Whatever it was, clearly one of the seals had intercepted it on the way up and had taken out its chest, stomach, and abdomen with one crunching bite.

Anxious to know if I had caught a rarity, I took it back and consulted a coloured fish chart I'd bought. I found it to be a ratfish, not unduly common but not rare either. Its most interesting quality was that its flank skin had bright rainbow hues, brighter even than a mackerel's skin. I felt if I stripped or mooched with a piece of that it might show up better than herring strip. I was sure too, that I had been using strips the wrong way. Holding it near the boat I had seen my strip turn around in slow spirals behind the dodger as I trolled. Surely, it ought to wriggle through the water, as would a small fish. Laboriously I cut two similar strips from the ratfish and sewed them together, giving a rainbow sheen to both sides of my lure. Then I experimented until I got it to go through the water in a straight path.

Late that afternoon as the sun began to sink toward Telnarko Island, I rowed out again to the ledge and tried my new bait. Again letting the boat drift over the reef, I mooched jerkily, let it sink, trolled a little, and was just about to give up at a fourth spot when I felt a sudden jag on the line. I flipped the rod tip – nothing there. As I wondered if it had just tipped a rock and whether I ought to take a look to see if the bait was still on the hook, the rod was almost pulled from my hand. The reel screamed, my rod tip shot below the surface, and all I could do was hang on – try to keep my fingers from the whirring reel handles yet still keep a slight pressure on the line so it didn't all unwind and get snagged up. On its first run the fish took out nearly fifty yards of line, then seemed to stop. Terrified it must have turned and might now be boring back and down to the reef and weeds to bury itself or cut the line, I reeled in frantically, ready to let the handle go at the first tug. When it came, the line was already travelling in the opposite direction. The fish must have stopped, turned upward toward the boat, passed it, and dived down again when my reeling in had caught it – for the loose line flashed to my right, slicing through the water with a musical swish. Then, unbelievably, the line started to curve upward again. Suddenly twenty yards away a silver giant shot clear of the water and hung in mid-air, shaking its head and whole body with a wet rattling sound. I just had time to see my hook embedded in the fleshy back part of its upper jaw and the lead weight sliding back, now loose, before the fish splashed down again and started to circle the boat. It dived twice more, the last one shallow, then I had it near the boat, gasping at the surface, its gulping gills forcing out jets of water as I held it there and luckily managed to gaff it the first time. My heart pounding more with excitement than with effort, I dropped it into the well of the boat where it snapped and jumped about so strongly I was afraid it would leap overboard again. I threw my coat over it and then, without even taking the rod down, I rowed home elated with joy.

It was my first salmon, caught with my own homemade lure – a great victorious day. I had no wish to stay and catch more. In my exultation I had a sudden wish to share my triumph with someone, even to have one of those ridiculous photos taken of myself, standing grinning beside the fish's inert body strung from a pole. But as I rowed back, my isolation was all too obvious. There was not another sign of human dwelling as far as the eye could see.

I got back and weighed the salmon with some fish scales I'd had since childhood – eight and one-half pounds. Was that all? I was sure it scaled at least twenty! I gutted the fish, removed its gills, then decided not to eat any until suppertime, when I'd be really hungry. I hit upon what seemed a cunning idea to keep it fresh. Instead of an indoor brine tank like Ed's, I'd hang it in the sea itself. Just as the old pioneers would hang a ham from a nearby branch, safely out of reach of marauding bears, so would I hang my salmon from a spar that projected out near my boat, midway in the water, safely out of reach of marauding crabs. Many times I had noticed when I'd thrown my cod heads into the ocean that dozens of tiny purple shore crabs with the charming

Latin name of *Hemigrapsus nudus* (sounding like one of the glamorous James Bond lady spies) would appear out of nowhere, scenting the fish heads from twenty yards away to converge upon them. I wrapped the salmon in a trouser leg and suspended it from the spar, weighting it down with a stone. Then I retired to sunbathe for what was left of the day.

Near the tent I had found a natural armchair formed by three rocks that faced due west. The rocks were covered in thick moss, a green carpet that softened the contours, and as I lay there on those blue and golden days, watching the ocean surface shimmering up into the balmy summer air, the seagulls wheeling silently above me, the distant ducks faintly spattering over the water, the moss seemed to pull the tiredness from my body. Around my inert form, the great yellow grasshoppers bounded upward into the air, then flitted about *zit zit zit* searching for their mates and flashing their pale green underwings before vanishing again into the grass. Even the mosquitoes and deer flies who would deliberately land out of sight under a knee or arm and probe furtively for a place to plunge seemed more amusing than annoying.

How ironic it seemed that I was now living with great joy on barely five dollars a week yet I was doing everything – sunbathing, swimming, fishing, rowing, trekking the wild places – that everyone I had left behind was slaving and saving for during their short holidays each year. Yet for me it was becoming just part of a natural way of life, not a brief frenzied escape when years of city life have so blunted one's senses one can barely understand the manifold subtleties of the wilderness. I had a lot to learn yet but what an open air university!

In the evening I hauled my salmon, deliciously cool, from its trouser-leg sea fridge, cut off a sizable steak to poach lightly in basil and marjoram for supper, and returned the rest of the fish to its bag. As the tiny purple crabs who had gathered beneath it but had found it far beyond reach scuttled away at my approach, I again congratulated myself on my brainwave. That night was unusually calm, and at times, half asleep, I fancied I heard faint splashings from below, but I took little notice. A morning earlier when peeping from my tent, I had seen my pack rat wobbling out of the kitchen and weaving its way over the rocky cliff. Following it quietly from above, I had seen it disappear into a crevice and had later examined the area. There seemed to be at least two nests in the crevice which ran back into a small tunnel between the rocks. The rats had hauled in sticks as thick as a man's thumb and lined them with leaves and shredded plant fibres. Outside, the rats' faeces seemed to have been deliberately dropped so as to make a short smooth black road over the angular rocks. And near the outside nest was a small store of fruit seeds, mouldy cheese rinds, meat scraps and vegetable peelings, all purloined from my garbage container. I resisted the temptation to burn out the nest. After all, if the rats could put my rubbish to good use it was as good as my burying it. They had as much right to be there as I had and they were not doing me any harm. In a way they were company. As I heard the splashings that night I imagined it was probably the pack rats having a nocturnal bath.

Next day as I sleepily walked down the rocky slope to my kitchen, I saw that the spar to which I had tied the salmon was twitching slightly. I hurried down the staircase

25

and hauled up the salmon while the snaky shadows, which I now saw were dogfish, sped off into deeper water. All that was left of my prize fish was its backbone, ribs, and head. The pants leg looked as if it had been torn apart by tiny sharks, which dogfish basically are. I had forgotten how, like little bloodhounds of the sea, dogfish can scent dead fish hundreds of yards away. No wonder Ed had a brine tank in his kitchen. I realized now, too, that seawater was not a strong enough saline solution to preserve fish. And it also had bacteria that would cause decomposition at a rate not much slower than fresh water. On my next visit to the store I sheepishly purchased some block salt. But I didn't give up the sea fridge idea entirely. The other pants leg kept clams, oysters, and mussels alive and fresh for many days, as their shells made them impervious to dogfish attacks.

The decision not to burn out the pack rats was perhaps the unconscious start of my desire to fit in with nature as far as possible. In my years there, I never built a boundary fence or cut any live trees apart from topping a couple of overcrowded pine that blocked sunlight from the platform. Even my little trail wound in and out around trees. Stumbling over root clusters seemed a fair enough price to pay for just having the trees that went with them still around the place. Slowly I found myself making friends with the animal life around me.

One day when I was cleaning codfish and throwing the entrails to gathering crabs, a group of seagulls landed. Straight away two big males began dominating the flock. There was a strict pecking order and, with wings up and beaks outstretched, they screamed at the others to stand back while they first ate their fill. But sometimes, I noticed, they slung out their throats and shrieked their unholy *keeyow keeyow ow ow* even when no other gull was near, as if for the sheer hell of making noise, Suddenly I felt a dab on my boot. A young brown-and-white speckled gull had waddled and belly-flopped over the rocks until it was right under the fish I was gutting, and was gulping down cod's tails, fins, skins as fast as he could, cramming one thing into his mouth before the other had gone down. He had a huge head, a soft duck-like beak, and I noticed his left foot was all bunched and twisted inward. As gulls are lucky if one chick survives to maturity from a nest each year, the chances against this odd runt surviving must have been fifty to one. I never saw its parents feed it although it peeped plaintively at any gull flying near. Clearly desperation had forced him to come close to me to pick up food the others dared not reach.

Gulls are the sheep of the sea-bird world, ungainly when not in flight and awkward over rocks and rough ground for which their webbed feet are ill-equipped, but Bert (I named him Bert because he looked like my concept of a Bert) was more awkward than any. After that first visit he took to hanging around the bottom of my staircase and he must have had a stomach made of steel, for he swallowed fish spines, heads, chunks of crust, potato peelings, decaying tomatoes, anything. My reluctant monthly fire to burn what little refuse I had left after the bushy-tailed rats had delved into my garbage almost ceased. I had little rubbish to burn when Bert was around. One morning after he had gulped down a particularly large set of fish spines, he suddenly flew to a rock, threw up the lot, and flew away, keeping to the side of the cliff. I couldn't understand it – until I saw a bald eagle gliding low over the water a mere two hundred yards away. Gulls often gulp down food in a hurry, regurgitate in a safer place, and eat again at leisure. And if there is danger about, they shed their load swiftly so they can fly away at top speed unhampered by the weight of the food. Sure enough, once the eagle was out of the way, back came Bert to gulp his breakfast down again.

Ugly and stunted though he was, nature had compensated Bert in one way – he had magnificent wings. They seemed almost a quarter larger than those of the other fledglings. Already he flew more easily than they and soared with less wing action.

As the other birds shunned or were actively antagonistic toward his efforts to stay part of the flock, Bert became more and more a loner. I had an odd feeling of kinship as I saw him by himself down there on the sand at low tide, stamping to bring worms to the surface or tossing over pieces of seaweed on the rocks as he looked for molluscs or baby crabs.

No sooner was I used to having Bert around than another guest arrived, also without a visiting card, and while he overstayed his welcome, he was the sort of guest one hardly asks to leave. Sitting at supper one night, I was astonished when a small black-and-white animal wandered straight into the kitchen, blinked at me in the candlelight, decided I was no danger, and promptly toddled over both my feet, sniffed at me again as if to say "Do you *have* to stick your big feet out in my way like this?" and started rummaging among the empty cans in my garbage box. I was so astonished I didn't move – which was just as well, for with its pointed head, broad lateral white stripes along its glossy black body, and its arched bushy tail, my new friend was a striped skunk. All I knew about skunks was that if you scared them they promptly discharged twin barrels of acrid oil at you that smelled so obnoxious the only way to get rid of it was to burn everything it touched. I sat there petrified, not moving a muscle, while His Lordship ambled about good-naturedly, ignoring me as if I were some lowly tenant on his estate and he was just making sure I was keeping everything in good order.

The skunk is the true king of the animals, for his stench glands have won him a unique respect and he knows it. Not even the coyote or cougar dares assail his dignity as he toddles about unless they're nearly starving in a harsh winter. So confident are skunks of the deterrent power of their twin anal guns that their biggest enemy is probably automobiles, for they trot along highways as arrogantly as this one was now inspecting my premises and of course they often get run over. Only the great horned owl and the golden eagle, who probably have no or little sense of smell, regard the skunk as a tasty dish. As my forceful guest retired behind my filing cabinet with some boiled fish scraps, I quietly sneaked up to bed. Halfway through the night I was awakened by loud snoring noises that seemed to come from right beneath me. I was sure the skunk was sleeping off his meal in the box of woollen scraps I kept on the cabinet. I wasn't going to disturb him, so I stuffed bits of handkerchiefs in my ears and went back to sleep.

Next day I paid one of my infrequent visits to the distant store and as there was no sign of the skunk at breakfast, I thought he'd probably moved on. One of the men who ran the store saw me stocking up with bottles of milk and asked if I'd like some

27

fresh, from their own cow. I jumped at the chance, for fresh milk was a rarity on the coast. Out back we went and he handed me almost a whole pail. I carefully placed the treasured creamy liquid on the truck floor by the seat, where I could hold it steady when driving, and went back for a tin of strawberries. I intended to skim off the cream when I got back and treat myself to a good, old-fashioned English country tea. Getting that pail of milk back to the tent was a tricky business. I even left the truck by the road so as not to jolt and spill it, then carried it down the old logging track and winding trail carefully.

That evening I had no sooner demolished two large helpings of my treat when His Lordship returned and, as before, ignored me as he waddled about helping himself. Cautiously placing my precious pail of milk between boxes on a high shelf, I quietly crept up to bed.

Next morning there was milk everywhere. Although the pail was still half full, black and white hairs told the whole sad story. The skunk, greedily drinking, had momentarily fallen in. It was no time to be finicky, however, for fresh milk was far too scarce to waste. I strained it through the treble thickness of an old sheet a few times, and apart from a slight muskiness, it tasted good enough.

For four more nights the skunk shared my home and was the epitome of good manners, apart from his nightly snoring. He was easygoing, amiable, and his motto seemed clear: "You mind yours and I'll mind mine. If you don't, look out!" Why the skunk is called the devil's child I don't know, for skunks never look for trouble. They even share their homes with a scared rabbit or woodchuck, amicably forage for food alongside porcupines or raccoons. Then he disappeared. Two weeks later an old retired logger was complaining at the store that a couple of skunks had set up home beneath his cabin three miles north of me, and he was going to smoke them out. I said nothing. His Lordship had clearly decided my dwelling was substandard – or his wife had.

Now I began to notice an odd thing on fine mornings just as the sun was winking through the trees – all the rocks below the cliff seemed covered in a sort of fur. At first I took it to be a trick of the light or the way the tide left the seaweed, but one day I went down for a closer look. As I drew near I heard a clattering sound and then all the rock surfaces were *moving* – thousands of little crabs had been sitting on them, basking in the early warmth, and the sound was made by their tiny armoured bodies hitting the shale as they scuttled away from my shadow.

Although the shore crabs always flocked to my feet when I was gutting fish, I'd never realized how vast were their populations until that moment. No wonder at times they appeared almost to wait for me to return from fishing trips, to compete for the scraps I dropped! There were crabs everywhere, none over one and one-half inches across the shell, and along with Bert and the other gulls, they ate everything I didn't burn.

That afternoon when the sun was at its height, as an experiment, I dropped a cod's head into the edge of the sea. There was not a crab in sight. In four minutes forty-two crabs had appeared from nowhere and were scrambling over each other, the bigger ones elbowing their smaller cousins out of the way. Grabbing what they could when they could and daintily transferring nips of fish flesh to their mouth parts, they looked for all the world like little jewellers delving into a bag of rough diamonds, squabbling and quarrelling, moving jerkily about, hiding in the thousands of stony crevices as my shadow moved.

Crabs are the most extraordinary creatures. They have chemical perceptors on their antennae, mouths, and legs so they can detect food at great distances and even taste with their legs as well as their mouths. If a fish grabs one of their ten legs they can snap it off at will and grow a new one. They can even grow new eyes. They have 180-degree vision, camouflage their bodies with dark and light pigments according to the twenty-four-hour rhythm of night and day, can bulldoze objects forty times their own weight under water, and are able to reverse their breathing systems so that they can hide under sand and still breathe if an enemy approaches. They have special wipers to keep their gills free of dirt, most can run over land faster than they can travel in water, and they can also breathe above and below water with equal ease. Unlike most marine animals, they take a good deal of time over their mating, and the male crab treats his girl friend, who can only make love when her new skin is soft after a shell moult, with exaggerated courtesy and care. Above all, most of the world's 4,400 species of crabs are perfect scavengers and, with man treating the oceans as an external disposal dump, they do trojan work filtering and breaking down pollutive sewage, offal, rubbish, and waste products. Over the summer weeks, I gradually learned such respect for the crab kingdom that I lost my appetite for crab dinners.

Occasionally, usually in the early morning, I saw the bald eagle flying low over the tent. Sometimes I'd hear the high-pitched *kri-kri-kri* first, an oddly squeaky sound for so large and powerful a bird, and I'd rush to the mosquito netting to catch a pre-breakfast glimpse as he set off on his regular hunting trip around his territory. It never occurred to me there might be more than one eagle in my area until one morning I was awakened by an odd drumming or flapping sound near the tent.

I hurried to the window to see an extraordinary sight. High above the bay two eagles, their giant talons interlocked as if in a fight to the death, were whirling down in a great spiral, tumbling over and over for several hundred feet, and as they fell their wing and snow-white tail feathers were being beaten backward and forward by the rushing air, sounding like flapping sails. Just as I thought they must fall to their deaths, they let go, and the smaller bird pulled out in a beautiful curve and effortlessly banked upward again, riding higher and higher, while the larger eagle flapped away to the south, also gaining height. As I watched spellbound, the smaller eagle angled toward the other and as it flashed down from the windless sky, great talons extended, the other performed a perfect somersault and presented its claws. Once more interlocked, they fell until again, just above the surface, they separated and the larger female set off to the north, with the male beating along, seeming calmer and more content now, in her wake. What I had seen was not a fight at all but a rare part of their courtship display, and as they flew over the last spit of land their faint metallic cries came back to my cars long after they had disappeared from view. It was the most impressive sight I had witnessed in the wild.

29

Now a swallowtail butterfly came hopping and dropping through the warm air before alighting on a leaf. As it spread the yellow sheen of its wings it was the very ornament of nature, a lovely insect that had changed from a heedless, insatiable grub to become a joy to the world. I suddenly felt as if I was back in the magical days of childhood. The memory of the eagles' display stayed in my mind for days, yet it perplexed me too, for by this time of year they would hardly be courting. It was late May and surely they must have a nest somewhere, with perhaps a youngster in it if they had bred successfully. I didn't think of looking for the nest. Eagles easily cover two hundred miles in a day of normal hunting and I assumed any nest they might have would be many miles away.

4 Eagles, Killer Whales, and Other Neighbours

*U*nconsciously, since Ed had left, I'd been turning more and more to the animals around me for a kind of companionship. After the unforgettable air dance of the eagles, I felt my keen curiosity about nature expanding even more. I knew bald eagles had been declining in recent years and it was strangely important that I now find out more about them.

It wasn't until June that I first thought their nest could be nearby. I noticed the male was flying south over my tent early each morning, returning around midday, and also flying over again before dusk. Such a regular pattern made it seem likely he was feeding his mate and one or even two youngsters, though I knew it was rare for bald eagles to rear two eaglets successfully in a season. Yet it appeared an impossible task to try and find the nest. Anyone who has ever tried to follow an eagle on foot over rough terrain knows how hopeless and clumsy even a fit man feels, for this great bird, weighing from ten to fourteen pounds, soars so effortlessly on its broad wings – which can span nearly eight feet – that it will cover twenty miles in a few minutes. Then at dusk one evening an extraordinary thing happened.

I was sitting idly in a clump of alders on the cliff edge watching my pack rats' nesting crevice. It was an oddly mosquito-free evening, probably between hatches, and I'd been there half an hour. One rat had already been out and had toured two tidal pools in the rocks below, and I wanted to see what it was up to. After another ten minutes, my perch was becoming uncomfortable and I was about to go when the rat came out again, sniffed the air cautiously, and walked off with its odd tottery gait toward the pools. Then a movement in the sky above the northerly land spit caught my eye. The male eagle had skimmed the fir trees and was coming toward me in a long glide. When halfway across the bay it banked and landed in a tree on the shore. For a few seconds it appeared to be staring hard in my direction and my first thought was that it had spied me. The pack rat, short-sighted as are all rodents, had seen nothing, of course, and was sniffing slowly along under a small rocky ridge that must have shielded it from the eagle's view.

The next moment the eagle had launched itself from the tree. It gave a few quick wing beats as it dropped low and came beating along the surface of the sea, it came straight toward me, swooped over the ridge at the last moment, dropped down with a rush of feathers and snatched my former raider in its talons, virtually pouncing on it, and flapped away transferring the rat to one foot and retracting the other like a jet leaving a runway. Eagles rarely use their beaks when killing small prey and one gripping stab of those two-inch talons had crushed the life from the big rat.

The most extraordinary thing about the attack, apart from my actually seeing it, was how the eagle had apparently planned it. It had clearly sat up in that tree and worked out that if it flew down low, keeping the rocky ridge between itself and its victim, the rat had little chance of escape.

Often now the eagles flew directly over my boat, sometimes quite low and without even looking down, as if I had become if not a friend at least a familiar and clearly harmless figure. They saw me long before I could see them, for their eyesight is at least three times as fine as a man's, and where a man might see a mere buff patch on a mossy escarpment half a mile away, the eagle would see three rock rabbits and even which way they were looking.

I still wonder what inspired the name bald eagle, for bald it certainly is not. Its strong, wedge-shaped head is covered with magnificent glossy white feathers, rightful apparel for the king of birds.

I began to have some extraordinary experiences with them. When fishing, often I'd bring up a red snapper too small to eat and would let it go. If it had come from a great depth its eyes would be popping and its air bladder distended because of the lighter pressure at the surface, and struggle though it might, it could not swim down again until its pressure system adjusted itself, which could take several minutes. This happened one afternoon when I was opposite a small government island, and I was leisurely rowing away from the fish flopping on the surface when I spied the eagle a mile away to the south. It seemed he had seen the fish, for he at once went into his long gliding stoop, covered the mile in less than a minute, paused briefly with a great rush of wings, snatched the fish up with his talons, then flew toward the island. I tried leaving a fish again and, within minutes, out from the island came the eagle again, missed the fish with its first swoop but plucked it easily with the second and again it beat back to the island.

One day I was astonished to see the male eagle stoop at a salmon rolling on the surface – and promptly disappear as the big fish dived in an effort to get away. The eagle did not let go, however, but actually tightened its grip, clearly piercing the fish's insides with its sharp scimitars, and presently both eagle and fish came up some five yards farther on. As I watched, stupefied, from a distance, the eagle then seemed to row itself and its prey ashore, half flying at first in a frantic effort to rise, then hunching itself along, swimming with half-folded wings. In the shallows it appeared to bounce on the fish as it again tried to fly but only succeeded in dragging the salmon onto the stony shore where it left it, still twitching, and flew to a low branch where it sunned its great wings. Eagles do not have oiled feathers like ducks or gulls and on the rare occasions, like the incredible one I'd just seen, that they get waterlogged, they have to dry out their wings like a cormorant. By now I was sure the eagles must have a nest nearby – they always seemed to be around the government island and I now realized it was dead in line with their frequent flights over the northern spar of land as seen from my tent.

It was on June 16 that I finally located the nest. I had rowed back to the island with the idea of feeding the eagles if I could. I caught a small rock cod from a deep hole and, just to see if it would work, I tied the horny lip of its mouth to some light fishing line, then, allowing the line to run off my rod and reel, rowed quietly away some two hundred yards. I watched the big trees carefully and after a few minutes, one of the eagles launched itself from a tall fir with an unusually flat top and began to soar to and fro above the fish, taking a good look at it. It was the female, and just below the top of the tree I could see a dark mass of sticks – the nest at last! Probably because her mate was away hunting, she had soared directly from it.

As she glided and flapped above my fish I was sure she would see the attached line, but finally she swooped down and grabbed the cod. The reel screamed. I tugged it lightly and instantly she dropped it again. But back she came, dived, and scooped up the fish. She could obviously see the line but either didn't connect it with me or reckoned she could get the fish off it without danger. Again I tugged, hoping she would fight for the fish, but again she let go immediately. Three times this happened, then the fish sank from sight. I hadn't anticipated this and by the time I'd rowed to the deep hole and caught two more, the male had returned.

Together the two eagles perched on low bushes and watched as I dropped both fish into the water and rowed away. It had been fun playing tug-of-war with an eagle, but I had no wish to disturb their nesting. More than anything I now wanted to find if they still had young and if possible to observe the eaglets.

Next day in the low dawn light I rowed back to the island, landed out of sight, and quietly stole through the forest until, some two hundred yards from the shore, the splashings of white droppings on twigs, bushes, and the ground beneath a giant fir gave the unmistakable clues. The tree was a good five feet thick at the base and as I looked up, the massive nest spanned a V-fork between two branches and hugged the trunk some 120 feet above my head. It was a good six feet across, and some of the twigs in it were branches almost as thick as a man's wrist. If the mother eagle was brooding right now I could not see, for despite being over three feet long, neither her beak nor her tail projected over the edges of her immense home.

The rocky ground rose steeply from the shore and fifty yards away I started to climb a small cedar and was only a few feet above the ground when the female eagle dropped down from her nest and glided out to sea, turning south. I hadn't climbed a tree since boyhood so I took my time, surprised to find I had to fight against a slight vertigo. At twenty-five feet, wedging my feet across two level branches and clasping the trunk with one hand for dear life, I took out my old pocket telescope and steadied it against the trunk.

There were *two* young eaglets in the nest. One was partly fledged, with wing and tail quills just starting to sprout, but the smaller one was still in the white downy stage. As I watched, it stumbled around the nest, its own large hind claw seeming to trip it up on the sticks of the rim. The other sat contentedly, fat and secure in the centre of the nest, and I judged it was getting the lion's share of the food.

It was an exciting discovery. Since World War II, bald eagles and some other birds of prey have been declining drastically, largely due to agricultural pesticides that are absorbed by the rodents the birds eat and that, washed into rivers by rainstorms, enter the tissues of their fish prey too. The build-up of poison induces sterility, and also causes them to lay more fragile, thin-shelled eggs, which break easily in the nest. So finding this nest with two young was a stroke of luck. I was just wondering how to build a small hide in the tree so I could occasionally watch their progress without upsetting them when I heard a rushing noise, I looked up – the mother eagle had seen me, had swung around in a large arc to come from behind, and was making great power dives over my tree. She banked, turned, and dived down, roaring past me with what seemed hurricane speed. Although she never came closer than seven or eight yards, probably because I wasn't near enough to be a total threat, I got down that tree as fast as I could. Above all, I didn't want to upset her so much that she abandoned her nest, though I felt this was unlikely now that she had hungry young. Indeed, before I'd walked more than a few yards she flew back to her nest, folded her great wings, and settled down to brood.

The hide gave me problems. I fiddled about for two whole days and ended with a three-foot-wide circle of wands, tied it to a branch above, and stretched the sacking "walls" from it. Three small driftwood planks would make a platform across two lower branches. On the fourth day, after making sure neither eagle was at the nest, I hauled everything up by rope and hastily got it into place.

Sitting on alternate haunches, propped up by one elbow for two hours or more, watching eagles through a wavering telescope held in the other hand became an endurance test. And when the sun rose and shone on the sacking, the temperature inside rose to over 100° F.

But the rewards were worth it. The beauty of a sacking hide, apart from its lightness, is that while you can see out easily through the walls (I also made a small view hole for my field glass), the bird or animal cannot see in. Twice the inquisitive female landed on a branch a mere few feet away. I was afraid she would try to tear the hide to pieces, but she didn't. She just perched there, great gnarled talons looking as if they were strangling the branch, and glared. Gazing into that mad dandelion eye, so fierce it seemed to peer into your very soul, its iris expanding and contracting like some magical camera lens as the bird changed focus on objects near and far, was awe inspiring.

Several times her smaller mate, who seemed to do all the hunting for the family, used the broad branch of a nearby tree to hold down and tear up his prey. Mostly he brought dead fish straight to the nest and dropped them before his mate. Sometimes she greeted him with a half-threat display of raised head and neck feathers and lifted wings, looking every bit like the great spread eagle of church lecterns and old carvings. At other times she treated him to soft nibbles against his beak, as if thanking him. I could see no reason for the difference, except she may have been hungrier when she looked threatening. But it was when he caught a rock rabbit or a squirrel that I first witnessed the eagle's enormous strength for its size. He brought the dead, furry body to the branch, placed both feet at opposite ends, and tore away the fur and flesh from the back until the spine was exposed. Then with but one or two powerful wrenches with beak and neck, he tore the animal in two. A man would have been hard put to do that. Then he ripped up one-half of the animal into smaller pieces and swallowed them, skin and all, before flying to the nest with the other. A clear case of me first, but in the wild it made good sense – his strength to hunt was of great importance when he was feeding four birds. Sometimes, as the eaglets grew older, the female would glare up and around at the circle of sky, then long before I saw anything she would fly off to meet her mate. Twice I saw her come back alone with food and feed the young but I only saw the male feed the young once, while his mate was absent. As far as I could see, the female never received food from him in flight, as peregrine or hobby falcons do, and usually she returned to the nest first, waiting for him to deliver the goods.

The larger eaglet was much more active than the smaller downy one, but the other remained out of things, usually near the rim of the nest. I deduced perhaps a week had passed between laying the two eggs, accounting for the difference in size, yet the mother made no special concessions to her weaker chick. She fed the nearest eaglet first, and that was nearly always the bigger one. It was an oddly moving sight to see this mighty bird, gentle with maternal love, ripping up the prey into small strips of flesh, then daintily offering them with the very tip of her powerful bill to the weak and gawky eaglets. She always fed them before eating herself.

I still fed the parent birds with fish some afternoons but while I fancied they might now recognize me as a benefactor, I didn't take any foolish chances at scaring them from the nest. Too often we humans read things into a wild animal's behaviour that just are not there, and no bird of prey, I knew, could have anything like gratitude in its make-up. My rule was not to visit the hide more than twice a week and usually in the dark before dawn. After the eaglets were fed they sank into a deep snooze and if the sun was out, the mother sometimes flew away for some exercise. Then I could leave. But often she also sank down and went to sleep, and I'd be stuck there until after the next visit by the male with food. Then she'd usually leave for a spell – and let me leave too.

In early July I became worried about the smaller eaglet. It was not growing proportionately as fast as its companion and twice almost fell off the nest rim, only regaining its balance by a weak flapping of its embryo wings and grabbing for dear life onto sticks with its beak. I decided to leave them alone a whole week.

One afternoon, giving the island a wide berth, I rowed straight out to the farthest islands two miles out in the strait to try for a salmon on the reef beyond. As I drew near, I saw a swirling in the sea just offshore. Some hair seals seemed to be splashing about in the shallows, then lunging at the smooth slab rocks and hauling themselves up with their odd caterpillar hunching movements as fast as they could go. They had an air of panic, blinking their sleepy eyes more rapidly than usual, and kept looking at the water, then at each other – a sure sign they were scared. Like sheep, young seals always look to their elders for leadership.

I could see nothing that could have disturbed them and was rowing smoothly past, some two hundred yards offshore, when my rowing boat gave a sudden surge. I caught a glimpse of something white flashing across my path and beneath my boat, and then a smoothly rounded, thick black object surfaced about thirty yards to my

35

right, headed toward the boat, rising up until it was some four feet high, then, at what seemed the last moment, turned away in a quarter circle. As I sat there, too paralysed with fear even to pull in the oars, I saw the triangular, curved-back-at-the-tip shape of the fin and the glossy streamlined body behind it. Then the double flukes of a vast tail came momentarily out of the water, gave two convulsive up and down strokes that drove the creature down again into the depths, and left my boat swirling in the eddy. Another broad, blunt-beaked black head like some enormous sparrow surfaced on my left, sank back again without a ripple, then re-emerged, completely perpendicular, higher and higher, until I saw the snow-white underjaw and throat and the bright, pig-like eye. Then, quite peacefully, it sank back down again. In those brief, terror-stricken moments, I became aware that other vast shapes were now swimming round the boat. I was in the middle of a pack of killer whales.

My one thought was how to get away without provoking attack. I didn't dare withdraw the oars in case the movement angered them. A professed agnostic, vainly contemptuous of most organised religions' view of God, I now found myself praying fervently to that God, the simple God of my childhood. I had never been so terrified. I didn't know what to do. As the killers circled the boat, I was all too conscious of the flimsy plywood between myself and them, my hands braced against the sloping sides for the shock of their first attack. My mind raced with stories I'd read about these voracious sea mammals: how they are the largest predators left on earth, whose males can reach thirty-one feet, and are capable of swallowing a man whole; how a group of killers can ram and batter the giant grey or bowhead whales, semi-paralysed with fear, into submission and tear out their tongues when still alive. Totally helpless, I had virtually given myself up for lost, my fear turning into a sort of stupor, when I realized the boat, bobbing like a cork in their circling and diving movements, had drifted within forty yards of the island. And as I prayed for it to go even nearer so I could try a sudden dash, it slowly dawned on me that the killers had no intention of attacking. If they had they would surely have done so by now. I was conscious too of an acrid, fishy smell, and as one killer surfaced near me again I heard a flubbery hissing sound, saw its quarter-moon shaped blow hole open and exhale a vapour that was slightly misty, even in that warm air, and the fishy smell increased. I noticed too that their movements were not at all violent, in fact became strangely conscious that perhaps they were merely playing and fooling around, for while one would hang perpendicular in the water appearing to look at me, another would do the same but facing away from me, as if idly surveying the distant ocean scene. It was perhaps the oddest part of the experience, the slow realization that they were not bent on destruction or eating me. When I was within fifteen yards of the rocky shore, I took heart, grabbed the oars, and flailing away like a madman, rode up onto a slab of rock and leaped out in one movement, muttering a heartfelt, thankful prayer.

Twenty yards up the shore I turned around. The killers were still lounging about where I had been, but none had followed my boat. Now that I was safe, I was shivering as if with shock. I wondered how I would get back. Yet it was clear they were merely sporting about for sometimes one would chase another, which would then smash its flukes flat against the water before surging down in a power dive. Then I realized that nearly all the horror tales of killer whales I'd read and heard occurred much farther north or south, in or near Arctic and Antarctic waters, where because of the cold and lack of sufficient food they were perhaps more voracious from hunger. Here, in the stretch of the Pacific between the Baja California and the Alaska border, and especially along the protected three hundred miles of island-studded straits between Vancouver Island and the mainland, the summer waters abounded with shoals of salmon and herring, with cod, halibut, porpoise, dolphin, and seals, and the many marine forms that make up their prey. I had probably been safe simply because they were not hungry. I remembered now, too, that not one of the fishermen I'd met while working on the salmon boats had ever vouchsafed a story of killers attacking men in these waters.

As I watched, what I took to be a large male surfaced beyond the others. His triangular dorsal fin seemed some five or six feet high and turned over slightly at the top, Whether he was their pack leader or not I cannot say, but he suddenly dived, re-surfaced farther out, and began to bore along the water, toward the open strait, travelling at great speed, and one by one the others ceased their circling and diving and followed him out. Soon they had all disappeared from sight. The sun was sinking before I plucked up courage to row back.

It was two weeks before I rowed as far as the salmon reef again, and I kept clear of the two outlying islands as they seemed places where the killers would feed when hungry, though I imagined they did most of their feeding around dawn, leaving the midday heat for rest and sport, then travelled mostly by night to new hunting grounds. I only saw killer whales twice more, once out near the reef when a small group swam by as if heading to some definite place up north, and once in the harbour mouth five miles up the coast, where again they seemed quite docile.

Killer whales are not true whales but belong to the toothed-whale family of dolphins. They have an array of teeth that is perhaps the most fearsome in the mammal world – from ten to thirteen pairs of sharp, conical spikes, up to three inches long, in both upper and lower jaws. When their mouth is closed, the teeth interlock perfectly with each other, like a giant steel, trap from which, once grabbed, nothing escapes.

The British Columbia coast, with its thousands of miles of etiolated coastline, is the last main stronghold of the killer whales. I have been in remote bars up and down that coast where someone will walk in and say, "There's a pack of killers in the bay tonight." And so common a sight is it, few bother to go out and look. Indeed the largest catch of killers – seven – was made less than ten miles north of me when some fishermen strung out three lines of flimsy salmon nets between them and the open sea. And the killers, well known for their timidity before strange objects, never once tried to escape. All were finally sold to sea aquariums where they became completely docile and trainable like the big dolphins they are.

Although killer whales have not been kept by man nearly as long as ordinary dolphins, the first surviving captive, Namu, in 1965, soon showed he had the dolphins' attributes. His owner, Ted Griffin, who often swam with him at his Seattle Public Aquarium, said the whale never made the slightest aggressive gesture toward him

37

and it was like "being followed by a large friendly dog". Since then, many other oceanariums have acquired them. Trainers claim they are even faster at learning than their smaller cousins. Some years ago at the Seaworld Aquarium in San Diego, a killer whale gripped the girl who had been riding him by the leg in front of a horrified audience and dragged her round the pool. Papers revelled in the story of her "miraculous escape". But the trainer was right when he said the girl had been dragged back simply because she had cut the usual game time short and the killer wanted to finish the routine. In fact his great teeth had not punctured her skin. Nevertheless it is hard to reconcile the proven docility of the killer in captivity with the blood-thirsty stories of its cunning, greed, and voracity in the wild. Certainly they were placid enough each time I met them in the open sea.[*]

Ten days passed after my experience with the killers before I went back to see how the eagles were faring. A forty-eight-hour deluge had forced me to spend a whole day drying out the tent, bedclothes, and books, and when I climbed up to the hide it had been so battered by the gales and rain it had to be reset. A brief glance had already showed me the mother eagle was missing and the nest looked strangely empty, though I could see something in it. Fixing the hide as best I could and wringing out the sacking around the frayed view hole, I poked the telescope through – only the feathered eaglet remained in the nest. Of the smaller one there was no sign.

I scrambled down the pine and rocky slope to the base of the fir, sure I'd find the eaglet's body. I searched the ground and nearby bushes but there was no trace of it, not even a wisp or two of down showing where it might have been dragged off by some fox, mink or raccoon. I looked up. No, it was not caught on any branch or spike of the fir's trunk either. It had completely disappeared. Whatever predator had taken it had been big and strong enough to carry it without dragging.

It was a sad discovery. It was uncommon enough for the eagles to have reared two young to the stages they had but clearly the second eaglet, smaller and weaker because of its later birth, had been unable to compete for food any longer and had suffered a harsh but common fate. I never saw the eaglets fight when the mother was present but occasionally when she had gone, the bigger would peck at the smaller, sit on its head or harry it around the nest, keeping the centre spot for itself.

No sooner was I back in the hide than the remaining eaglet roused itself from sleep and began to stagger perilously over the vast nest, still tripping over its own disproportionately large talons. But its feathers were well-grown now, white down clinging only here and there in isolated wisps. The bird stood up and flapped its wings weakly, clinging hard to the sticks, then stared up at the sky, appeared to see something, immediately went into a crouch and started to squeak. I looked up too, saw nothing, but in less than a minute one of its parents came into sight with something in its talons.

The mother eagle landed with a large, dead rock cod, momentarily hovering as the eaglet, cheeping and prostrating itself in its eagerness to be fed, kept blocking her

[*] This was long before modern studies of the animal, and the *Free Willy* films.

landing spot. As soon as she was down, the youngster started pecking at the fish, while from the other end the mother trapped it with a talon and hauled off skin and scales, flicking them away with her beak. At times they seemed to be having a tug of war, probably good for the eaglet's developing muscles. It was one of the few times I'd seen the mother return with prey and alone. Maybe she had met the male a few miles away, taken her nest share from him, thus allowing him to carry on around his territory. It made sense. By now the eaglet was big and feathered well enough not to need daytime brooding.

I didn't think the male was having as much trouble feeding his family as some naturalists believe. Eagles hunt mostly at early morning and dusk, when small mammals are more often out searching for their own food and live fish are more inclined to be lolling around at the surface. They never kill for pleasure, will take a dead fish rather than pursue a live one, and do not need food every day. One rock rabbit or marmot or a four-pound fish will satisfy an eagle's appetite for two days or even three. They do not waste time or take unnecessary risks nor do they pursue their quarry into forests where their wings could get damaged. Their bodies, light for the size of their large wings, need minimum effort to change angle and area and to glide in shallow stoops upon prey at speeds up to ninety miles per hour. This, plus their incredible stereoscopic eyesight and powerful talons, enables them to size up their chances of a kill and to make it with the least delay. They usually kill in the open and at the height they fly they can probably see several prey at once, decide which is easiest, and go for that one alone.

When its mother had flown away again, the eaglet tramped around the nest rim, sometimes looking perilously over the edge. Then it would sink into a stupor or even roll over on its side like a playful dog and doze with its neck outstretched on the dirty nest sticks. By now it was eating some of the fur, skin, scales, and bones of the prey and regurgitating the indigestible bits in pellets that were gradually trampled into the nest structure. The nest must have smelled foul for as far as I could see none of the birds made any deliberate effort to drop their pellets overboard, though some fell off naturally.

Half an hour later the eaglet woke, stood up, tramped about again, flapped its blunt wings a few times, then started peering anxiously at the sky. But its mother did not appear again in the hour I remained. Instead the eaglet picked at some rabbit remains and, to my delight, once trapped them awkwardly with one foot as it tugged at the tendons. Its foot didn't hold too well, the rabbit slipped out, and the eaglet fell over backward, but it tried again and again, finally pulling off a morsel to swallow.

After another week the eaglet was spending most of its days alone. Once I saw its mother return with what looked like a half-shredded chipmunk that I presumed had been given her by her smaller mate, who would be better adapted to catch such small, rapidly moving prey. She dropped it by the eaglet, saw the youngster stumble over to it and mantle its wings as if protecting it from her; then she flew away, making no attempt to feed it herself. I saw the male return to the nest only once more – and the female immediately crouched threateningly, spread her wings, and screeched at him.

He looked quite abashed, landed in a nearby tree, and started looking out to sea as if embarrassed by his mate's attitude. Three days later I returned. The nest was empty. I looked round the area and saw the eaglet, now fully fledged, sitting on a thick branch close to the trunk of a big fir. It must have made its first short flight and now it stood there for over an hour as if afraid to move. The sun was dying behind the islands in the strait when the mother returned to the empty nest. She landed there and stood with an oddly lost look, like the parent of an only child who has just left home for the first time. Then she looked at the eaglet and it looked back at her. It lifted each foot slowly and moved inch by inch along the bough toward its home. It looked at the sky, down at the ground, and its face had an almost fearful expression, as if not only wondering how it had got there but how on earth it was to get back. The mother eagle did nothing. The eaglet started to flap its wings, harder and harder, jumping up and down on the bough but clinging to it as if trying to break it off, then suddenly it leaped up into the slight wind and flapped without any difficulty straight back to the nest, landing so awkwardly it cannoned into its mother. The eaglet was now three months old and he was ready to face the world.

Two days later as I performed my usual scramble down the rocks from the tent to my kitchen for breakfast, I was startled by a massive, mottled light-brown-and-chocolate-coloured bird that leaped, half-flying, from one rock to another, across my beach. It was the eaglet. It was the first time I'd seen it from above and it seemed larger than either of its parents, fatter and with bigger wings. I decided to try to feed it, and perhaps get it used to coming to my beach for food. I took a cod fillet from my brine fridge and gingerly worked my way down the log staircase. By the time I was halfway down, the eaglet still had not moved but was watching me intently. I threw the fish with a minimum of movement so it landed near the eaglet, but the flop of the fish on the rocks scared it and immediately it leaped into the air, half-inclined its body against the westerly breeze, and flapped in this odd, sideways fashion right across the bay, over the spit of land, and was lost from sight. But the thought it might return of its own free will if it knew I would provide food was an exciting one.

When a golden eagle escaped from the London Zoo in February 1965, attempts to catch it attracted more headlines, plus radio and TV coverage, than any other single event in Britain that year. In the thirteen days Goldie was free, thousands flocked from all over the capital, others sent parcels of scraps and drawings of suggested traps and starred him in advertising copy, political cartoons, stage jokes – everyone unconsciously paying homage to the proud, fierce, solitary king of birds whose desire for freedom reflected their own needs. My flat had been near the park and twice seeing this great bird perched in the trees had been just another incident prompting my own escape into the wilds.

It was a week before I saw the eaglet again, and now I was certain it was a female, judging by its great size. She came flapping toward my bay while her parents soared and circled high in the sky, as if keeping an eye on their progeny. The first weeks of a young eagle's life are its most critical. No one knows if bald eagles actually teach their young to hunt, but they invariably stay with them for a few weeks. If the youngster could fly some of the way on their hunting trips, she would certainly pick up the few tips she would need to survive. I threw out another piece of fish, hoping she would now see it for what it was and take it. But no, she landed on a large rock, looked at it briefly, then took off again following her parents to the south of my land. And then I was glad.

In the past twenty years, bald eagles had been on the decline and I felt that to have just one more soaring free in the skies was a far greater reward than having it half tame, a mere enhancement to human ego. I only saw her once more, one day when she beat her way across the bay, the mottled light and sooty brown streaks on her chest glittering as if burnished by the morning sun. She had now learned to glide and seemed to be revelling in her new-found skills.

I am convinced eagles actually enjoy their powers of flight, that they often spiral upward, wafting around on thermal air currents, for the sheer sensual pleasure – just like a man on a bicycle down a long gradient amid beautiful scenery, only more so.

As I dismantled the hide and the platform, though, I remembered the only sad note from my days of eagle watching, the death of the smaller eaglet. Its complete disappearance, so sudden and with no trace, seemed yet another reminder of nature's harsh unconcern for the weak.

5   The Bad and the Good

A man living alone in the wilds soon finds the "harmony of nature" is a mere myth, and the "divine plan" is rather a callous system in which each species struggles to survive against others. In nature the individual life is of little account.

The inexperienced man in the wilderness survives only by trial and error. He must learn fast for there are few second chances. He needs to develop a monumental patience, for he cannot hurry the seasons nor change the weather. He is forced to capitulate to nature's forces, to bend with the gales, to shelter from the rains, to learn to make the most of the calmer periods – and all the while to maintain eternal vigilance, which must become part of his subconscious.

The high cliff path I had walked a hundred times was perhaps even more dangerous than the first time, for one careless step born of familiarity kills just as surely as chance. One morning, by now well used to my log staircase and feeling extra joyful that overnight rains had been replaced by a brilliantly blue sky, I hurried down it to catch some fresh fish. My right heel hit some loose bark and skidded inward on the wet, slippery wood, and down I went. Only a shale-covered ledge projecting from the cliff six feet below prevented my being dashed onto the rocky beach. Groaning with pain, my shirt sticking bloodily to my back, I crawled up the staircase on all fours. The only way I could apply a dressing on the two-inch gash near my spine was to stick it on one of the log pillars of the kitchen, back onto it with the help of a mirror, and tie the ends of a strip of old sheet around my chest. As I couldn't row the boat without reopening the wound, I became a vegetarian for ten days! Two days after the accident a high spring tide, fanned even higher by a stiff westerly, floated a huge drift log into the back of my boat and knocked it off its wharf. Trying to haul it back up a cedar pole runway at an angle of forty-five degrees, even with the aid of gin-pole pulleys, and at the same time to keep my back straight to keep the wound closed was difficult to say the least. But my boat was my lifeline, and I never took foolish chances on the staircase again.

In the wild one is constantly reminded of one's own mortality. I remember a morning when I was resting and heard a thumping sound, followed by a bang on the platform just outside the tent and a crash on the beach below my cliff. I hurried out to find a rock above the tent had become dislodged, part of the gradual erosion process, and had hurtled down, missing my dozing form by less than two feet. It had made a six-inch dent in the veranda before bouncing down to the shoreline.

I noticed for the first time that there were many rocks perched on ledges above my home, and after that they *all* looked dangerous. By expanding and contracting in the heat of day and cold of night, rocks 'walk' down slight slopes over a period of years until one day they thunder down. So without stopping for breakfast I grabbed the crowbar and climbed the slope. For an hour I started jamming loose rocks behind more secure ones or tossing them to the side of my platform until one escaped my crowbar's control, went bouncing down, and to my horror smashed into the tent itself. I hastened down to find it had torn the canvas and wrecked my precious hurricane lamp. From such accidents I learned never to do things on impulse but to plan first. I also recognized a danger I had not seen before. The rest of that morning was spent on a nearby beach finding a huge eighteen-foot slab of timber, floating it back, hauling it up the cliff, and nailing it between two trees as an effective rock barrier above the tent. It was a laborious process for one man, for having hauled one end up by pulley, I had to tie it securely, then swing up the other end, secure that, and so on, until the slab was on the cliff.

Time and again I went up or down the log staircase only to find I'd forgotten something at the other end and had to climb back. It was the same with the long trail through the forest to the truck. Written lists thus became part of my way of life, and I learned never to waste a journey, to go always with hands full, whether it was merely empty kerosene cans, spare supplies, books or any kind of useful building material.

One sunny afternoon, bored with typing, I took the crowbar down to the beach and started clearing a gangway through the rocks so that my boat could float in and out at medium tides. By levering with the bar resting on adjacent rocks and kicking smaller rocks under the one to be moved – to keep it from dropping back – I could move rocks weighing more than eight hundred pounds without difficulty. But it wasn't until one rock had rolled back, gashing my foot, and the tides had come in again, that I realized rocks were lighter and thus far easier to shift when under water. In two days, working with water up to my backside, I had a thirty-yard gangway with a bottom of small pebbles and along this I laid a ladder of cedar poles, wedging its long crosspieces under side rocks so it couldn't float away. By the time I finished I was working by moonlight, but it was immensely satisfying to look back and see how many big rocks I had managed to heave out of the way with no one else's help. Such days left me with a lusty appetite so that the simplest food tasted delicious, my subconscious mind worked on writing problems often producing in a flash lines I needed, and at nights I slept like a log.

Keeping clean after such sweaty daily work was a problem, but by hanging a large bucket of seawater from my staircase and letting the water siphon out through a rubber pipe and tin with small holes in the bottom, I had a serviceable shower. I found washing my hair in seawater especially invigorating. Like many men of forty, I'd found my hair thinning on top, but at the end of that first summer, after scrubbing my scalp in seawater's beneficial salts – iron, calcium, potassium, phosphorus, sodium chloride – my hair was a good deal thicker than it had been in the spring. The open-air life and better blood circulation through enforced exercise may also have been contributing factors!

The biggest problem was fresh water, as important in the wild as food and shelter. While I had discovered cooking in seawater gives vegetables just the right salty tang, I needed fresh for drinking. Every time I left the tent for supplies I hung a gallon container from what I called my "water finger". I filled it from a creek about half a mile away from the cabin as I carried other stores along the trail. I could usually, with care, make a gallon last nearly a week. But when this third finger of my left hand seemed to be getting a permanent crook, I decided to dig a well. In two whole days I had dug, pick-axed, and shovelled four separate holes three or four feet deep through the rocks and tree-root tangles without finding a trace of moisture. Exasperated, I gave up. And though I didn't have a well, I had four fine, unpollutable refuse holes in which my waste tins would in a few years decompose harmlessly. I hadn't wasted my time.

I had formed a rule about dumping rubbish in the sea in my first days on that coast. As my rowing boat weaved its ramshackle way among the luxury pleasure cruisers one fishing weekend, someone inside one of them pulled a lever. As the accumulated debris floated across the calm Pacific I rowed like hell to get away. But my rule wasn't based on mere prissiness. For too long too many countries, with their total populations of several billion human beings, have regarded the world's oceans as a vast refuse dump, a universal global sink. Yet our seas, along with trees and vegetation, are the lungs of our planet. Their microscopic phytoplankton release a major part of the oxygen vitally needed by everything that breathes with lungs and gills. They cool the tropics, bring warm currents to cold areas, and make much of our earth habitable. They provide the water that, drawn up by the sun, falls as rain upon our fields. And yet man is so short-sighted, the oceans still receive vast amounts of harmful industrial waste concentrated in the coastal regions. And it is precisely the coastal regions that are the main nurseries for the eggs and young fish of many edible species. A depressing picture but, while there was little I could do, I was sure the Pacific at least could do without my waste products. It's like everything else. If you don't like the world, the only way you can really help change it is by changing yourself. It is the only beginning.

Meanwhile, I still had no fresh-water well, only blistered fingers and an aching back. So I wrote to Ed. In a few days his terse reply came, written in a neat, open hand. "Find a big alder or willow where the roots are thick and go straight down, and dig there ..." Next day I did so and after hacking around and through small rocks, at six feet the ground grew mushy beneath my feet. Another two feet down and I had water pouring in. With trousers soaked and my hands half-skinned from heaving out the sharp rocks, I felt only elation. I made the hole as large as I could and, to keep the mud out, lined it with sea-scoured yellow cedar split on the beach. Then with two plastic hoses joined together, I got a siphon system working. I made a rough board top for the well from drift lumber, covered it with rocks, earth, and moss so it was indistinguishable from the surrounding terrain, and reckoned now my "water finger" could return to its normal size.

Then I stood in my kitchen and twisted the hose nozzle, and the water spurted ten feet - beautiful, crystal-clear cold water. It was my second big triumph in the wild after felling the staircase tree.

The astonishing thing about living wild and free by the sea is that eventually nearly everything one needs comes drifting up onto the beaches. On most fine days, after mornings working at the book, I wandered along the shore lines looking for any new drift lumber or useful logs – to be stacked on the cliff for when I built my cabin. Walking over the rocks well north of the eagles' island one fine day I heard a clinking noise and saw a bright reddish object bobbing against some rocks in the gentle surf. It was a large copper tankard and, though its sides were slightly dented, it had a plate-glass bottom that, oddly, was neither scratched nor damaged. I'd found more than a mere drinking container. For some time I'd been meaning to write away for a face mask so I could see clearly under water. Surely the tankard would do just as well – I could hold its handle like a crude lorgnette! I tried it out when up to my waist in the sea and it worked perfectly – several little crabs were heading over the seabed toward my naked feet.

So now, on every fishing trip, the tankard came with me. But it wasn't until mid-July that it really came into its own. I was heading out past the far islands to the best salmon reef when I saw what looked like small, square-faced dogs sporting about in the calm swell. As I rowed nearer there was a sudden splashing as one surfaced from under the boat and I had a brief glimpse of a pair of bulging eyes, long greyish whiskers on a bear cub's face, and bent forepaws. Then with a snort halfway between a sneeze and a cough, it reared backward and swam away on its back a few yards, then looped and dived. And as it went I saw its rear feet start to kick out. They were webbed as fully as a duck's. I grabbed the tankard, glued it to my right eye, and jabbed it under water to find the animal again. But in my hurry I almost overbalanced the boat and shipped the tankard and my eye full of water.

There were five of them on the surface. They looked like otters but were huge, and two of them seemed almost five feet long. They were all around and underneath the boat, some swimming with undulating movements like otters, others idly doing a sort of dog paddle, their webbed rear feet giving them great thrusts through the water. And as they all stared back at me, more curious than scared at this quiet invasion of their watery world, I realized what they were. They were a small group of sea otters, a marine mammal that spends nearly all its life in the sea off rocky islets and which, although once common, was almost exterminated by fur hunters in the early 1800s for its dense, beautiful pelt.

They were rare creatures and I felt elated with discovery. I stayed still and after some five minutes – I was surprised they could stay under water that long – they began to pop up around me. Often sea birds and animals are not afraid of a man in a lone boat if he is silently rowing and has no noisy outboard engine, but the moment they feel your eyes on them, actually looking at them, they dive or fly away. I stayed rigid, only moving my eyes as the boat turned, irritatingly slowly, in the eddying currents. They gained courage when I didn't move. One, a little fatter than the rest, seemed to have something tucked under its arm, like a portfolio. When it swam

45

within my full vision I could see the object was a baby, a tiny replica of its mother. She held it in her left forepaw much like a child carrying a doll, and its little mouth was reaching downward for one of her teats. The nostrils on her puppy nose wrinkled with curiosity as she passed and she was such an endearing sight I involuntarily stretched out my hand and made a soothing, chuckling sound. Instantly she gave a whuffling snort, tightened her clutch on the dozing baby, and dived. It was hard not to laugh and I wondered what would have happened if the poor little mite had breathed inward just as she dived!

The mother's sudden disappearance didn't alarm more than one of the others. They weren't like sheep but seemed to make up their minds individually, which is rare in a herd animal. As I continued to sit silently, again motionless, they started scudding around the boat keeping about fifteen yards away. On the perimeter I saw one sculling along on its back holding what looked like a piece of white biscuit in one paw. Then I heard a loud cracking noise. It wasn't a biscuit, naturally, but a whole clam, and the otter seemed to crack the shell with its teeth alone. As he opened up the clam with the claws on both stubby forepaws, he looked just like a baby does when seated in a high-chair working on its supper – completely engrossed. He ripped off pieces of shell, tossing them away like a monkey peeling an orange, and started chewing into the clam, giving the boat a few cautious sideways looks.

As I reached for the oars they all dived at once and it was as if they had never been there. I rowed away from the island, wondering whether to fish or not, and had gone about half a mile when up popped three of the otters. They must have followed me under the water.

Gluing my tankard spy glass to my eye I again watched their antics. I was now on the edge of the salmon reef and below me great fronds of kelp waved in slow undine rhythms, echoing and copying the slow-flowing currents, while the sea otters wove their graceful, sleek shapes in and out of the sandy green caverns, like mermaids in a fathomless dream. I was transfixed, envying their delightful, silent water world. Now I saw one hold the tip of some broad tangleweed against its side and roll over and down so the weed folded round and round its body, until it was all but hidden. Sea otters are said to do this to hide when killer whales are about and to sleep at night, but as I watched it darted out again like a torpedo, still holding the tip of the weed and drawing it out like the spiral of a spring when pulled from the centre. As the otter let go again the tangleweed swirled round and round like a snake, unwinding into its original shape. Nearby were two more otters, one twirling and spiralling up around the other, perhaps its mate, which seemed to enjoy the curving caress of its companion's moving body.

Dusk was beginning to fall when I finally stopped spying on them, too late for fishing now. But as I reached for the oars for the long haul home, I stopped. About twenty yards away a large grey otter had surfaced and started lazily swimming on his back. He looked as if he had a bald spot on his chest, but as he came nearer I realized it wasn't a hairless patch at all but a small flat stone. Intrigued, I saw he had a clam in his paws, which he turned over and over. To my surprise he didn't bite it, but instead held it a few inches from the stone and brought it down with a hefty whack. He smashed it twice more against the stone, cracked it open, and calmly picked out the mollusc's flesh with his tongue and teeth and tossed away the shattered fragments like a man tossing away an oyster shell after swallowing the contents. I reasoned the otter's greyness meant he was older than the others, that he had devised this method to save wear on what few teeth he had left. The stone served as his anvil cum lunch counter!

In recent years British Columbia has made brave attempts to reintroduce more sea otters into its coastal waters, and this heartening try at last reversed the trend of two entire centuries in which man regarded the animal world as merely useful for his own profit.

Nature, while she will take away with one hand, often bestows with the other. Among the bountiful handouts delivered to me by the sea were first my tankard spy glass, but also a log wharf, a complete window frame, a pot of white paint, tins of motor oil, an antique whisky barrel, half a mahogany boat from whose boards I made good shelves, a desk top and cabin lumber. I was writing my book upon a flimsy plywood table when a large five-foot-wide, three-inch-thick round, which someone had cut off a drift log to remove its timber mark, came bumping along the rocks. By axing it into a kidney shape I made a superb natural desk top that I covered with a piece of velvet bedspread; I put the typewriter above the recess and used the two "arms" of the kidney shape for resting my elbows. Although I now had the window frame for my future cabin I did not have a sill, which had to be L-shaped to prevent rainwater flooding in. Sure enough, a few weeks later, up drifted the right piece.

My platform veranda often became slippery in the rain and as a fall over the edge would result in a forty-foot drop onto the rocky beach, I cut a safety rail from a cedar pole – but I had nothing to which I could attach it and I wanted something decorative. One morning I woke to a hollow banging sound. A large, smoothly scoured spar of fir with a tangle of roots that looked like a giraffe's head and neck was nudging the rocks below. Curve-notching it to the front log pillars, I had an impressive corner post for my safety rail, and from the sea it made the front of the platform look like the prow of a Viking ship.

One day on the far land spit I found two huge logs twenty feet long and more than two feet across, which were joined together by a thick crosspiece. It had obviously been part of a wharf. At high tide I levered it into the sea, sat astride it, and with oarlocks made of rope, rowed it to the beach below my staircase. I cut in notches and set more crosspieces found on the beach, and by nightfall I had my own floating dry dock for the boat. I beached the dinghy onto it at every high tide; then when the tide went out again, instead of the boat being in danger of holing itself on the rocks through the flimsy pole ladder, the big logs took all the pounding and the boat stayed securely lashed on top. As the prevailing winds blew onshore and there was very little pressure to take the assemblage out to sea, I just tethered it with light ropes. It was free to float but not float away. And at high and medium tides I also now had a fine diving board!

When such free gifts come wandering up and idyllic weather has set in for days, it seems impossible not to believe in some benign wilderness power. Every day the hummingbirds whirred among the honeysuckle surrounding my platform and the yellow swallowtail butterflies came hopping and flopping through the balmy air. Hawk moths darted here and there, extending quivering proboscises into flower trumpets, and now and again I could hear the soft splash of a salmon leaping over the kelp beds.

Then I'd wake one morning in semi-darkness and the drumming of a million raindrops on the sides of the tent told me another two-day deluge had arrived and life was not all ease and enjoyment. Twice in mid-July the platform held pools, and everything in the tent was soaking, including me. But after the second storm I saw what looked like a glass whale in the sea. I launched the boat and found it was a mass of thick plastic sheeting that must have blown off one of the scows pulled by tugboats down the straits to Vancouver. Towing it back to my beach, I found it was sixty feet square and in perfect condition. I spread some on the platform and built a frame to lift it over the tent when the next downpour came. I thought this would keep me from being bothered by rain anymore until my cabin was built.

In early August my well dried up completely, the occasional downpours being absorbed by the parched earth before water could reach bedrock level. And I was back once more to carrying a gallon of drinking water down the trail. An attempt to collect rainwater in a plastic sheet laid over the rocks and angled so the water channelled into a bucket soon came to grief. The first time the plastic blew away and got stuck in a tree; the second time I found the bucket half-filled with water but also a dozen assorted beetles and one feebly swimming mouse. As I tipped them out and saw the sodden mouse totter weakly away as if on tiny stilts, I gave up that idea.

A few days later I was asleep in the tent when I woke to the sound of mewing, like a child whimpering. Puzzled, I poked my head out of the tent flap without lighting the oil lamp. Immediately there was an odd coughing noise, then a scuffle of branches, I waited a minute or two but hearing nothing more, I felt it was probably a raccoon up a nearby tree and went back to bed.

Next time I was at the distant store I remarked on the incident and described the sounds to the brothers who ran the place. "Cougar," they said without hesitation. This was a shock to me, for I'd understood mountain lions only came to the shore regions in the height of winter, when harsh weather and lack of prey forced them down from the snowy mountains.

Wildlife books had told me that of all the big cats, the cougar is next to the cheetah as being the least threat to man. And while it was likely to be a sick or old beast with worn teeth to make it forage near a human dwelling in summer, I still felt nervous as I stumbled down the trail with my back pack and hands full of supplies and my water can. In fact if I'd known then what I found out later – that there had been twenty-six authenticated attacks on humans by cougars since the turn of the century in British Columbia alone – I would have been even more scared. As it was, when I reached the spot where I estimated it had been, I set down my load and searched around. Sure enough in the drying mud near the path were two paw prints and they were a good four inches across, though I could see no claw marks. It was small comfort over the next few nights to reflect cougars are basically afraid of man when all there was between me and that marauding animal was the thickness of the tent's canvas. I transferred the contents of my garbage box to a large plastic bag to lessen the scent, and washed the box thoroughly in the sea.

I now began to think seriously about building the cabin for the forthcoming winter, when another item floated up on the tide, almost as if to help me prepare for the time ahead – a forty-four-gallon oil drum. With crudely cut doors and some stove pipe and asbestos fibre and collar, I could make an incinerator, extra cooker, and winter heater. These big fuel drums make ideal heaters, once you've mastered the smoke problem, for every part of their metal exterior becomes piping hot and throws its heat all around.

One night I returned late from a fishing trip and was sitting on my veranda in the moonlight when I heard a scratching below. Instantly thinking "cougar!" I reached for my newly purchased spirit lamp, whose bright glare I was sure would scare off almost any animal, and looked cautiously over the edge. There, sitting up in a begging position like a dog and waving its long-clawed hands like a shadow boxer, was a raccoon. Its black-masked face looked owlishly up at me, blinking in the strong light. I'd heard that coons sometimes come around houses in the evening looking for scraps. This one had clearly smelled my fish, so I gently threw him a piece. To my delight he instantly dropped on all fours, went with a wobbly, cat-like gait to the fish, and cautiously reached out for it, then hurried furtively into the undergrowth, where he ate it with an audible smacking of lips. Then back he came with much more confidence. Lonesome as I was since Ed had left, I encouraged him and before long he was prowling around almost every night. I looked forward to his visits, hearing his scratch on the logs if the kitchen door was shut, seeing the strange red glow from his eyes in the lamplight as he sat, waiting patiently for scraps. Apart from knowing he would hardly wander abroad with such impunity if there was still a cougar within striking distance, I was glad of his company.

6 Autumn – and a new companion

I nicknamed him Spooks because he always came at night, appearing so quietly if the door was open it seemed he had materialized out of the air. Although he was heftily built and some three feet long, a foot of which was bushy, black-ringed tail, he was a comical-looking character. He seemed half dog and half cat, with long sharp claws on all four feet. He was covered in grey fur and his face, with bright button eyes, erect ears, and sharp nose, looked alternately owlish or foxy. The black bands across his eyes gave him the air of a brigand, a highwayman, which, I soon found out, also coincided with his nature.

I had heard a lot about coons during my first months in Canada and while they can be easily tamed, even house-trained if taken as just-weaned pups, wild adults can be as dangerous as wildcats if cornered. Hunting coons has long been a favourite North American pastime and a challenge, for they lead even specially trained dogs on a merry dance once they decide to run. They can shin up trees faster than a squirrel and outrun any dog over a short distance. They are so cunning when chased they have been known to mark trees as they pass to delude the dogs into believing they have gone up the trunks. They run along the tops of fallen trees and along creek beds to break their scent line. If caught by a dog in open water, the coon tries to leap onto its head; from there it can hold the dog's jaws shut with its claws and bite with its four sharp canine teeth, as well as weigh the dog down until it drowns.

The raccoon is a redoubtable beast, for it combines the qualities of so many animals in one – the near nocturnal sight of an owl, the fighting abilities of both cat and dog, the climbing speed of a monkey, and the cunning of a fox. It dens in old woodpeckers' holes, in hollow or broken parts of trees, in rocky ground crevices, even sometimes in old enlarged rabbit burrows.

First named *arakun* by the Algonquin Indians, the early British settlers mispronounced the name, turning it to raccoon. It became yet another animal to benefit man, for its pelt not only supplied him with warm coats and hats but became accepted barter. Although the craze for coonskin coats in the 1920s reduced its numbers, it soon reasserted itself, and even the 1955 craze for Davy Crockett hats failed to dent its populations. Today the coon positively thrives on man's encroachment and, like the persecuted European foxes, it has learned to live near urban man, raiding his garbage bins and stealing his chickens.

Within a couple of weeks Spooks was semi-tame. He even began following me up to the tent after his meal and while he refused to step over the threshold, he often sat licking his claws near where the spirit lamp warmed the side of the tent. Once he got used to me his movements were quite slow and he sat still for minutes at a time. If I held out food and said things like, "Here you are, Spooks, come along and eat it up," in a soft, soothing voice, he approached cautiously, extended both hands at full reach, took the morsel with great delicacy, then hastily retreated a few feet away and ate it.

The raccoon's Latin name is *Procyon lotor* and *lotor* means "washer". The old belief that coons dip everything they eat in water because they have poor saliva glands is largely discounted today. Spooks never made any attempt to find water for food dipping but he always made a lot of lip-smacking noise when he ate, chewing everything into the tiniest pieces before swallowing. Still one day I left a shallow bowl of water nearby to test the theory. For several nights he ignored it, but once, having no fish, I gave him a piece of dry brown bread, He took it, sniffed, examined it carefully in both paws and then, to my delight, hobbled over to the bowl, dipped the bread in, and started chewing more noisily than ever. I never saw him actually drink from the bowl.

Early one morning in the predawn twilight I heard a sudden scrabbling sound on the trunk of a large fir near the tent. I looked out and Spooks was clawing his way up the tree, tearing away little pieces of bark as he went. I realized then how powerful he was, for his baggy back legs seemed all muscle as he shot up the trunk. Sure he was being chased by something, I looked down on the forest floor, but saw nothing. It seemed sheer high spirits that made him dart about madly. As I watched he galloped along a branch and came hurtling back. Then, with ears flat, he calmly backed down the trunk and slowly tottered off through the woods. Hastily donning shirt, trousers, and gym shoes, I followed him. After about half a mile, mostly uphill, I saw his grey rump and banded tail disappear through a salal thicket by a higher reach of the creek where I filled my water container. I dodged round and carefully peeped over a lichen-covered rock.

Spooks was standing up to his belly in a gravel pool, his bushy tail high, moving forward furtively, reaching under the bank and turning over small stones. About three yards in front of him I saw a small movement under water as a crayfish scudded over the sandy gravel, flicking out its long claws and scooping up water larvae. Surely it would detect Spooks heading upward? It did, swiftly darting under the overhang of the bank, making a little cloud as it went. But Spooks kept coming, feeling more with his feet than searching with his eyes. He reached the overhang, delved in with both paws and came out with the crayfish secure. Then he dashed to the bank and, holding it in both hands like a person holding an ear of corn, he ate the luckless kicking creature.

I said in a normal voice, "Hello there, Spooks!" Instantly he leaped about six feet sideways, hissed louder than a cat, and dashed up the nearest tree. I thought once he recognized me he would calm down. But no. He did not associate me with the bush, his own domain, but only as the creature of the tent and log kitchen who sometimes gave him scraps.

51

I thought I'd seen the last of him then, but two nights later he was back, acting as if nothing had happened. The odd thing was that I came out of the kitchen after supper and found him sitting by the tent above in exactly the spot where the lamp used to be when I was *in* the tent. Coons are said to have good memories and here was ample proof. I went into the tent and put the lamp in its old place, but having no fish or bread I handed him a piece of chocolate. Out went his hand and after a brief sniff he nibbled away as if he'd been used to chocolate all his life.

It was over a week before I spotted him in the daytime again. As I was heading up the back of my land, I saw him resting in the sun on a broad branch, both his hind legs dangling as he warmed himself. He heard me and darted down the tree, then scampered off at a trot. Keeping well back I lumbered after him. Now and again I caught glimpses of his little fat backside as I toiled in his wake in a direction I hadn't been before. I saw him cross the forest road and keep on going, so I did too. Puffing along, I decided after another ten minutes this was a fool's game. He could easily tire me and I was about to give up when I came into a small parklike area. As I came from the forest some little animals that I took to be rock rabbits scattered in all directions. Of Spooks there was no sign. I started searching the rocky edges of the clearing. Some of the boulders were huge and had stopped on this flat area in their tumble down the mountain slopes in a bygone age. Keeping to the right of the park area, I saw a dark hole in front of me. It was a small cave. Wondering if this was one of Spooks's dens, I stepped inside.

Once past the first opening I was in a large dark chamber with its roof some three feet above my head. As my eyes grew accustomed to the gloom, I saw clam shells and small bones on the cavern floor. This was probably his den.

By mid-August Spooks still came to the tent at night – but only occasionally now because the bushes were thick with red and yellow salmonberries and the acid red huckleberries and he could eat his fill of them. Once, seeing something grey in a bush about seven feet off the ground, I approached stealthily. There was Spooks clinging to the thin twigs with his rear feet and picking berries with his long, thin fingers. Indeed he was stuffing berries into his mouth and crunching greedily so that the juice ran down his lower jaw.

One evening when I'd forgotten to close the tent flap, I found Spooks inside. His curiosity finally had got the better of him, for everything on my shelves had been pulled onto the bed. Wrapping paper from my few chocolates was strewn about and Spooks himself was sitting oddly upright in a corner, like an old drunk asleep outside a restaurant kitchen's doorway, his fluffy tail held between his forepaws. Charming though he looked at that moment, I didn't want him moving in as an unpaid guest and so I shooed him out with the broom. He woke with a rasping snarl, and scurried out and up the nearest tree.

When two nights later he began scratching at the tent as if to claw his way in, I felt he was becoming too much of a good thing. He puzzled me too, now, by sometimes taking the fish, bread, or other food, and dashing off into the night with it. I thought he was probably storing it somewhere for future use. But one evening the problem was solved. As he waited outside the kitchen, where I was now feeding him, I was aware of several pairs of redly glowing eyes watching us from the trees. Four more coons! One, far larger than the others, a female, was clearly Spooks's wife, and the other three small ones, who hissed and squabbled with each other, were the three surviving members of their brood, probably born in May.

Five coons, while not likely to gang up on a man, could soon reduce my tent to strips of canvas while searching for food when I was fishing or on a supply trip. For the next few nights I threw scraps well away from the platform into the bushes, and I cut down on the fish dish. But the problem was solved for me.

About 2 a.m. one morning I was awakened by a fearful racket – a cacophony of hisses, spits, barks and growls. I rushed out with my spirit lamp and there in its glow, cornered between the rocks and the log ends of the platform, was Spooks, his teeth bared in a snarl, slashing away with his claws at a large blackish-brown animal that promptly shot away from the light and disappeared into the forest before I could see it clearly. It must have been a dog, for no cougar barks or growls, but I'd never seen a dog in the area before. As it fled crashing through the brush, Spooks glared up as I stood on the platform, then with a reproachful look he scrambled up the sheer face of the rock, shot up the corky bark of an old fir, and disappeared in the top branches. I never saw him again and the slight loneliness I'd felt before his arrival returned.

One September afternoon, as I struggled down the trail with heavy groceries from the distant store, I realised it was time for me to prepare for winter. As I walked down hill, half sliding on the loose shale of the steeper parts, the wind increased in force and when I came out above the platform, the westerly winds off the sea, with nothing to impede them, were blowing a fair gale. My log wharf had snapped its nylon rope moorings and was banging against the cliff in the breaking waves. The boat had slipped under its light lashings and was overhanging the wharf, full of sea water from the waves crashing over it. I hurried down the staircase and managed, after frantic bailing, to heave it onto the higher rocky landing, where I hitched it to the gin-pole rope. Both oars had gone but a mad dash over the rocks revealed one two hundred yards away and the other some thirty yards beyond it. They had been battered on the rocks but were still usable.

That night was the worst I'd known living in the tent. The wind tore at the canvas as I drove large nails through the log crosspieces of the platform to hold the guy ropes and filled the shelves inside the tent with rocks to hold it down. My plastic sheet awning against light summer rains was completely destroyed. I could have given up and gone to sleep in the truck up on the old logging tracks but I was determined to stick it out. Besides, my weight was needed to help hold the tent down!

In the darkness as the wind punched against the canvas, I sat staring miserably through the small net window at the black sea. It raged like liquid mountains on the move, forming ranks of waves far out, then marching relentlessly, their tops foaming with fury, toward my shore, there to snarl and pound as if to beat the very air itself into submission. A streak of forked lightning hit the dark, jagged shapes of the rocky headland, lighting up the scene as if to give a last stark look at the world to a drowning man.

Next day, as the last of the storm clouds scudded over to the southeast revealing glimpses of bright blue sky, I hung my sodden clothes and bedding to dry and rowed out to try for some much-needed fish. As the sun hit my face, it felt like the blessing of survival after being close to death. Slipping between the feathery grey islands with their flashes of jade, purple flowers, and orange rock, I caught four ling cod in under an hour, the last weighing over twenty-five pounds, and as this was more fish than I could keep fresh, I gaffed the hook out of its mouth and let it go. When I returned, I hastened to my well. The bottom of its shaft was dryer than the land around it. Although a good inch of rain had fallen during the night, it had not been enough to soak down to the bedrock to replace the water that had drained away or evaporated in the long hot summer.

That storm had been my last warning. Winter was on its way. The few poplars higher up were turning yellow and alder leaves, the first to fall, now swirled around the platform. The birch were losing their rich greens. There were gaps appearing in the trees to the north so now I could see the tiny bay next door that formerly had been hidden by the foliage. As I walked the trail, the falling leaves were opening up the landscape. Trees losing their clothes are rather like humans when naked – their weaknesses show up and you soon see their real character. Although the temperature drop was gradual, I now noticed my feet were cold until well after midday unless I was doing strenuous outdoor work.

It was time to think seriously about my cabin. I skinned my hands turning the old oil drum into a reasonably smoke-free wood stove, laboriously cutting in a door and a smoke outlet with a metal chisel and hacksaw blades. On all suitable days I scoured the neighbouring beaches, sometimes rowing a dozen miles, stacking useful lumber and straight drift logs above high-tide level and towing home what I could. I always tried to ensure I would be half-blown home by the prevailing winds. These were stronger now but I felt I could not afford an engine. To complicate things even more, the boat had begun to leak. However, I patched it up as best I could with plywood and thick paint.

All around me now nature seemed to be showing its wild creatures that harder times were ahead. The great parasitic jaegers, known in Britain as great skuas, had suddenly appeared out of the west. They flashed in on wings of burnished steel, powerful, sleek birds with mighty, intermittent wing beats, flying with contemptuous ease as they chased the unfortunate sea gulls until they were forced to regurgitate whatever they had eaten. Then the jaegers would swoop down and gulp the half-digested food, often before it hit the water.

Occasionally I still fed Bert, but he was more wary now that he had learned the full use of his large wings. One day I saw a jaeger chase him and, as he twisted and dived like most gulls to get away, I thought, "Poor Bert, still getting it from everything around." But to my surprise, as the jaeger drew near in level flight Bert suddenly performed a tight upward loop, came down where the jaeger's tail had been a moment before, sheered off to the right, and by the time the jaeger had recovered its wits, was forty yards away heading in the opposite direction. It seemed such a neat little lesson.

Bert had been forced to compensate for his infirmity on the ground by perfecting his other skill, flying, and in doing so he now had an advantage over the other gulls who had despised him.

One day at the distant store as I was picking up bolts, hinges, nails, stove pipe, and paraphernalia for my cabin, I recognized a familiar chunky figure. It was Ed Louette, all neat in city clothes. He had just arrived on the bus with his inevitable bag of tools, and apart from his square, outdoor face, he looked more like a prosperous businessman than the tattered old carpenter I remembered. It was I who felt like a hobo now.

Ed had rented a small trailer four miles up the coast near the broken old wharf I sometimes used but before winter set in he intended moving back into his rented cabin. On the land behind me I'd discovered an ancient cabin site with five acres of land. Many years earlier an attempt had been made to homestead the place but the pioneer had left, unable to stand isolation, and the lease had lapsed. I had an idea – and a brief battle with myself. I didn't want to lose my idyllic privacy, but if ever I was to have a neighbour, I wanted a man like Ed. With his skills he could soon erect a cabin and no longer have to pay rent from his pension. I told him about the place and a few days later brought him back to look it over.

To my astonishment, after viewing the gently wooded site, he turned it down. He shook his grey head. "If hi was a young man of sixty I'd do it. But at nearly seventy – well, hi like some comforts now, and sometimes my courage leaves me." Yet I knew he thought nothing of rowing fifteen miles a day when fishing! The truth was he had phobias about dealing with officialdom and it would be too much of a hassle.

As we explored the top end of the land, Ed suddenly cried out as his foot went into a fold in the earth and his leg was soaked halfway to the knee: "There's a water pipe here. Look!" There was, too. We scraped away the earth and overgrown debris and found a thick galvanized metal pipe that was still exuding water, "It must go back under the road to the creek that runs down from Halsam Lake," he said. "How far is your place down from here?"

"About a quarter mile."

"Well, get yourself some plastic pipe, hitch it up, and you've got a water supply," he said. I'd already told him about the well drying up. To buy so much plastic pipe, get it to the site, and lay it through the dense brush alone seemed a big task, but Ed regarded it so lightly, I decided to have a try later.

As we walked down to my tent Ed again started scraping about in some thick salal scrub. "Now what have we here? Good God, it's a whole Yukon chimney. And hit's in fine condition. Look!" He wrenched it out of the tangle and thrust the three-foot-long metal contraption into my hands. "Just what you want for that oil drum stove you were talking about. Not a bit of rust hanywhere!"

Looking at my platform, the log work, and the curved notches of which I was so proud, Ed hid a smile and said I was doing all right – for a beginner. Then he saw the pools of water left on the platform from the rain.

55

"Well at least you got it level," he said, "but you ought to shim it up so the water drains off. Does your tent get wet underneath?"

I laughed. "It sure does."

He looked around. "Hand me that crowbar there, and get a couple of four-by-twos." I did and he went to the back of the platform, levered up the rear logs where they were hooked into the rock folds, and stuck in a four-by-two at each corner so water would flow away.

"You know something," he said, "you should have built a cabin on this platform. Winter will soon be here." I said that had been my idea too, and that I'd been gathering materials.

He looked directly at me, staring intently for a few seconds as if summing me up.

"Well," he said, "hisn't that strange? I was down on my beach this morning and up drifted the finest red cedar spar I've seen for years. Ideal for roof shakes." He paused, looked around the area noting the log staircase, the beach, the trail. "Right," he added. " *We'll* build you a cabin, professor. Yes sir, we'll build you a nice little house and we'll start tomorrow!"

Ed Louette was one of the world's finest and last-surviving log craftsmen. I could only blurt out some awkward words of thanks.

7 Ed and the Cabin

Shortly after dawn next day I lazed idly in my warm bed wondering if Ed really meant to help me build my cabin, when suddenly there was a loud crash on the veranda outside the tent.

"We're here!" came a ringing voice. "And look at that fine clear sky!" Ed had hitched down on a logging truck and had walked the entire trail with a heavy toolbag. "Are you hup yet?"

"Of course I'm up," I shouted, leaped out of bed, pulled on my underpants, socks and boots, stood up, realized my trousers were still on the floor, got a boot stuck in a trouser leg, and was just taking off the boot again as Ed peered in the tent flap.

"You shouldn't sleep in boots, professor," he said, taking in my predicament at a glance. "Bad for the feet." He turned away and slapped on the side of the tent. "Now," he said as I pulled on my trousers and tied up my boots again, "har we going to take your tent down? It will be easier to frame the walls on the platform first, then stand them up."

"Eh? Yes. I mean … no," I gasped as I pulled on a shirt and smoothed down my hair. "I was *reading*," I added fatuously, as I scrambled down the cliff. "Do you want a cup of tea?"

"Heck no. I had breakfast," said Ed, throwing stray timbers off the platform as I boiled my tea, guiltily crammed some cereal into my mouth, and then hastened to join him.

"Well, we'll build your cabin around the tent," he decided. He slapped his palm with a metal tape, an eager light of battle in his eye. "And we'll make it simple. A shed roof, I think. And we'll build it back to front."

"How do you mean?"

"The winter winds can be terrible here." he replied. "So we'll make it eight feet high at the front hand twelve feet at the back – must have a four-to-one drop, so snow can slide off. Yessir, that will mean the smallest area to the west and when the wind hits the roof it will sort of press the cabin down, not blow it away."

I should have known he would have had it all figured out. It was the start of an extraordinary nine days. That man, sixty-eight years old, worked at a pace I could barely match. He refused all short cuts, insisting we mortise-joint the corner posts and use plumb line and level. He taught me how to measure and cut the wall studs, stagger the wall bridging, notch the roof beams, make a template, and cut the "birdsmouths" in each log rafter so all would be the same size to fit the beams, how to cut shakes from the red cedar spar, and even how to scribe logs so each fitted into the other, a most complicated procedure.

One morning he turned up late, at 10 a.m. – he had already spent four hours tying up drift lumber he had found and rowed to his beach, ready for us to tow away at high tide. And he had even borrowed an outboard engine. Back at his beach Ed thrust a spar of wood into the rope loops he'd made around each end of the timber pile, twisted the loops so tight moisture spurted, then nailed the spars down. The whole mass then floated like one solid log – a trick I would never have thought of. Towing his boat behind the lumber, we stopped off on the way back and loaded into it two more red cedar spars Ed had found.

"Come on," he shouted, as I stood on the cliff top with a rope and he timber-hitched load after load of wood for me to haul up, "we can get another lot up before lunch!" Later we cut the cedar spars into two-foot bolts and quartered them with his sharp froe and homemade mallet from a six-inch alder trunk, Ed split off the shakes like an assembly-line guillotine. Turning the block each time so the shakes would taper, he whacked the froe, twisted its handle, and each shake sprang off with a musical pop – a perfect two-foot by eight-inch wooden roof tile. But most times I tried it, I had to drop the mallet and break off the shake with both hands on the froe.

As I watched Ed's tough old hands working with such apparent ease, I felt a mounting envy. For him, none of the introspection of the writer. Those hands were proof of years of healthy craftsmanship, of creative endeavour that had made Ed a happy man.

"So many people seem unhappy because they're not doing something *himportant*," Ed said once. "But what does it matter what a man does, provided he gives, contributes? You must make yourself love what you do, and do it as best you can. What other reason for life can we ever really know for sure?"

As we sat on the rocks each lunchtime, Ed treated me to much of his homespun philosophy and told me a little more about himself. He explained his blood was Scots and French, related on his mother's side to the writer Alexandre Dumas. This was a surprise, indeed, but it helped explain the literary works I'd seen on his shelves in French – a language I now learned he could speak and write fluently. Some of his views that I had regarded as cranky were the result of a highly original, if untutored, mind. Another day he told me one of his last paid jobs had been as a foreman on the log palisade building of a well-known lodge at the head of Jervis Inlet. "I had forty-five men under me but I didn't really like it. Hi like to do the work myself, my life is halways with the tools." Unable to stand by as an overseer, Ed started carrying the heaviest logs to the site and ruptured his back. His next professional job, building a log house up north at Kitimat, proved to be his last. "My back went again, and I could not go on." Back in Vancouver a doctor put him through some exercises, told him his back was only sprained, and awarded him three weeks' compensation. Hiring a cabin on our coast while he looked for a small lot on which he might retire, Ed agreed to top two trees for his landlady while she was on vacation. On the second he hit into a hornets' nest and the treetop twisted as it fell, knocked the sapling on which Ed was braced, and down he went fifteen feet onto a rocky patch.

"I felt my back was broken. I dragged myself into the cabin and my bed, but couldn't walk for five days. When I got hup it was Sunday, the store was shut, and no one in the nearby cabins would help. But hi got a bus to Vancouver – and the honly seat left was over a wheel!"

After a month in the hospital the doctors told him his back would always be weak, that hard physical work was out for good. That did not fit in with Ed's own ideas.

"Now, what had made my back bad in the first place?" he said. "Being *compressed* with the heavy logs! So hi made a trapeze from the ceiling. I hung onto it and cycled in the air with weighted boots. I did that for weeks. Well, that stretched my spine and heverything must have gone back into place. A year after that hi was carrying heavy logs again and my back has never bothered me since!"

For lunch Ed devoured sandwiches made of brown bread, honey, and molasses, sprinkled with wheat germ. They looked almost as atrocious as another dark red mixture that he munched with great enjoyment. I asked him what that was.

"Bull's hearts!" he answered. "By God, they're good for you! Years ago the old Indians made pemmican from buffalo and moose meat, pounded it to fibres, mixed in dried berries, and then sealed it all with the fat. This is like that. You know, a few years ago I began to feel bad. Hi went to a doctor and he examined me and said I had a weak heart. Hi had always to walk hup steps, not run. Well, hi came out of there and hi ran hup the first steps I saw! The heart is a muscle and can be made strong. But hi changed my diet, yessir, I changed my diet. A man is what he heats, I'm sure of that."

"Now the heart is the centre of an hanimal," he reasoned. "No fat and hall the good blood! So hi cut the heart into strips and shove a strip into a small grinder. Then a carrot, then another strip of heart, then a carrot. That way it doesn't need much cooking and most of the goodness is left. Then I put the whole lot into a plastic box. When I want to heat I put some into a fry pan with some vegetable hoil and lots of honions and cook it lightly. Then you really have a pemmican, a meal with lots of strength!"

He broke off a piece and handed it to me. To my surprise it tasted delicious.

Walking up the trail one day to cut cedar poles to make a long ladder to the cabin roof, Ed pointed to a small tree with large leaves. "Cascara! If you hever get bound hup, take some leaves from that tree and boil them and drink it. Good for the stomach. You always tell cascara by these big white veins hunder the leaves, see?" And he turned a leaf over.

One thing Ed never ate was salt. He shrank in horror when he saw me putting some on my food one day and I asked him why. At first his reply seemed to have no connection.

"When hi was a child back in New Brunswick, we lived in a Garden of Eden. There had not been a crop failure there for two hundred years. Lobsters lived under the rocks and heverywhere you saw their claws sticking out. Cod followed the little caiplin fish into shore, got confused – maybe the bright sand dazzled them – and the sea was so thick with fish sometimes they were rolling up in the waves onto the beaches. All you had to do was pick them up by their tails and put them in a barrel. And yet" – he pulled a long, surprised face, his eyes wide open – "there were still people starving …"

"Starving?"

"That's right." He gave a vigorous nod. "Starving! And hi believe it was mostly the fault of salt."

"Salt?"

"Yessir, salt! The old folks buried everything in salt. In New Brunswick in those days you could buy a gunnysack full for fifty cents. Pork was kept in salt and herring, and other fish they cut in half and filled with salt. Every damn thing we hate was salted. It was a Scots habit, I think. And I believe over the years that men and women's brains were destroyed by salt. We were living in a Garden of Eden and we didn't realize what was really there or how to preserve it better, you know.

"In winter we almost lived on salted fish, and the women never took the trouble to desalt them by soaking them overnight. It was too easy to take them out of the barrel and put them straight into the pot. At six years old, eating those fish was the same as sticking me in the guts with a knife. At fifteen they were pulling my teeth out and hi've worn false ever since. Every kid at school had a runny nose, heven the Indians, and coughed from fall to spring. What other reason could there be? I'm sure too much salt poisons the brains, makes people stupid. Well, I haven't touched a grain of salt for twenty years now – and I'm getting younger all the time!"

If Ed was a crank, he was the strongest, healthiest, happiest crank I ever met! At the end of each day I was ready for my bunk. But Ed refused ever to let me run him home by boat or truck. He preferred to walk the trail, then hitch, and if no one came along, he ambled the five miles to his trailer.

One day I tried to bring up how I was to pay him for his help for I had little money to spare. Could I pay in instalments?

"Ho, I don't want to be paid!" he said, almost in disgust. "Hif you have money, pay the rate. If not, and I believe in you, hi will work for nothing."

It was Ed's approach to the wonders of nature that attracted me most. His view seemed that of a marvelling child. Yet his knowledge of animal, bird, and insect life was considerable. In his cabin I'd noticed books about animals and trees, even ancient copies of Audubon's *Birds*, from which he fed his constant curiosity. I mentioned my days with the bald eagles. He knew the nest well, had known it for several years, but he had not told me about it because he wanted the great birds to remain undisturbed. "We are killing hall the eagles," he said then with a trace of anger. "When hi first came here, you could see an eagle every hour of the day, but that pair are the honly ones I've seen here for three years, apart from that young one. It's the farmers and forest men with all their pesticides, you know. Yes, hall those chemicals." he went on. "And now everyone wants their own darn summer cabin too, taking more of the wild land. More food, more wood is needed. The farmers put chemicals on their corn, the forestry service sprays trees to keep of pests. But what happens? The birds that heat the pests are poisoned, the mice that heat the corn are poisoned, the rain washes chemicals into the creeks, and they take the poison to the sea. Fish breathe and swallow the poison, and animals and birds like the eagle, who take the fish and mice, get it worst of all..."

I was surprised that an old man like Ed Louette felt so concerned about such matters. For several lunchtimes, in breaks from strenuous work, we talked of our wild, lovely place. We both agreed that in this last truly abundant wilderness of the northern hemisphere, the superb scenery would soon pall if the glories of the wildlife all around us were not there too.

"What do you think of hunting?" Ed asked one day. I said I wasn't sure. As sport I was basically against it, but for food, if a man was hungry, I saw little wrong with taking an occasional deer if there were plenty around.

Ed suddenly fished a well-thumbed booklet from his pocket and handed it to me. "Read that. Don't you think that's wrong? It is sick when men kill so many hanimals as that, don't you think?"

I looked through the booklet. It was headed *Inventory and Evaluation of the Wildlife Resource of British Columbia.* Compiled by the British Columbia Fish and Game Branch, it had been presented at the ninth British Columbia Natural Resources Conference. One table that caught my eye showed the yield of wild furs caught in British Columbia from 1931 to 1963. The figures seemed astounding for the year 1962–63 alone: 26,529 beavers, 1,919 of the uncommon fishers, 12,570 lynx, 8,099 martens, 1,363 otters, 10,821 weasels, and even 40 of the rare wolverines. My surprise increased as I read a second table compiled by two eminent British Columbia biologists that showed numbers of big-game animals shot by hunters that year: 68,000 deer, 4,900 elks, 600 mountain sheep, 2,100 mountain goats; but the figures that staggered me most were 18,722 moose, 400 grizzly bears (plus an estimated illegal kill of 25 percent), and 3,000 black bears.

Ed watched me intently as I thumbed through the report. The apparent attitude behind the writing shocked me, "... it is estimated total expenditures by hunters exceeded $23.6 million. If the market of fur bearers in 1962, amounting to more than $900,000, is added to this sum, then the harvested 1962 value is estimated at $24.5 million. The value to nonconsumptive users (i.e., photographers, tourists, observers) is considered to equal this sum, hence the total wildlife value is $49 million ... The wildlife resource is relatively unexploited in relation to potential yield so an increase in the number of users will result in a greater harvest ... each game animal will become more valuable as hunter competition increases. In both ways the value of the wildlife resource will be enhanced by increases in the size of the province's human population."

I stared at Ed in amazement.

"Oh ho ho," said Ed, trimming yet another shake. "Hi thought that would interest you! It seems, to them, that hanimals are honly meat, honly money, dollars."

"Eighteen thousand moose, four hundred grizzlies and a hundred killed illegally," I said, hardly believing what I'd read. "In a single year, in just this one province? I thought grizzlies were dying out?" All I knew at the time of my talk with Ed was that there were fewer than a thousand of these last great monarchs of the north woods left in the contiguous United States. And yet here, just over a man-made border, they were killing some five hundred a year for sport.*

"They are," said Ed emphatically. "Mark my words, the big bears *har* rarer now than when I first came here. Men want to be heroes, go home and say, 'Hi killed a big bear.' You know, when hi was in the Yukon after the first war, there was a big row going on because the Alaskan farmers could kill any bear they saw within a mile of their livestock."

"If they killed sheep or cattle."

"No, no. If they just *saw* one near their farm. There was a big row. But in 1930, they were protected again. Protected! It's like that today – that report says they're 'protected' too, but they're only 'protected' so they can be shot in the spring and fall by hunters. How do they know how many to kill, know how many cubs are being born, how many survive? Hit's not only hunting – all their land is being taken away. If something isn't done, the grizzly will be extinct in fifty years."

Soon Ed was talking volubly about bears, describing how a black bear weighing four hundred pounds or more could climb a tree like a squirrel, yet a mature grizzly, with longer, flatter claws, could not. "The grizzly is just about the most intelligent hanimal in the world," he said. "Every one is different, like humans, acts different in the same situation. You never can tell what hit will do. And strong? I reckon a big grizzly could heasily kill a lion. You hear many stories, but they rarely attack man, you know. Hi've walked through thick swamps and tidal flats with grass four feet high, with grizzlies lying in thickets all around, so close I could smell them. Just like hogs!"

" Yessir, they usually let you go. Hi was only once charged and hi got up a tree – had to stay there three hours before it went away! But I didn't mind – hit gave me a chance to see one real close. I had a gun but I wouldn't shoot it."

"No use running, I suppose?"

"Heck no. A grizzly can go as fast as a racehorse for sixty yards. And it can run sideways along a steep mountain faster than a dog. People say they're clumsy and because they have short legs they'll fall if you run downhill from them. Boy, a grizzly

---

*Twelve years after this book was first published the B.C. wildlife authorities told me they were stabilising their grizzly population at more than 5,000 animals, hunting had been reduced by 60%, and all nursing females and young up to two years old, were now protected.

can go hanywhere a man can go! Hand with their claws they dig into rocks and roots better than a goat."

When I asked how he knew so much about bears, Ed told me they had fascinated him as a younger man. On vacations he had trekked alone into wild mountains south of Bella Coola, nearly halfway up the British Columbian coast, to study them. Once he had trekked with a pal named Pappy Tihoni to a place they called their secret valley, where they had seen more than two dozen grizzlies in three days. What little he told me that day of that adventure sounded incredible, but when I pressed him for exact information about the secret valley he suddenly laughed, as if to disguise the fact he didn't want to tell me much more.

"Listen, hi've come here to help build your house," he said, "so let's get hon with it. We don't want to waste this good weather sitting here just jawing."

As we began work again, I asked how old he had been when he made his treks into the wilderness of the valley.

"I set out on the first on my fortieth birthday," he said.

"I moved into this tent on mine," I returned. His laugh was not one of derision, but not one of total approval either. "This? This his nothing," he said. "You know, professor, you should go on a trek like that, maybe hin the spring. Yessir, a man like you should go and live in those mountains awhile, go through that wild place. You'll learn a lot, especially about yourself. But it will age you, mind, it'll sure age you!" And with a strange quizzical look at me, a look I never forgot, he went back to work.

By noon on the ninth day the entire cabin frame was up, including a beautifully finished golden-shake roof that, from the sea a mile away, glowed like an amber jewel amid the forest green. And it had cost me little but the price of nails. Ed ate his lunch, brushed the crumbs of his homemade shortbread from his knees, and stood up.

"Well, hi think I'll go and do some fishing now." He looked up at the sky. "Not many good days left. Yessir, a fine afternoon's fishing and tomorrow I move back into the old cabin again."

"I'll come and help you move, Ed, with the truck."

"Ho, thank you, but hit's not necessary. Hi've only two bags of tools, some clothes and I have all day. You get the sides on. Get your sides up while it's still dry!" And off he went, knowing I could see to the rest myself.

I had run out of logs and drift lumber and had no time left to collect more before the late Indian summer ended, so I compromised. I would plywood the walls and cover them with shakes later. It took another week to buy the plywood at the small town to the south, haul it by sea or down the trail two sheets at a time when the wind was high, and scribe the unwieldy sheets to fit the studs and log rafters exactly. I also bought secondhand windowpanes but smashed one getting it down the trail. At times I balanced on primitive scaffolding high above the rocky beach, not daring to look down. It was a partial cure for my slight vertigo. I *had* to do it. By knocking in a large nail to hold onto with my left hand, and taking smaller nails from my mouth and driving them into place by holding them against the hammer head with my right, I finally had all the sheets in place. I blocked in the windows with straight cedar slivers, cut a hole in the back wall for the stove pipe and its asbestos collar, then took down my tent and stowed it on the rocks in the pie-shaped kitchen below.

For a bed I nailed four planks onto crosspieces and set them across my two primitive sawhorses in a rear corner. This not only kept the sawhorses dry and out of the way but gave me a high bed under which I had plenty of storage space. I put the kidney-shaped desk below the front window, giving me a view over the islands that I hoped would be an inspiration as I wrote throughout the winter. Dragging the solid two-foot-six-inch mahogany door, given to me by a friend in Vancouver, from its storage place in the kitchen, I hung it from the rear southeast pillar, then nailed felt strips around its frame to make it draught proof. The first time I swung it, it closed with a solid, satisfying, and silent clunk. Nailing the three-tier wooden shelves I'd made for the tent to the studs of the south wall and filling them with my books and sea-scoured ornaments, I was surprised at how much room there was left in the twelve-foot-square cabin.

Proudly I descended the log staircase and walked down to take a good look at the results of all the hard work. As far as I could see in every direction there was no sign of human habitation, but there, in the midst of the virgin forest green, rose my new home. With its single window in the front, like a Cyclops eye on the world, it looked like a quaint wooden garage on stilts. Suddenly, I began to laugh. While in my former city life I'd never believed 'the apparel oft proclaims the man', I'd certainly thought a man's home proclaimed his character, and therefore a smart area mattered. What foolish masochism it seemed now. The nearer the maelstrom – the busy, noisy, nerve centre of the city – the costlier it is to live, and the harder you have to work, amid the greater din, in order to stay there!

As I lay on my bed that night, with the candlelight playing on the golden walls, the air heavy with wood fragrance, and my superb view, framed by the window, I felt an extraordinary exhilaration. Nothing had ever given me more pleasure than working with Ed and making this simple home in the wilds.

My joy was short-lived. Overnight, as if it had co-operated only until the moment I was safely inside, the weather broke. A cold wind, bringing low dark clouds from which big blobs of rain spattered onto the new roof, came in from the northwest, probing its fingers into every crevice and gap like some building inspector appointed by nature. There's nothing like a blast or two of wind to show you your gale-proof cabin is not! I spent hours blocking tiny holes from poorly-aimed nails and slight warps in the roof boards, and scribing extra bits of wood around the inner sides of the log rafters.

It was much colder the second night, and next day I hauled the old oil barrel, in which I'd already cut a stoking door and smoke outlet, into the cabin. This combined heater, cook stove, and incinerator was a great idea, I thought, and as it was going to be sorely needed, it had to be right. I was hammering away when I heard shrill chatters and squeaks coming from outside. Sitting on the curving fir's branch a mere four yards above my head was a cheeky Douglas squirrel. I had seen him previously, scuttering around his treetop estate, making little showers of dried moss and chittering shrilly at anything that moved, but he had never come so close before. Now he was clinging to the rough bark with little claws, jerkily flirting his bushy, yellow-tipped tail, and scolding me for all he was worth. I wanted to be friendly, so I tossed a crust of bread onto the cabin roof, went back to work, and forgot him.

A few minutes later he was back, scolding again. I stopped hammering and waited, dead still. Soon there was a clonk on my roof, a patter of clawed feet, then nothing. Slowly I inched out and climbed onto the big rock near the door, and sneaked a look over the roof. He was sitting on his little haunches, his long bushy tail curved like an S above his head, and in his delicate hands he held my bread up to his mouth, nibbling away with his buck teeth. "Hi, Douglas," I said softly. Instantly he bounded about six feet, hit the edge of the roof, and shot up the fir, then turned and cursed me roundly for disturbing his meal.

That first day hardly boded well for a friendship with my new neighbour, but apparently Douglas' demanding stomach enabled him to overlook my thoughtless hammering – next day he was back. Around dawn he landed on my roof with a thud that belied his weight, which can't have been more than a dozen ounces, and scampered around looking for an easy breakfast. He came for lunch, tea, and dinner too – for he was hard at work. All day he gathered fir and pine cones, standing on one branch and reaching up on tiptoe to haul down the one above with both hands to see if it had a cone or two on it. Then he'd bounce down to the forest floor with tail-flipping, jerky movements and hare off with his booty – where to I never knew. He must have been stuffing them in his nest, under roots and stones and hollow logs for his winter hoard, for he often came back with his face grey with dust and his whiskers sparkling with white and amber crystals of resin. Douglas worked even harder than Ed Louette. It really cinched our relationship, however, when I found him drinking rainwater from a dish I'd accidentally left out near the kitchen. From then on I filled it each morning and put it on a projecting beam on the leeward side of the cabin. Now he didn't have to do his little Tarzan act through the high foliage to get to the creek to the north of my land. He became tamer and tamer, going hoppity-hoppity over my roof, scrabbling down the log pillars, stopping every now and then to give a little warbling song.

8   Winter Solitude

*F*or three mornings Douglas had failed to appear. The wind had been roaring around the cabin, and as I lay abed, reluctant to swing my bare feet out into the new cold day with its dark cloud masses racing above the little window, winter arrived with a rattle and a bang. The rattle came from the hailstones hitting my roof, sounding as if someone had climbed the curving fir beside the cabin and, was hurling down buckets of gravel. The bang brought me out of bed with a leap, and as I reached the side window I saw a tall white snag tree forty yards south of the cabin, which I had intended to fell, hurtle down the slope point first like some medieval battering ram and then shoot over the cliff in a shower of rocks.

There were a fair number of those old snags around me, but I'd been reluctant to drop them as they made special homes for all kinds of moths and beetle grubs, and were sometimes used by wood-peckers for nesting holes and I wanted a few of these gay black, white, and red birds with their odd looping flight and mad laughing cries about me in the spring. What I hadn't figured was that these branchless snags, their bare trunks made slippery by rain, would fall forward. One, tobogganing down like some runaway ballistic missile, could easily go straight through my cabin and, or, me.

After breakfast I climbed up with saw, rope, and axe but found only one about a hundred yards up that seemed on a possible collision course with the cabin. To make sure it didn't go forward I reached up as high as I could and roped it to a nearby fir. It was like axing and sawing through stone, but finally I had it rocking. I heaved on the rope until the last ominous crack, then a heavy pull brought it down as I leaped out of its way. As it lay on its side, prevented from sliding down by the rope on the fir, I realized I'd found another way of keeping fit through the winter. By now I had it all figured out – my survival in the wilderness winter. My biggest problem would be loneliness. I could combat that by escaping into my novel – the characters would be company of a sort, and weaving incidents together would help take me out of myself. But as every writer or desk-bound office worker knows, sitting down for hours dulls body and mind, fat settles around the middle-aged waist, the blood meanders sluggishly through the veins, and even the brain grows lethargic. But I had two basic needs – food and firewood. I'd been alarmed by how much wood my oil-barrel stove could burn up – a whole tree of one-foot logs would roar away in a day if I wasn't careful. Well, the moment I felt writer's cramp I could at least come and hack away at old snags like this. Or I could row out a few miles and tow back drift logs from the beaches. And I could fish at the same time.

This part of my fine plan soon came unstuck, though. In the rough seas my rickety little boat sprang several new leaks and was soon beyond any patch-up jobs with paint or plywood for winter use. I could not buy a bigger one because I needed to conserve finances. So I laid night fishing lines. Walking out at low tide and anchoring a stout nylon line to a rock, baiting a few dozen hooks with half-cooked mussels and odd bacon and kitchen scraps, I managed to retrieve a few small fish on the next low tide. Any big fish that took a bait had ample time to break free and tangle the line among the seaweed. I tried hauling the line back at high water and on the few occasions it didn't snag on rocks or weed, I did harvest a few fish. But as the days grew colder and the fish deserted the shore for deeper and warmer water, I often caught nothing at all.

My quandary seemed solved when I met Ed on his beach one day in October. He told me he was leaving in a few days to spend the winter in Vancouver, where he could read for hours in the fine new library or observe the foibles of his fellow man in the public gallery of the courthouse. "If you will give me and my tools a ride to the ferry next week," he said, "hi will leave my boat behind for you." It was a fine, sturdy mahogany rowing boat, kept in spanking condition. Fishing on good days would help me solve the food problem, and the rowing would keep middle-aged spread at bay.

On my way to the store a few days later, Ed's cabin seemed ominously deserted. The red cotton curtains were drawn and it stood forlornly in the rain, a padlock on its door. On a sudden premonition I ran across the road and looked over the cliff. A large eighty-foot fir that always had grown seaward at an alarming angle, its branches streaming out from the winds like a girl's hair in a storm, had fallen down. And one of its largest limbs had driven straight through the bottom of Ed's boat and also had split the log wharf on which it rested. The dinghy looked like an agonized shrimp impaled on a gigantic cocktail stick. For a frightening moment I thought Ed might have been trapped underneath and I hurried down to check. But there was no sign of him. Relieved, I then realized he would have completed any work on the beach before locking up the cabin.

At the post office hut I found a short note from him. Two days ago he had been walking down the cliff path in a high wind to turn his boat when the tree had crashed down. Had he gone down half a minute earlier, he would have been killed. He regarded this mishap as an act of God, felt he had overstayed his welcome, and when a logger friend had stopped by on the way to the ferry, he had accepted a lift. He was sorry not to be able to say goodbye.

Now I had no boat at all for the winter. I felt oddly lonely as I walked down the trail, the white-capped sea crunching into granite hollows, dragging rocks back into the deeper waters with a loud clacking sound. The tall alders near my well had lost nearly all their leaves and their slender grey-green trunks swayed rhythmically in the wind. They looked like great eels, their tails wedged in murky roots and bushes, rearing their heads as if waiting for some passing fish to seize and devour. The dogwood bush was now bereft, its lovely white flower bracts a mere memory. Only the deep glossy leaves of the tough salal and the thick, glabrous green-and-violet leaves of the red huckleberry seemed to be standing up to the onslaught of the wind among the bushes on the more sheltered outcrops. Here and there twisted arbutus trees stood in clusters, their red bark peeling and fluttering in ribbons, revealing bright green skin beneath, their long, dark leathery leaves rattling against each other as if reluctant to let go and die.

As I stood on the forest edge, sheltering beneath the drooping wet sprays of a red cedar and saw a few broad red leaves clinging to the topmost twigs of a solitary maple, I reflected how profound were the changes now going on around me. The leaves, glowing scarlet as if with anger, shimmered and shivered as if loath to leave their vantage point of summer. No, no, they shook their heads, but one by one the relentless wind plucked them from their perches and sent them swinging to the forest floor, where they joined the twin-winged seeds they had once sheltered.

How often we stand alone in a forest when all seems still and feel nothing is happening, that it is at peace. Yet all the time the forest is changing, through birth, growth, death, decay, and rebirth at a pace too slow for us to comprehend. Now, I thought, in the autumn nature is quickening her pace. As the sun's trajectory lowers and its powers wane, the warm air rises from the summer-heated land. Cold winds rush in, the sap ceases to rise, leaves lose their food supply and their waterproof coats, and rain soaks in, making them heavy. Winds tear them away as frost and hail complete the task. Down to the forest floor the leaves float, adding to the humus of the ages that one day will form the food for new plant life. The storming gales snap old trees, leaving the stumps as homes for insects, or blow them down so the upended roots provide safe dens for smaller mammals, new nest sites for birds, and yet more shelter and food for other insects and their larvae. Now the creeks and the rivers swell, gouging out small, loose rocks, wearing away their courses, sweeping away the accumulations of summer – old leaves and dead branches – mulching all together and leaving some as silt upon the low surrounding land, while the rest spreads out in the sea forming new beds and food for weeds and thus nurseries for young fish.

It is easy sometimes to stand thus, a simple smile upon one's face, feeling how beneficial nature is overall, that even at her most cataclysmic – when lightning, forest fires, avalanches, and rock slides do her more dramatic work – she bountifully bestows more than she takes. It is tempting for man to be an optimist. An avalanche may completely flatten a degenerate forest but in following springs this area will encourage new lichens, bushes, and grasses for many animals. Yet the avalanche has destroyed animals in its path too. Lightning may strike a dry, dead tree and burn a few around it, creating a clearing where new bushes can grow. Yet lightning can also cause fifty square miles of virgin forest to burn to ashes and can kill scores of unwitting creatures trapped in the holocaust. A prolonged downpour may water and irrigate parched land to the benefit of some, yet may cause such flooding it takes years to set the damage right. Nature is bountiful only to those species strong enough to survive her unselective whims and to take advantage of the good.

Shelter, warmth, and food were now my prime concern. For days I wandered the beaches and forests carrying and stacking drift and fallen wood for the primitive stove, making a woodshed from the plastic sheet held down behind screening cedars by logs and rocks. I pickled oysters and mussels in vinegar. I boiled the free berries of fall and fruits like plums and oranges bought at the store in sugar syrup, then bottled them in old honey jars with screw top lids. I remembered my mother telling me as a child, "Make sure no air is left in. The hot liquid shrinks, making a vacuum that keeps germs out." I brined beans, tomatoes, and carrots with salt on the same principle. And I stacked apples and root vegetables in layers of hay and sawdust under my bed.

Until now the wilderness life had been largely idyllic, but in the early winter days I began to find that land untamed or uninhabited by humanity flays the mind, throws it back upon itself. Alone, when the great eagles, ducks, gulls, and other birds have flown south, when animal friends are partly hibernating, or like my skunk, raccoon, and squirrel, have often moved nearer civilized centres for the urban spoils, when the sun hides behind dark cloud on the low horizon day after day, the world becomes an emptier place, almost devoid of life. One is left alone, face to face with no one but oneself, and it can be an unnerving experience.

I didn't know it then, but the loss of Ed's boat was the start of a series of winter mishaps that had me doubting my sanity in leaving my affluent, comfortable, and highly social life in London for a more 'real' life in the Canadian wilds. For three months it seemed nature itself was conspiring against me for my audacity. Ever since I had first found my place in British Columbia I'd had no wish to tame it. I wanted only to live on my land simply, to erect just sufficient shelter for reasonable comfort but not to rape or significantly alter the look or the ecology of the place. Primarily for that reason I had refrained from using rock drills, bulldozing in a road, or blasting out a large well.

Now I found that in winter my well, which had started to fill again, became the home of three dead snakes and four bloated mice, all half-eaten by maggots, whose dead bodies also swirled in the putrid milky water. One glance at that horrible pit and I abandoned the well. I decided to try and use the water from the pipe Ed Louette had found behind my land. I felt I no longer needed the power saw since I had gathered most of my winter fuel, so I sold it to raise funds for over four hundred yards of plastic pipe. Anyone who has ever tried to carry, lay, and half-bury such a length of semi-rigid piping on his own will understand what that project meant. I had to cut it into rolls of a length I could manage, then join it all up later with bits of thicker pipe and metal clips. This alone took a week. Then one day after climbing the three hundred yards of rocky slope to where the hose ended, wedged between two high rocks, I found the water flow had dried up completely!

It took two days of stumbling around in cold rain to trace the pipe's path and find the trouble – a joint had come undone right in the middle of a culvert. Back I scrambled to the cabin for a rope and some clips and only by anchoring myself with the rope against the icy swirling waters in the culvert, after hauling the lower end of the pipe back up from the ravine, could I join it up again. The water was so cold I twice had to climb out and run up and down to get warm. Once I'd made the repair I had to find the head of the pipe higher up in a pool in the creek. It had been ingeniously located behind a deflecting rock so leaves and debris could not enter. Holding it at head height, I had to pour canfuls of water down it for two hours to get the siphon system working. Twice more that winter I had to repeat this procedure to break air locks – just to get what in cities I'd always taken for granted by turning on a tap.

About a week later, as I lay abed listening to a miniature tornado moaning in the log eaves and rattling the windows and door, a distant crash resounded through the forest. It felt like a minor earthquake. I walked up the trail to find a large fir had blown down, missing my truck by less than a yard and completely blocking it in. It was a good two feet thick with many branches. How I cursed myself for selling the power saw! Well, at least here was some good exercise. I went back to the cabin for my bucksaw, sledgehammer, and a sharp stake. By tying one end of the saw to a strip of old inner tube wrapped around the driven stake, I made a rough "sawing partner" and managed to cut the trunk into sections. I felt great pleasure levering the huge chunks of tree to the edge of a rocky escarpment and watching them disappear downhill in a cascade of rocks. Now I could at least get the truck out again.

It seemed ironic when I received a letter from a friend in London. "What on earth are you doing, still out there on that rock alone, dodging reality?" he wrote. I pictured him at his desk writing for popular magazines, wrestling with articles he did not believe about people he did not admire, feeling murderous towards his neighbour for letting their dog bark in the garden, worrying about the rising costs of his heating, petrol, taxes, seeking solace at night in smoky bars where inconsequential chatter became a boon for it prevented too much thinking. I ... dodging reality?

Grey day now followed shorter grey day as November crept past. Dark lowering clouds rolled by overhead, and the sound of rain hammering on the roof and against the cabin walls became so much a part of everyday life I hardly heard it anymore. Rain does more than wet you somehow. It rains on your heart, your spirit, dampening down even the process of thought. I rose each morning and half-slid down to the kitchen, holding onto the guy rope of my gin pole, its water running down my armpits, to stop myself slithering over the muddy rock faces and over the cliff. As I cooked and ate breakfast in the cramped space, door tightly shut in the half-dark, and heard the ceaseless pounding of the waves against the cliff, I wished I had built the cabin farther up the slope. Reason told me it would take maybe a thousand years to wear away such durable granite, yet at times it felt the great rollers were battering into my very foundations. Then up the slope I scrambled, a spare log under each arm to dry by the smoky stove, shut the cabin door fast and worked on my book for another eight- or ten-hour stint.

Until now consciousness of my complete isolation had been allayed by all the joys of outdoor summer life, by fascinating experiences with the animal life around me, by building my platform, by meeting Ed and building my cabin with him. But now, imprisoned by bad weather, immersed in my book, I felt the real pangs of solitude. I found myself becoming more and more reliant upon the mail as a kind of emotional anchor. About once a fortnight I returned down the trail clutching what few letters I received, relishing the thought of reading them. Then I hoarded them for hours. Putting them on the desk, I'd find jobs to do, prepare supper, *anything* rather than actually read them and have nothing more to look forward to. Then as the simple meal bubbled away, I'd sip a glass or three of homemade wine, arrange the letters with the least interesting at the top and the more intimate ones from friends at the bottom.

The first reading of a personal letter was always quick. I skipped words and sentences deliberately, to tease myself with the promise of the second reading, which was always after supper. Then, with the dishes washed, pipe drawing well, the logs popping in the stove, I would devour the contents avidly, often finding meanings that were not really there.

When a postal strike lasted five weeks, my previous dislike of the modern curse of strikers – who think nothing of paralysing essential services with their too-frequent demands for more pay and shorter hours, a symptom no longer of human rights but of laziness, greed and social decay – became an irrational hatred. I maintained a tight courtesy in my dealings at the distant post office and store, but I tied a rough sack of sand to the fir tree nearest my cabin and gave it a few hefty wallops if I returned home letterless! At this time I could hardly believe I'd had such a busy social life in London, Paris, Madrid, Rome and Hollywood. It had all faded in my memory and now seemed unreal.

At last the strike was over and I returned home with a whole bag of letters. In anticipation, I cooked myself a three-course meal, put a bottle of wine on the desk, and happily went through all the mail. It was early in the morning when I got to the letter I was cherishing until last. It contained the worst blow I had received all winter. The girl I had believed might join me in Canada, once I'd established myself in my new life, wrote that she had fallen in love with someone else. The disappointment drove me in upon myself more than ever.

By late November loneliness had become a powerful enemy. I needed human company now, if only for a short while. Twice I tried walking up the trail and driving to a beer parlour near the town. I knew some of the men from my previous fishing work and short logging experience – good, mad, simple characters. Struggling, albeit a little pretentiously, as I then was with what I felt to be momentous issues in my book, I felt little kinship with the raucous beery talk of big fish and trees, or the tough horseplay. I sat in the smoky haze, the lost emigrant, with little to contribute for my interests were not their interests.

On my second and last visit I was invited home by a tough, scarred old logger to meet his family. All night Floyd had been the cynosure of the bar, telling outrageous stories, arm wrestling everyone with ease, a rough, happy-go-lucky, hard-drinking character. I was certainly surprised when I entered his cabin to find he had five fine-looking children. All were well-dressed and polite, the room spotless. Proudly his wife gave me their youngest baby to hold – it was the first child of two I'd ever had on my knee – and in response to a compliment I paid, Floyd began expounding his unsentimental theories of fatherhood. As I listened to this uneducated man who could barely read and write and held his lovely child, aware of the love that existed among them all, I was suddenly overcome by an appalling sense of desolation. Compared with this simple man, I had nothing but my fancy ideas, my private search for a life of meaning. It seemed that all I had ever really wanted was here, now, in this room. I felt old for the first time in my life, a complete failure in human relationships. The baby giggled against my cheek and tweaked my ear with her tiny pink fingers. "She likes you," said the mother.

"A man like you should be married," Floyd responded, laughing in his hearty way. "It's not natural, living down on that cliff, all alone like a hermit." I tried to speak, to form some affable reply but was suddenly conscious of a look, a bashful downcast glance from his eldest daughter. She stood by her mother's chair, one hand on its back while with the other she gracefully moved a lock of raven hair from a small oval face with skin like roseate alabaster. Her eyes were so deep a blue they seemed almost violet. She was beautiful, like the young Ava Gardner. In that second, in every unconscious curving pose of her young body, the power of early womanhood seemed trapped in all its devastating, teasing innocence. She was barely half my age.

Managing some fatuous remark about being too old, too broke, and too cranky, thanking them for their hospitality, and trying not to appear in a hurry, I made some excuse about its getting dark and took my leave. As I stumbled down the trail, I cursed myself for a fool.

For the whole of that winter, my novel now became what no book should ever be – my entire raison d'être. And a prop, the last and only prop, against an increasing spiritual as well as physical isolation. Naïvely, perhaps absurdly, the theme of the novel was one at which even a Tolstoy, Mann, or Kazantzakis would have balked. I was trying to redefine creative love at its highest concept, to strip the Christian ethic from all its supernatural myths and to try and show how it could be lived today.

The anti-hero trend in the literature of the day bored and irritated me. We could laugh at Lucky Jim, Billy Liar, Portnoy, Sebastian Dangerfield; we could love their weaknesses but we could never *admire* them. I wanted to create a true modern hero – a return to romanticism perhaps, but to a new kind of romanticism without illusions – a man who lived his ideals come what may. It was, of course, a grandiose concept and, for me, perhaps a foolish one. But I was here. I was alone. Therefore I was committed.

As I recorded my protagonist's wasteful, hedonistic years, I found myself forced to dip into my own experiences. In the long, aching winter silences, broken only by the clacking of the typewriter, I raked through the embers of my own past fifteen years and the disturbing realization that I had become a shallow and selfish man. This was driven home most forcibly one day when, still sad at the rejection by my girl in London, disturbed by the logger's description of me as an unnatural hermit and the lingering memories of his beautiful daughter, I decided to try and recall every single woman I'd ever known. By thoroughly investigating this aspect of my past, not only might I recall a few amusing, sexy, or tragicomic anecdotes that might serve as a basis for some parts of the book, but I would perhaps discover what influences women had had upon my life. I doubt if there is a man alive who can honestly say women have had no significant influence on his life!

I wrested my old address books from the filing cabinet in the kitchen, sat at my desk and stolidly typed them all out, every woman with whom I'd had an affair, long, short or extremely brief. After the months of celibacy, I was astonished by their sheer numbers. Some of them had been, still were, famous names regarded as among the world's most beautiful women. Where once one might have felt an enormous boost to the ego from the sheer sensual feast one had apparently enjoyed for so many years, I now stared at the disembodied list with dismay. I had become accustomed to being loved – but how little real love there had been. The picture I now saw of myself was not a pleasant one.

I recalled some words of Ernest Hemingway, 'Nobody knows what's in him until he tries to pull it out. If there's nothing, or very little, the shock can kill a man'. I knew now I could write little of what I was attempting until I understood my *self* clearly. The past now returned to beguile, to reveal significant aspects that were often unpleasant, to force guilt upon the conscious mind. And it did so with a power impossible amid the day-to-day distractions of city life. During this enforced self analysis, it seemed as if the ultimate salvation of my protagonist was running side by side with my own.

The work *had* to be done if ever I was to respect myself again. And it was here the attempt at patience began, the monumental patience any man needs to survive emotionally alone in the wilds.

On fine days I rowed my battered boat to the nearest rocky islets, filling my bag with mussels and oysters. These now had to be scooped up by a homemade wooden scraper as even the low tides covered most of them. And I reset a night line, anchored to a float some quarter of a mile out, but I was lucky if it produced a fish a week. Most evenings I huddled round the stove, reading by oil lamp and candlelight all those great philosophers and thinkers of the past so many of us say we'll read one day. I immersed myself in Nikos Kazantzakis' magnificent autobiography, *Report to Greco*, and searched deeply into the works of Nietzsche, Jung, Radhakrishnan, the Upanishads, Maritain, Schweitzer, Madariaga, Sartre, and the Buddhist, Moslem, and Jewish religions, seeking arguments, insights, and inspiration. Arbitrarily approving and rejecting in the light of my own thoughts and experiences, I'd never done so much pure, sustained thinking in my life. At times I felt triumphant surges of mental and spiritual growth as new insights came, but at others I felt my head would burst if I absorbed any more, as if one new thought would send me insane. Even knowing my own intellectual inadequacy, I persevered, not through courage but because to give up would have meant surrendering to the pangs of loneliness, to constant and perhaps unendurable awareness of my personal isolation.

I tried to assuage depression by physical exertion, sawing firewood, digging out rocks and making steps up from the kitchen, running along the logging tracks. I thought too of some great creative figures: Van Gogh in an asylum; Rembrandt dying in poverty; Byron and Shelley drowning; the final despair and persecution of Tolstoy; Nietzsche struggling with insanity. I thought of the assassinations of Lincoln, Gandhi, Kennedy, and of how both Hemingway and Fitzgerald died believing they were defeated men. If such exalted lives could end so, if there were millions of people

73

starving, dying, lying sick in hospitals all over the world, what in hell's name did a little loneliness in the life of a fool like myself matter? Not a jot.

"About time you suffered a bit, lad," I told the white face and black-ringed eyes in the piece of broken mirror. "You had your fun, so get back to your desk and *work*!" I said it aloud for I had now started talking to myself. It's said when a man talks to himself he is nearing madness. I think I would have gone mad if I had not. "No man is an island, entire of itself," wrote John Donne, but John Donne committed suicide. The words came to haunt and taunt me continually.

One ploy I used to stave off the crushing pressures of solitude was to try and live in my imagination outside the book as well as when writing it. If I could not have old friends or a woman I loved about me, then I could *imagine* their presence. At night, my work over, I would deliberately project myself into a fanciful world, creating scenes, conversations, situations, where everything that happened could either be romantically ideal or awful. It is surprising how this art can be perfected and can take the edge off loneliness.

But I was not yet free of the old fetters, and some nights I would lie tortured by images, particularly of women I had known. I had strange dreams of fantasy, half awake and half asleep, when I was struggling along in flowing streams of lips, breasts, and thighs, the faces flying above, below, and all around me, laughing, scolding, crying, jeering, mocking, teasing, withdrawing.

I did have some companionship, however. No sooner had I climbed into bed most nights than I would be disturbed by the mice, twice the size of British mice, who galloped around the cabin floor which, in the still, dark night, reverberated like a drum. They had discovered in the kitchen a perfect labyrinth of posts, shelves, and rock ledges along which they could run, jump, slide, and leap until they reached the food. Now and again I heard a plop as they fell onto the tar paper below the washbowl. Once full of my food, they sneaked through tiny hidden gaps into the cabin to play in the warmth from the embers of my stove. At first I shouted, threw things, and set a trap that cracked their spines. But the trouble was every time I heard the trap snap, I lay there wondering if the bar had just injured and not killed outright, so I had to get up, finish the mouse off with a sharp blow from a stick, and empty the trap outside.

Why was I killing them, anyway? I asked myself. It seemed they were the only forms of life near me, so, like a convict in solitary, I began to cultivate their friendship. To stop them from possibly fouling my blankets, I tore an old one into strips, built them a long, compartmented box from drift tree slabs in the far side of the kitchen, and stuffed it with the strips, torn-up newspaper, and dry brush. To allow them access to the cabin floor from the kitchen, I punched out a knothole above their box, covering it with a piece of tin before I went to bed so they wouldn't get back to wake me with their thundering around. And I put all my dry stores into a tin box and at suppertime after feeding myself, doled out their rations on the cabin floor.

Now I realized what beautiful little animals they were, with their black sparkling eyes, long whiskers, soft white bellies, and engaging, timorous habits. Rats and mice carry germs, say folks with horror. Yet these mice, far from human sewage and habitation were forever grooming and washing themselves like little cats. They were not house mice, tough little town terrors, they were deer mice, with spotless white boots on their feet. If they ever had to walk across mud or wet ground, they raised themselves up high, sort of on tiptoe, hurrying across into the dry again. Often I heard them squeaking, but sometimes they made an oddly sweet singing sound – a song the male makes when ready to mate.

I began looking forward to our little dinner parties and gave each one a name, sitting dead still while they cavorted and chased each other over the floor. One Saturday night as they all sat around my circle of crumbs and cheese, I realized I had created a miniature Round Table, that the large one nearest their knothole who seemed to be looking at the others rather than eating could have been a mouse King Arthur. "Not might is right," I quoth at them, waving my wine glass. "But might *for* right!" And as they scuttled for cover from the din of the human voice, I realized maybe I was doing rather more quaffing than quothing. But they were soon back, nibbling away and wiping their long whiskers clear of crumbs, snatching titbits from each other like children at a party when left to their own devices.

Early one evening I saw one of the larger mice, distinctive for a kink in its tail, sitting on a branch of the curving fir near the cabin, busily chewing a conifer seed. Suddenly another mouse hared up the tree and ran toward it. Off they went, flattened out like a pair of lizards along the branch, leaped on the cabin roof, down the rear log pillar, and vanished under the cabin near the long box. A few days later I looked through the knothole and saw Kinky Tail, her mouth stuffed with a square inch of blanket, making a nest almost the size of a small melon. And she was a good deal plumper than I'd last seen. "Thanks, boys and girls," I said as I replaced the tin covering. "Thanks a lot for reminding me." As if life alone wasn't tough enough!

One fine morning in early December as I wandered through the forest before visiting the store down the coast, I realized how much I was dreading the coming of Christmas. Spending Christmas alone is all right if it's a change to be alone, but to be solitary throughout the festival without a break from long months of nothing else but one's own company is something else. I wished for a moment I could hibernate for a while, at least until Christmas was past and gone.

Suddenly I stopped – straight before me, half hidden by a high clump of salal growing on some rocks, was a naked body. It looked like that of a woman and it was somehow draped, head down, over a rock. My heart missed a beat, then started pounding loudly. Was I about to become witness to the results of some foul murder? Was she – perhaps she was still alive? Fearful, wondering what I would do when I got there anyway, I ran toward it.

I found myself staring at a deformed arbutus tree. Its red-brown limbs had grown into the shape of a naked girl, with twisting legs, buttocks, waist, breasts, and elongated arms but no head, only the trunk where the head should be. I sat down to recover myself. Was I really going crazy? Is this what isolation was doing? I climbed into the truck and drove to the store. At the meat counter, the owner finished serving a woman, then turned to me with a smile. I pointed to a dish of ground beef.

"Haa," I said. "Haa—ha—wan—" With sudden panic I realized I could not speak. I knew what I wanted to say, but my mouth refused to work in co-ordination with my lungs and vocal cords.

"Are you okay, Mike?" said the owner. "You look kind of white." "I'm okay," I said suddenly. "I'm fine." I coughed. "Just not used to talking." I passed it off with an attempt to smile. "I want two pounds of ground beef," I said slowly, deliberately, and loudly. I was all right after that, but I was conscious as I spoke to people then that there was an odd gap between what I thought and wanted to say and the exact moment when my lips would actually form the words. I felt as if my mouth were half-stitched or made of thick rubber. And I had developed a definite lisp. When I got home that day I started a daily programme of reading aloud to myself, passages from Shakespeare and some favourite speeches from *Cyrano de Bergerac.* After a page or two my throat was sore from so much talking! If anyone had happened to walk past my cabin and heard some of my monologues, he would doubtless have returned to his friends and told them there was a mad old hermit down near the beach.

As the days crept on toward Christmas I was not too sure he would not have been right. All my little ploys to stave off loneliness – talking to myself, dinner parties with the mice, hard physical exertion, losing myself in work and imaginary mental arguments with thinkers of the past – were losing their effectiveness. Day after day the low sky seemed to lean heavily upon the earth and upon my spirit. Damp and cold waited in the cabin corners with inexhaustible patience, ready to creep back into the bed coverings, the books, my clothes, even into my bones, when the fire went out. Some days were mere grey hushes – a scarcely noticeable difference between the long nights as I sat huddled in three sweaters, two pairs of trousers, three pairs of socks in my boots – and the flickering candlelight made the typed words jump and twitch before my red-rimmed eyes.

A strange inner sadness grew as Christmas loomed nearer. I seemed to stand apart from myself, and as I looked at all around me, having been so long without social intercourse with fellow humans, I unconsciously began to invest the inanimate objects with thoughts and feelings. It no longer seemed odd to touch the trunks of the great firs and cedars and speak to them, promise I would never cut them down and would protect them if they would shelter me. The logs now trapped in my cabin walls – had they not once been live, growing trees, holding their crowns to heaven, reaching out with delicate sprays of green to greet the early spring? Did they now mind being so imprisoned, or would they have preferred to lie freely upon the beaches, drifting on the tides to new places, new log friends around them! As I lay in bed at night looking at my huge fir-root ornament on top of my bookshelves, its writhing golden arms formed the shape of a Spanish galleon and in the tortuous light appeared to move, breasting the shadows and sailing away into the night. The face of Leonardo da Vinci in a painting Eva Bartok had bought for me in Florence, now lit by the moonlight through the window, broke into a sardonic smile, and once it seemed the eyes looked up from their eternal work and looked into mine with a fathomless yet critical stare.

One windless night, just for a change I made a small fire outside to cook my supper and was sitting there watching the light from the flickering flames. Suddenly I saw faces everywhere, in the whorls of trees' bark, in the crevices of rocks; and the branches above me were like twisted human limbs trapped forever, yearning for freedom. As I stirred the vegetables in my pot they rolled upward in the simmering water, as if trying to escape the agony of its boiling heat, each bean and pea a sacrifice to my arbitrary human need to eat and live. I remembered once in the summer when feeding some animals around me while having lunch how I suddenly had become conscious of the act of eating. Without food there is no life, no higher thought, nothing. As those know who have seen the trance-like state of starving thousands in India and Africa, without food there is no mind at all. We are all compulsive eaters or we die. I recalled now, this winter night, how I'd read that even plants have feelings, that those living close to nature had found by speaking to plants, treating them with loving care, the plants flourished far beyond the normal, yet these people finally consumed the plants to live themselves. What kind of creation was this that could survive only by destruction, what life, that was supportable only by consuming other life! What terrible trap were we in? What deity had created this cruel system? And as the light from the flames danced the thousand faces into life and they seemed to draw ever nearer, as if sensing my weakness now, I felt there was an incarnate, malevolent diabolism in the very air about me, that I was wrecked in some Stygian hell, with no one but myself to blame.

Two days before Christmas I'd had enough. Now the feeling of utter isolation, the sense of deserting and being deserted by all we call normal life made me fear for my reason. And a wretched feeling had come, too, that I had become nothing more than a misfit solitary, the book merely an excuse for wishing the world into a private state that suited myself. I had stocked up with some drinks in the hope of chance company, so that night I stopped work, had several glasses of wine, and set out to look for people – any company would do. Most of all I longed for female company, just one sweet smile on a girl's face.

It was a fitful night, full of a stormy hell, with the moon emerging now and again from behind the dark, scudding clouds. On the horizon Telnarko Island was like a giant purple crocodile, its mouth ready to engulf any ship foolhardy enough to venture up the strait at such a time. I walked up the trail by torchlight and as I reached the truck I found a note tucked under the windscreen wiper. Some friends had come on the ferry boat from Vancouver for the three-day holiday and, looking for me, had eventually found the truck but, faced with the thick alder thicket in the dark, had not known where to go next. The note said, they would be in the beer parlour. How wonderful!

I climbed into the truck, started it, and set out to drive fast along what seemed to be the old logging track where it ran along the top of a steep inland cliff. There was a loud bang, the front of the truck went down, then dropped sideways over the cliff. It hit the slope with its side, then its roof, then went on down, the banging becoming louder and faster. I thought, *This is it, God help me, and what a foolish way to go, rolling down a cliff.*

Instinctively I put my hands on the roof, my feet spread-eagled so I was like a starfish pressing back against my seat waiting for the one big final bang when I would know no more. But it never came. The truck suddenly stopped, hitting a tree and a huge rock simultaneously, the right way up, on a mossy bank. Then my door slid back gently, as if opened by a chauffeur. Not until I got out did I feel the pain in my neck, a wrenched arm from clinging to the wheel, and a bump on top of my head where I'd hit the roof on the first bounce. I climbed up the cliff, curiously elated at my escape, loudly and defiantly singing a tune I'd never heard before. Thunder broke out overhead as I walked back down the trail as if in a dream. Back at the cabin I lit the lamp and looked into my piece of shaving mirror to see if I was still really there, and apart from a face as white as the lightning now illuminating the dark woods, I looked perfectly all right. I sat down, drank two bottles of wine staring at the raging seas, and collapsed into bed.

The next two days remain a blur in my memory. I walked out and met my pals from Vancouver and other people. We visited several beer parlours, were in and out of strange houses, and I had a great deal to drink. I found my sweet smile on a girl's face, for the second sleepless, hard-drinking night was spent with a woman. As others retired from the festivities the third day, I recalled later only a mad desire to carry on, that I sank a final tumblerful of neat whisky in the last house, fell asleep in someone's truck, and soon after was in a brawl of my own instigation.

My first normal memory after those strange three days was of sitting alone at my primitive desk, knowing only a desire to finish the book. I swore, as a man will at such times, that I'd never touch alcohol again, and with trembling hands emptied every bottle I had over the cliff. Then I hiked out and apologized for my behaviour to all and sundry before they left for town again.

I felt a new strength then. If I could not in fact live what I was attempting to express, then my work would be baseless. If I could now beat loneliness in this wilderness, its own battleground, I had perhaps beaten it for ever.

One evening, returning from below with my supper, I found Kazantzakis' book lying open at an early page I had not read before, apparently turned by the breeze from the open door. There was nothing on the page but these lines:

Three kinds of soul, three prayers:
I am a bow in your hands, Lord. Draw me lest I rot.
Do not overdraw me, Lord. I shall break,
Overdraw me, Lord, and who cares if I break?

To a man whose soul was drowning, those last wonderful words were like a lifebelt and my heart reached out to thank the great Cretan.

A few nights later I awoke suddenly from a deep sleep and the whole cabin was filled with a strange new light. Grey shadows flitted across the now white walls. The unearthly silence was only broken now and again by a barely discernible hissing sound. At first I wondered if I was dreaming, but finding I was truly awake I got up and looked through the side window. Great snowflakes were falling from the low bank of clouds above, blanketing everything with a white shawl, while to the east wisps scudded across the face of a rising moon. Tiny wind eddies drifted grey phantoms across the clearings under the fir and cedar trees; they leaped from behind rocks like ghosts of men who had been crouching there. I shivered. Now I would have to slog through the snow to the store and I had no snowshoes. As I climbed back into bed I was thankful I'd made a trip two days earlier.

Well before dawn I woke again. The moon was now at its height in a clear sky and the snow had stopped falling. I dressed and took a walk as I was sure another fall would be on its way and I had a sudden desire to see the white-mantled woods before the snow became unpleasantly deep. After crunching through the powdery new carpet for a quarter mile I found myself deep in a cedar grove punctuated by the huge trunks of a few firs with their deeply fissured russet-brown bark. Delicately, as if interlinking them all, the long green sprays of the cedar branches flowed from one to the other, drooping from their shorter grey and crimson fluted trunks as if to form naves in some giant cathedral. Through an opening in the screen canopy against the inky black sky, shafts of moonlight filtered down as if coming through a stained glass window. As they struck the myriad upturned cedar branchlets with their thin covering of snow, they turned them into radiant candles, and now and then they lifted upward as the white crystals fell from them and shimmered down to the forest floor. Clumps of dark salal seemed oddly arranged in rows, like pews waiting for their worshipping occupants. From the near distance came a faint musical sound as the creek, now fed by melting snow along its banks, hastened through its pebbly course to reach the sea. I stood for some moments in silent awe, healed by the balm of this wondrous scene. Then I heard faint footsteps scurrying along – some small creature scuffing through the snow. Now I caught a glimpse of it between the salal. It was a raccoon. Was it Spooks I wondered, but I only saw a flash of its black mask and striped tail, then it was gone again. I stole over to where it had vanished. There in the snow were the tracks of a grouse, and behind, partly obliterating them in places, were the footsteps of the coon, like those of a tiny baby. Why had I never come out like this before, at night in the moonlight? The forest, the world about me, was not dead after all. Some animals were still coming out, even in the cold and snow. I had been so caught up in my work, living inside myself, I just hadn't looked hard enough, or at the right times.

That moonlight walk gave a great lift to my morale and revived my interest in nature, which had somehow gone into hibernation, too, during months of wrestling with the book. Now I resolved to finish the book as soon as possible so I'd be ready, to seek fresh adventures in the spring, maybe even make the trek through bear country that Ed Louette had once suggested.

Although the loss of my truck meant I now had to walk to the far store for essentials and carry them back, a day's work in itself, I found the long hikes wonderful for clearing the mind. I was glad, too, that the snow had melted after a few days. Often I paused in the cedar grove to make notes on a pad – thoughts that would never have come when just sitting down. So in that way I turned the handicap of the long walks into a gain. As the end of the book came into sight and I knew for the first time I could actually finish it, I felt happier.

9 Wild Dog Booto

*I*t was a raging February night. And as I sat at my desk, the rain beating drenching tattoos on the cabin roof, in counterpoint with the cracking of logs in my barrel stove, a movement made me look out of the side window. Two large, green eyes glared in from the darkness, moving from side to side. Suddenly I remembered an old man living alone down the coast who had been attacked by a cougar that came through his window one winter night. A jagged streak of lightning briefly outlined ferocious jaws and the large brown body behind the eyes.

Scared, my heart beating fast, I backed slowly to the rear of the cabin for my torch and axe. At least I'd try and get one good chop at it if it came for me. Keeping well away from the window, I shone the torch – to find myself looking at a large dog! And the reason its eyes were moving from side to side was because its tail was wagging wildly with desperate hope. It was a fearsome-looking dog, nevertheless, a cross between a Labrador and a wolf, with powerful jaws. I opened the door slightly and he seemed to go mad with delight. So I let him in.

He came slithering into the cabin in pools of water, soaked to the bone, wagging his tail so hard his hind legs skittered from beneath him. Despite his wide head, he was as thin as any dog I'd ever seen. The bones showed through his black-and-brown coat, and down his back was a five-inch scar. The look in his eyes said, "I only want to be friends, but please may I have something to eat?" I gave him all he could swallow – the scraps from my supper and two cans of the best chunky steak – and he wolfed it all down as if he thought it the last meal he'd ever eat. Then he spent the next half hour trying to find different ways to thank me – whining, pawing at my legs, burying his wet head in my lap, poignantly responsive to every look or movement I made. As I wiped him dry with a towel, I realized this was probably the animal that had scared away my raccoon, Spooks, in the summer. But now, every time I looked up from my work, I found his deep brown eyes upon me, and his tail thumped the floor to signify friendship.

So Booto, the wild dog from the forests, came into my life. From now on I had a companion for my long tramps. In truth I was more grateful for his company than he was for my food and shelter. I started by calling him Buto because he looked so brutish and I couldn't very well call him Brute. But as I discovered his lovable nature, Buto seemed too harsh and so his name became an affectionate Booto, or sometimes just Boot.

No one I spoke to knew exactly where he had come from. He had been a stray since his puppy days. To win scraps from the loggers and fishermen, he employed a number of cute performances designed to melt the flintiest heart. He used them all with me. He would scratch at a door and when it was opened, he'd sit up and beg in the most endearing way, crossing his white-booted paws with an appealing look. Or he'd roll on the ground and cover his eyes with a paw. Or he'd chew grass suggestively, giving me a look of agonized hunger. The first time he treated me to his little act was the morning after his arrival. Hearing a scratch at the kitchen door as I made lunch, I opened it and there he was, high up on his haunches, boots crossed, and suddenly just the tip of his pink tongue appeared before his face broke into a big grin. It was the way he did it – no awkward rearing up as with most big dogs, no quick push-up with a paw; he just swung up like a jack-in-the-box as if on a spring and stayed there, steady as a rock. I smiled, then roared with laughter, and as I did my face felt strange and I caught a glimpse of myself in the shaving mirror. My smile looked odd, like a grimace of fear, and I realized it was the first smile my face had felt for many months. What a difference a smile makes, I thought, as I gratefully stroked his thick chestnut ruff and spoiled him with two fried eggs. I smiled again – at the sea, the islands, the trees – and soon everything around seemed to become a smile. I went back to my book that afternoon with renewed optimism.

Booto had engaging ways of making his wishes known. One morning when I'd forgotten his breakfast, he brought an old dry bone and dropped it at my feet: *clonk.* When I offered it back to him, he gave a whuffing sneeze of disgust and shook his head. Booto's sneeze, I slowly learned, always meant, "No, not that. Think again!" Sometimes I'd find him sitting up begging silently near my chair. I'd go to the kitchen to get him some food but he'd sneeze loudly – he didn't want food but a walk.

He soon let me know his favourite dog biscuits. One morning while I held out packets of the three types I'd bought, he suddenly begged. "Which one do you want then?" I asked. He let out a deep-throated bark so loud it rang through the cabin like gunfire. "This one, eh?" I said, rattling one packet in particular again. His second bark dislodged a picture from the wall.

"Sssh!" I hissed. "Not so loud. Bark softly. *Softer!*" And I made a little bark to show him. To my astonishment, hungry and anxious to please, he imitated me. Finally we had his "please" bark down to the merest whuff – which actually sounded like "yes."

Over the next few weeks on visits to the store, I tried to find out more about him. It seemed he was everyone's yet no one's dog. Mostly he was fed by some folks who were starting a cafe near the fishing village, and a retired bulldozer driver and his wife three miles from me. Booto's early history, as far as I could piece it together, was that he was part German shepherd, part Labrador (which explained his thick jaws and gentleness with people), and one-quarter wolf, shown in his low hindquarters and long, curved, bushy tail. He had come from the north as a pup with a couple who had mistreated and later abandoned him. Whenever I told him off, he'd put on a hang-dog look, standing still with tail drooping and head almost touching the floor, perhaps in memory of his days of ill-treatment. Various cabins and the cafe knew him by different names, among them Zeke, Prince, and Butch.

What surprised me most was that an animal with such an insecure background could have such a kind nature. Here in a simple dog was living proof of how intelligence can outshine early environment. One quality that had helped save his life on that wild coast, where scores of stray dogs had been shot over the years, was that he never ganged up with other strays to run down deer. He preferred to hunt and walk alone. It soon became clear he was a doughty scrapper, for on walks to the store any male dog that saw him coming would either give him a respectfully wide berth or vanish altogether into the bushes. I saw him fight once, when a summer tourist let his large, barking Airedale out of his car to see what would happen, and Booto shot underneath like a wolf, flipped the Airedale into the air, and raked its stomach so badly it was glad to escape back into the safety of the car. It was just as well Booto could handle himself for he was, without doubt, the most ardent canine Casanova on the coast. He had a coterie of female admirers in the summers and though I heard two of their owners had threatened to shoot him should he show up again, they never got around to it – mostly because Booto made his romantic dates at night, when he couldn't be seen, which seemed pretty good thinking.

One of my fears in adopting him was that he would, if only by his scent and presence, keep away all the wildlife friends I hoped to have back in the spring. But if the mice were any indication, it seemed I'd have no problem. One rainy night as I was working toward the end of the book, Booto lay with head on paws, glaring disconsolately at the downpour through the windows, when the mice came up through their entrance hole into the cabin. They certainly weren't put off by his scent and soon began skittering around the floor as usual. To my surprise Booto just lay there, dead still, his eyes darting as the mice ran about like pond skaters.

But he couldn't stand the sight of mink. One sunny morning a mink ran across the beach and Booto turned into a raging beast. Growling deeply, he ran down the slippery, uneven log staircase as fast as if it were a regular flight of stairs and cornered the mink in a rocky crevice. As Booto whined and scratched the rocks – he didn't dare put his paw inside – the mink snarled and spat. Then after a while, when Booto realized he couldn't get it out and relaxed his guard, the mink shot out like a small brown arrow, dived into the sea, swam some twenty-five yards under water like an otter, and shot up the beach and vanished into the trees. The only other animal that induced belligerence in Booto was a raccoon. One afternoon I took my axe into the forest to cut a couple of cedar poles to repair my boat slipway when Booto, nosing along the ground, stopped, with hackles raised, by a tall fir. He whined, scraping at the tree with his claws. I looked up, saw nothing unusual, so I hit the tree a hefty, ringing swipe with the flat of the axe. Immediately the owlish black-and-grey face of a raccoon appeared. It looked down at us, saw Booto, hissed loudly, and retreated back into the hollow of the cleft. For the rest of that day Booto just wanted to wait by the tree for the coon to make a move. It was with great reluctance that he agreed to leave at dark and return home.

Booto soon became a fine wilderness companion and I learned much forest lore from being with him. On long treks he could cover four times as much ground as I, sniffing out interesting items I'd have missed, like a squirrel's hoard, a vole's burrow, fish remains left by otter or mink on the shore, and once a rare marten's scat. He could follow deer trails over rocky ground, trails that no human eye could detect, showing me how deer usually follow the line of least resistance and, with this in mind, that one can easily pick up their trail on the far side of a long rock face. He never ran about wildly as some dogs do upon being let outside, disturbing every creature within hearing. Several times, miles inland, he led me upwind to small groups of blacktail deer, their trails thickening into heavily mulched paths where they had walked again and again in their own tracks to keep them open in the snow around their yarding areas, so they could browse the low hanging balsam fir branches. Once we were sitting in a thicket when a fine buck came into the clearing ahead, put its hoofs against a balsam trunk, craned its neck, and broke off a spray of foliage. Only if I had been near-starving could I have shot such a lovely creature. Booto, however, stood up, his floppy-tip ears cocked forward, and I think *might* have moved out but for my restraining hand and the whispered command, "Keep back," which he usually obeyed. The buck heard me too, leaped upward, looked round briefly, then bounded away into the trees.

It is hard to explain the pleasure I derived from such successful stalks of wild animals. Maybe it had to do with the hunting instinct that lies latent in most men, though I prefer to think it was more the sheer pleasure of seeing such creatures in their own kingdoms. I remember that day I was wearing an old suit I'd bought for my first columnist's job in London, a grey wool dappled with green and brown threads; it proved ideal for blending in with the soft shadows of the woods. Ever since then I've deliberately bought only clothes that can be ideal camouflage for stalking.

Early one March morning Booto and I were walking up the back trail when there was a rustling in the salal and salmonberry bushes. Booto, ignoring my command this time, went crashing through the undergrowth. A few minutes later he caught up to me with a hen bush grouse held lightly in his jaws. Although blinking rapidly with terror, the bird was quite unharmed. "Drop it!" I commanded. But Booto just stood there wagging his tail and looking terribly proud of himself. Stern orders had little effect now and only after several minutes of patient coaxing did he drop the grouse at my feet. It lay there on its back, its speckled breast pumping in and out like tiny bellows. But each time I went to pick it up, Booto also darted forward. Only after I'd said the final word of disapproval – "Bad dog!" – did Booto look guilty and, clearly restraining himself with great difficulty, allow me to set the trembling bird free. I made a big fuss over him after that. For years he had hunted minks, frogs, snakes, and grouse for food. I had no wish to stifle his natural instincts, but he also had to learn to obey.

Booto made himself useful in several ways, not only in the woods. In summer, partly to raise cash and partly because it had gone haywire for the umpteenth time, I dug up and sold my water pipe. Now I was reduced to carrying fresh drinking water down the trail again. One day I heard Booto lapping away from a rock pool that I'd always thought was full of seawater. But he knew better. It was fresh, filled by an unseen natural spring in the cliff. From then on this spring became my handiest water supply – and the flow, when channelled by a small, wooden flume, made a wonderful cooler for drinks.

One calm night as I typed away, Booto suddenly stirred, then gave a short little *whuff.* He occasionally did this when he heard anything suspicious – his ears would prick up, then he'd make the gruff sound as if to warn me there was something outside and also, I think, to tell me to keep quiet. Usually it was only a coon up a tree. Now he was on his feet, ears cocked staring intently through the window. Then I heard it, a short coughing sound, then a mewing noise that I'd heard here once before – cougar! Instinctively I moved toward the door, but Booto growled warningly and stationed himself in front of me. When I opened the door he didn't rush out immediately but only took a step or two outside, raised his lips in a stark smile and growled, catching his breath between growls in a menacing way. It was the most frightening combination of look and noise I'd ever heard him make. He was staring up into the large arbutus tree near the cabin. As I moved out, the large, dark shape of a cougar leaped out of the tree, landed on a flat rock, and sped off into the night, whereupon Booto launched himself like a rocket, chased the cougar into the bush, but didn't pursue it far. Then he came back, grinning and wagging his tail.

Some days later on our next walk to the store, a front-page story in a local paper caught my eye. A male cougar had been shot when found prowling around one of the settlements down the coast; it measured nine feet, three inches from the tip of its nose to the end of its tail. It seemed likely it was the one near our cabin, for a transient male cougar can easily cover twenty miles in a night when looking for a home ground of its own or for females in heat, for, unlike most animals, cougars don't mate only in spring or summer. I was sorry it had been shot, yet I also felt relieved. Although the chances of its actually attacking a grown human male were probably thousands to one, Booto could have been in danger. Bigger dogs than he, even trained guard dogs, have been taken by cougars when really hungry.

I had always admired and respected animals in their natural state more than any domestic pet, so it came as a slight shock to me to realize I now loved my new companion so much he came first in my affections. Booto became more an equal than a pet, and certainly one of the best friends I ever had. True, he could offer no intellectual opinions, but the last thing I wanted now was a pal who broached such topics. His affection was unlimited and without strings. When I was unhappy, *he* was unhappy. When I was glad, he wagged his tail, begged, jumped, or rolled on the floor with a big, white-toothed grin. I wouldn't have exchanged him now for a thousand dollars or the highest pedigree dog.

Despite Booto's traumatic life, if he had any neurosis at all, he kept it well-hidden. The only thing he really hated was taking a bath. Once a month I'd boil water in a big metal pot that had drifted onto my beach and do my laundry, and sometimes I would use the fairly clean rinsing water to bathe Booto, especially if he was scratching more than usual. As soon as he saw the papers on the floor and the pot come off its hook, he knew what was coming and tried to sneak away up the trail. I would make him sit near me while I got things ready and he'd start to shiver. He shivered all the time I bathed him with the warm water, despite the clouds of steam. And if I turned away to reach for something, he would quickly and quietly step out of the pot and stand dripping on my nice clean floor, still shivering away. His dislike and distrust of water was so strong it even extended to the sea, for he showed no desire to swim, as will most dogs, even on warm days. I wondered perhaps if someone had tried to drown him as a pup.

His mistrust of water apart, Booto was so bright it seemed perfectly natural to talk to him, but if my "dog talk" ever degenerated into those silly gobbledegook phrases people who live alone with a dog often use, Booto would swiftly signify his impatience. One idiotic phrase, half-sung to a rhythmic tune, went, "Booto the Mooto is a nice boy and a good boy, is a good boy and a nice boy is Booto the Mooto ..."; I'd just be going through it for the third time when with a colossal groan of disgust he'd drop on the floor, rub one ear into the floorboards, and cover the other with his paw.

Occasionally he let me know he disapproved of my behaviour too – like on the day I finally finished my novel. As I put the last page in my typewriter and pounded out the last words of what I hoped was a romantic yet realistic ending to the book, I felt a curious euphoria, almost tearful. I was elated that I'd now completed the long haul, yet sad that I would have to bid all my characters goodbye and that I had nothing ahead but the world of reality – a world that, when I reckoned my remaining assets, looked somewhat grim. But I'd long ago planned that final day. First I would put away the huge pile of pages for a week before reading through the entire book and sending it to a literary agent. Second, I would break my resolve about drinking and celebrate. Third, I'd start looking for a job. And to achieve the last two I'd go to the beer parlour. This wasn't as odd as it sounds. On my first arrival in Canada, I'd got two outdoor jobs from beer parlours – one as a salmon-boat deckhand working the tiny coastal fish camps, the other as an assistant blaster helping to dynamite old stumps from the route of a new road.

Now I tried the beer parlour again, leaving Booto tied up outside. That night, with only a halfhearted offer of a job as a second joiner on two plywood cabins "sometime next month" and having imbibed a little too much, I came out with some noisy loggers and was about to climb into their car for a hillbilly party at one of their homes when I felt a sharp tug on my jacket. I looked down, Booto had clamped his jaws firmly into my jacket hem and, growling slightly, refused to let go. The loggers roared with laughter. "Looks like old Butch reckons you've had enough!" shouted one. Booto's grave disapproval was clear in his eyes.

"I reckon he's right," I said. "Good night, lads." And with that Booto and I walked the long, dark miles home. I'd forgotten my torch and instead, because like all dogs he could see far better in the dark than any human, I held onto Booto's tail down the forest trail and within an hour we were safely home. As I ate some bread and cheese, too tired to cook, I felt that rather than compete for odd jobs on the coast, I'd better get back to my old craft.

That week as I read through the book, I really felt I'd got it right, that the lonely nine months' slog had been worth while. I punch-holed it all together, wrote a covering letter, and with a fervent prayer mailed my baby to a leading literary agent. Next day, leaving Booto with the bulldozer driver and his wife, I hitch-hiked south down the coast and caught the ferry to Vancouver to try for a newspaper job. It seemed the only sensible hope to restore my finances.

It was another world. Two editors in grand offices gave me cordial interviews, talked of their own days in Fleet Street, but offered no work – not to a dishevelled-looking hermit. My former international expertise, my work on papers with thirty times their circulations, counted for nothing here. They wanted men with expert *local* knowledge, *young* men. I was soon out in the street, the smile dying on my face.

How small I suddenly felt as I walked the streets of the bustling modern, cosmopolitan city. Big, sleek cars rolled by and well-dressed, hearty men greeted each other and disappeared into luxury restaurants. I recalled my Jaguar and Aston-Martin days with an ironic smile. I felt an alien, a being from another world. I found myself by a drugstore counter where the glossy magazines stared up at me as if mocking my former life. From old habit I bought two and walked through a residential area to the seashore.

At English Bay I sat in a sandy cleft by a rock in the pale wintry sun, wondering, now what? Being turned down by the provincial papers was an unexpected humiliation. I was strangely tired and lay back and closed my eyes. I opened them again a few minutes later as wings swished above and I saw a seagull sail overhead to land awkwardly on the sand nearby. As it took a few steps forward to worry a piece of seaweed, it limped. I blinked. Could it be … no, it was too small and grey-looking. It suddenly stopped pecking at the weed and regarded me with a supercilious yellow eye. I broke off a piece of the small pizza I'd bought for my lunch and tossed it over, and as the gull dived, scooped it up, and flew away, I seemed to see my friendly white gull, Bert, all over again. And then into my mind's eye came the great eagles and their nest, my fright with the killer whales, the amusing nights with Spooks the coon, the cheeky little skunk, and dear Booto, sitting up like a jack-in-the-box, his brown eyes full of trust. As the traffic thundered by with a dim roar behind me I suddenly thought, "What in hell am I doing down here anyway, trying for a newspaper job in this alien city?" I'd be back in the old trap of rents, taxes, mortgages, credit payments, appearances – enslaved in order to do the work. Maybe the truly rich man is one who doesn't need much.

I realized at that moment what an extraordinary life I was living on the wild coast. The smooth young editors had done me a favour. I saw again the burnished golden seas at sunset, the islands and bays thick with oysters. Had I, by slaving day after winter day on my book, wrapped in my own spiritual searchings for a work that was centred upon Europe, now become blind to all this incredible land had to offer, its vast untouched fastnesses, its wonderful wild creatures?

My happiest moments since I had arrived in Canada, in fact, had all come with animals, or at least while watching them in natural surroundings. With a shock I realized this had been true nearly *all* my life – as a child at six different schools I had often sought solace, a refuge, in the wild lonely woods and fields. The only lessons I had really looked forward to were biology and woodwork. "All British fish have two dorsal fins," the biology master had said at my last school, and up had shot my hand.

"Pardon me, sir, but I think the pike has only one." And in the silence that followed, I'd added nervously, "Er, could I show you?" The master had looked at me in surprise. "Hmm, then do that, Tomkies. Perhaps you'll do that?" And that night I had walked to the lake a few miles from my home and caught a small jack pike to show them all next day. It was the only time in my entire schooldays where I'd shown myself ahead of the rest of the class! And in woodwork I had spent one a half years of lessons carving a hawk from a piece of walnut, trying to fashion each feather perfectly. How strange it was to realize now that that wooden hawk, now resting on the bookcase back in my cabin, had become unconsciously my most treasured object, for it was one I had somehow kept through all the cities and countries I'd known.

That hawk, a symbol of freedom to me as a child, now seemed to represent so much more – the only truly constant interest in my life. But where as a boy I had used nature merely as a refuge, it could now become something far deeper – a fascination with the natural world and all it can teach man for its *own* sake. If I could no longer now be part of any city, maybe I could, in some way, truly become a part of the wilderness itself. I would not be negatively fleeing *from* society but *to* something, a world that for me seemed finer, and one to which I could really relate.

Perhaps now by truly understanding what interested me, I would find out what I wanted to do with the rest of my life. So far I'd only made my stand on the more benign shores of the Pacific coast and, while there had been the rare brush with the cougar and a few black bears were known to be in the vicinity, the great untouched wild places, among the last in the world, lay farther north. Now I recalled the long talks with Ed Louette when he told me I should go on a trek into the mountains, into the world of the grizzly, moose, and caribou before I died. I remembered his piercing, challenging look as he had said, "You'll learn a lot, especially about yourself. But it will age you, mind. It'll sure age you."

There and then, sitting on that windy city beach, I decided I *would* make that lonely trek this spring. I only needed to raise some money. That afternoon I made an unsuccessful attempt to find Ed. When I visited the address he'd given me, I was told he'd left two months earlier. It was disappointing, yet I felt sure our paths would cross again.

Sitting in the ferry lounge on my way back (north), I idly flicked through the magazines I'd bought. In one was exactly the kind of story I used to write. Then came the best idea of all – back at the cabin I had files stacked with unsold material. Surely I could sell some to magazines here? I now had a good reason for temporarily going back to the writing I no longer valued. I could use the money to finance a deeper experience of the wilds. With new heart, my mind made up, I hitched home, claimed a happy Booto, and within a week had written and mailed two stories. And as I typed away, Booto occasionally pushed his head onto my lap and wagged his tail, as if he approved of the idea, too.

10 Spring – and a Bad Scare

*F*rom high above, the shrill, metallic *kri kri kri* sounded through the still air of the April morning, and as I hurried to the cabin door I thought, "They're back, they're back!" I looked out and saw the huge female eagle soaring aloft on her spread pinions, sailing with glorious ease in a great circle, the sun peeping from behind the mountains to the east blazing her white tail and neck feathers into golden flames. With a few lazy flaps she glided again, far over the northern land spit and toward her old nesting place.

As I turned back, a new spider's web in the arbutus branches hung spangled with dew like a lacy necklace of diamonds, while beneath the umbrella of a dark leaf the little pirate sat, his feet on his master thread, waiting for the sun to dry the droplets. Now I looked out over the motionless Pacific and heard a whistling sound. A small flight of mallards was winging in from the south, the females in front quacking faintly to each other as they glided down into the next-door bay. Five goldeneyes arrived on the same flight path, twisting and turning with their wings bent down to slow their speed, and then slooshed into the water near the oyster island. Within a minute two drakes were showing off to a brown-headed female, bobbing their high black crowns and flashing their white circular cheek patches. Soon they would be pairing off, then away they would all go again, flying to inland lakes to nest and rear their young.

It was a good day, the first real spring morning, a time to be out amid the new-stirring life. I would go to the post office and see if the agent had sent word of my book. But first I'd go fishing, just sit out there and dangle my line, for it was too fine a morning to waste. I heaved the little old boat into the sea for the first time that year and as I went down the log staircase I heard a scuttering in the trees above. I saw a squirrel leap from the top of a pine to a fir branch, only a glimpse, but I was sure it was Douglas, and as he chattered away I knew I'd now be awakened fine and early in the mornings. As I rowed away from shore Booto suddenly ran down the staircase and up and down over the rocky beach, whining with distress, perhaps thinking I was deserting him. At the same time I noticed tiny rivulets of water seeping in through the cracks in the boards. All right, for both reasons I'd not go out too far. Four hundred yards from shore I let down my bright jigger, jerked it up and down, and within two minutes caught a four-pound green ling cod. Then I heard a strange huffing and puffing noise behind me. I looked around and there was Booto – gasping for breath with each stroke, his brown eyes wide with both fright and determination! For a dog who hated water this was quite an achievement. "Good boy," I said encouragingly, "there's a good boy," as I tried to show great delight at his brave effort and pretend it was the most natural thing in the world to haul a sopping-wet eighty-pound dog aboard a small leaking boat in thirty fathoms while it tipped up so alarmingly it threatened to send us both to Davy Jones's locker.

I was strangely touched by Booto's desperate affection, for his loyalty now seemed steadfast and beyond question. But this was no moment for too much sentiment. With Booto's extra weight, water cascading from his thick coat, water gushing up through the opening cracks, the boat was rapidly filling. By frantic rowing I managed to get back to shore before it sank beneath us. But as I bailed out the boat and hauled it up the beach, a sharp rock gashed a hole where one of the boards had become completely rotten. As it lay on its side like a stranded grey fish, I knew my dinghy had come to the end of its days.

After lunch we walked along the forest road and there at the post office in the fishing village was the airmail letter I'd both hoped for and dreaded. At least he hadn't sent the book back, I thought, as I took the thin envelope and walked back in the watery sunshine, unable to read it until I reached home. Continually now I had to call to Booto who, judging by the number of romantic scents he was finding, was also feeling spring. At my desk I opened the letter with trembling hands. The words stared up at me starkly: "… you have attempted too much. You have produced the equivalent of one of those huge Tintoretto canvases when the modern taste is for the miniature or small etching. The tone of the writing is also too strident, too declamatory, for present-day tastes. (I am inclined to think if Thomas Wolfe were alive today and just starting as a writer, he would find it impossible to get a publisher.) There is something of Wolfe in your conceptions and the heroic scale of your story." He did not want to handle my book.

It is said trouble comes in threes. The final loss of my boat had been one blow, the rejection of my book the second, so when I hiked to the post office the next day and was handed a letter from the magazine to which I'd sent my stories, I had little doubt it would be the third. I was now so broke I would soon be in real trouble. As I walked back up the forest road under cloudless skies, I decided to take a long time to return to the empty cabin before reading yet more bad news. Strangely, the steadfast image of Ed Louette again came into my mind, his kindly patient face, his hours of selfless workings, and again I heard his words about the untouched wild lands to the north he had exhorted me to visit. But such a trek now seemed doomed, at least for this year.

Well, I had the whole day before me. We live only a day at a time, rich or poor. If I couldn't make the big trek this spring, I could at least go for a really long walk right now. I decided to make a good ten-mile semicircle across the mountain slopes, then back down to the cabin.

As I called Booto and we climbed a rocky face and headed into the dark forests, the female eagle passed over our heads. She was beating steadily toward the peaks to the southeast and as I watched her go, I realized I had yet to see her mate. Was she actually looking for him, I wondered. *Woof, woof, woof* went her great wings as she passed above, her flight taking the same line I was to follow.

By the time we were a mile inland, the morning sun had cleared the mountain tops and behind a thick cedar a pocket of frost huddled forlornly, trying to escape the weak but melting rays, hoping to survive a little longer. Alder branches clicked in the warmth and here and there pushed out tiny sticky green buds. Yellow fronds of new needles adorned the drooping tips of hemlocks and the dark branches of balsam firs, and the deep olive leaves of the wiry salal dripped moisture from their ends, freckling the hoary grey on the bed of old leaves. Here, as everywhere without man's interference, nature had been her own thinner, for what old trees had not been mown down by avalanches or cleared by lightning fires had been hurled down by the storms. And I now saw that their tenderest tips, along with other branches and litter blown down that winter, had been heavily browsed by deer. So nature had not only added to the eventual humus in which new trees could grow but had provided the small herds with vital food through the harsher days. Twice I broke off the thick stony-hard resinous centres from fir snags – there are no finer natural fire lighters in the wilderness than these inflammable chunks. From atop a bush a robin sang its first sweet song of spring and by my feet I saw a crumb of dark brown earth fall from a fern sprout as it shouldered its way into the light, its top bent over like a snake's head.

Within three hours I judged we were high above the area of the cabin and as I broke through the forest into a clearer space ahead, I heard the faint rushing of a creek, its waters babbling now, swelled by the first melting of the high snow. Behind me, as if it had waited until I'd passed through, I heard the faint drumming of a wood-pecker's beak on a rotten pine snag as it sought to find the softer places where beetle grubs tunnelled under the old damp bark.

I walked down the rocky escarpments beside the creek, my knees braced against the steep angles and granite faces. Somehow it always seems harder going *down* mountains than up them – one pounds the heart, the other wilts the knees and they crack ominously. Then I came to a small black lake in which trout were leaping at the few early-morning flies. I wished I'd brought some fishing tackle, for in such unfished lakes these juicy one-pounders are easy to catch. At the far end we came to a flat area where the outlet creek spread into a small swamp. The air was heavy with a pungent scent like skunk and all over the swamp grew clusters of huge deep-green leaves, rather like heavy lettuce, with bright yellow pokers thrusting up through them. As we tramped through some between the skirting alders the smell increased, and I realized then it was coming from the plants themselves – this was skunk cabbage and I'd never seen any before. Some of them had been torn up, their roots cut through.

Suddenly Booto stopped, nosed along, and paused about seven yards away, scraping with his paw on the ground. I went over and found some greeny-black droppings. Some were large, almost two inches thick, while others were much smaller, not much larger than those of deer, but they were in short, blunt-ended sections, not like the oval pellets or occasional whorled cakes deer leave. Puzzled, I walked on, wondering

A rainbow touched the nearest island, as if showing this was the good place.

Enough drift lumber for a dozen log cabins.

For a long time my house was a cavernous old milk truck.

The sea provides – enough fish for a week in one hour of fishing.

The twin log staircase made it easier to haul up building logs.

Plywood sheets were best for the floor.

For the summer I lived in a tent on the platform.

On fine days the views were idyllic.

Bert, the lame seagull, became very tame. His wings were larger than the other gulls'.

Ed Louette, master log craftsman, helped me build the final cabin.

FACING: *It looked like a quaint wooden garage on stilts.*

The cabin's interior – by candlelight.

Topping a small pine tree that obscured the sun.

The young bald eagle I had watched grow up adopted the area around my cabin.

I was terrified when killer whales encircled my rowboat.

Floating log berths were vital for my boat on the rocky beach.

As far as I could see, my cabin was the only human habitation.

The sunsets were idyllic, and varied from day to day.

Wild dog Booto adopted me one wild winter's night. He loved his grub!

Booto had some endearing tricks – like begging with crossed white 'boots'.

Boating to the cabin with toolbox and Booto.

Searching the dumps for food, black bears lose their fear of man.

Boating into truly wild terrain in search of grizzly bears.

I had to fight a sense of fear when finding the first grizzly tracks.

A big grizzly has been rooting for grubs.

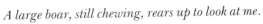

A large boar, still chewing, rears up to look at me.

A mother grizzly with two well grown cubs.

A grizzly fishing for spawning salmon.

Cubs run with their mother for two years, while she teaches them to hunt and fish.

The wilderness had shown me a path to a higher understanding.

what could have made them, as Booto, whining oddly, followed behind me. I should have heeded Booto's whines, I realized later, for the answer to the strange droppings wasn't long in coming.

Suddenly I was conscious of a new reeking odour, rather like iodine. There was a crashing in the thick bushes and salal nearby, and a small brown bear cub stumbled across the track in front of me, just as the head and shoulders of a mother black bear emerged like some vast golliwog from the underbrush near some upended tree roots. She saw us and began making strange *oofa oofa* aggressive grunting sounds. Terrified, my eyes instantly taking in the power of her shoulders, the sharp black claws of her heavy forefeet, I stood rooted to the spot. I remembered Ed's advice, "A black bear will never attack you unless you get between a mother and her cub. Even then she'll probably send it up a tree, make a mock attack, then dodge around you. Keep still, don't show fear, and above all, don't run." Paralysed, my heart pounding, I somehow kept still. Of all the stories told by wilderness Canadians with whom I'd fished and logged, none had been wilder or caused more merriment in the beer parlours than outlandish bear stories. But they didn't seem amusing now. There wasn't a tree between us that the cub could get up, I realized with increasing fear. I was never more conscious of my own puniness than in the second or two that powerful, sharp-eyed animal and I looked at each other.

She first seemed undecided between going for me or following her cub, then she dropped down and started to run in my direction. Booto took charge and barked at her, and she appeared to change her mind and go for him. He was far faster on his feet than the bear and, making strange, half-whining barks, he dodged about in front of her, luring her away from me. As I heard them crashing through the brush seaward, I quickly gathered my wits and hurried toward the cabin. Once there, I slammed the door. From all I'd heard I knew I ought to be safe now but for some minutes I stood there feeling very unsafe.

After twenty minutes Booto returned, looking not at all frightened but extremely pleased with himself. He came running up to me wagging his tail, then licked my hand and gulped down two bowlfuls of water as he regained his breath. I gave my rescuer the best supper he'd ever had and that night I wrapped all my food in plastic bags. It was a foolish idea, I learned later, for bears have noses like bloodhounds and the smell of my food would have lingered long after being wrapped in plastic. I realized then just how flimsy my cabin really was, for if that big mother bear did come around, her great strength would easily rip through the studded plywood walls of my kitchen.

So excited was I by the incident with the bear I completely forgot the envelope in my breast pocket until after supper. I took it out, resigned myself to the inevitable contents, and opened it. I could hardly believe when I read: "... as you say, the facts in your first story were the basis for the one published in Britain, we are buying what is virtually second rights for $600. But for your second story, exclusive to us, we could pay a fee of $825. Would you please let us know if this is satisfactory? As for your third idea, we would also like to commission this and, again, as it would be exclusive to us, it would command the full fee ..."

91

My joyful whoop and leap into the air startled Booto, who dashed to the door with a gruff bark, thinking there must be something outside. I grabbed him for one of our playful wrestles on the floor, but he was tired and groaned as he often did when he thought I was making a fool of myself. No matter. I got up again and hammered out a reply to the magazine editor. I was free! Now I could make the big trek I'd promised myself. Then I remembered the black bear.

There was an odd humiliation attached to the incident. After my months in the wilds I'd begun to feel I had an affinity with the natural life around me. I'd subscribed to the old theory that a man need fear nothing in nature in the North American woods if he himself has no evil design. But had that sow bear been of a more touchy disposition and had Booto not been there, I felt sure I could have been in trouble. There's no room for sentiment in nature and if I was now to go into wilder parts alone it would clearly need to be a calculated risk.

Over the next day or two I tried to think clearly. From all I'd heard, attacks by black bears were extremely rare, usually occurring at garbage dumps where they had lost their inherent fear of man, or on foolhardy youngsters who had thrown sticks or stones, had approached too close, or had fed them at permanent camp sites. As for the unpredictable grizzlies, more humans were killed on North American highways over the average vacation weekend than had been killed by the big bears since the turn of the century. Mauling attacks were more frequent than with black bears, but again mostly around garbage dumps or where they had been wounded or had been protecting their cubs. A careful, thoughtful wanderer of the woods should be able to avoid all these circumstances.

The more I recalled what I'd heard about the bluffing tactics of black bears, the more likely it seemed I'd not been in the danger I imagined. She had not really launched an all-out attack on either myself or Booto. Seeing us suddenly like that, her cub too near us for safety, she had grunted a combination alarm and warning, and as the cub had been unable to tree and could not rejoin her without crossing our path again, she had been forced to run toward it. She could easily have felled me, but she had, if anything, curved slightly around me. And I had been in her back yard, after all! It was an encouraging thought; so was the fact that I'd managed to freeze successfully. Over the next few days I felt increasingly drawn to the wilder lands, to experience the real wilderness Ed had described. When the first two cheques arrived, I made up my mind I would go. There had been something challenging in the way Ed had looked at me, too, which spurred me on.

To carry equipment to a starting point for the trip, I needed my truck back, if it could be salvaged. I was also sick of having to walk to the store and back for supplies, for I was limited to what I could carry on my back (Booto's cans of dog food seemed to weigh heaviest!) and until I found a new boat, also needed for the trek, I couldn't easily supplement my diet with fish.

Thus the next morning I climbed down the inland cliff over which I'd crashed for a new look at my truck. The body was wrecked but the engine and wheels seemed undamaged. On previous trips to the small town to the south I'd noticed a grey truck like mine, which had been parked ever since I'd come to the coast. I hitched down to see the owner, who after warning me the engine and two of its tyres were about finished, sold it to me for $180. Reluctantly admitting the task of retrieving my old truck was one I couldn't perform alone, I hired a garage owner with a winch crane. Towing my new truck, we somehow manoeuvred down the old logging tracks, and after much cursing, perspiring, and resetting of its front wheels, we managed to haul my battered old ruin up from its mossy grotto with his fifty-yard cable. To my great relief, although shaky on its mountings, the engine worked fine.

His bill came to $110, mostly for mileage, but having spent $180 on the new truck, I settled my debt to him with some effective wilderness bartering. Part of the now useless equipment under my cabin was a TV set and a tape recorder, which, shorn of electrical power, were now idling away in plastic bags. So in return for both plus $25, his claim was amicably settled.

Over the next two weeks I manoeuvred both trucks into a forest clearing and laboured to make one good vehicle from the two semi-wrecks. Naturally it rained most of the time, and as I toiled away rebuilding all the wooden structures inside, converting a six-volt system to a twelve-volt, linking up hoses, universal joints, changing the generator and gear boxes, painting the new truck under a hasty canopy of plastic sheet, making the scores of adjustments, it seemed I was never dry. Booto hated the entire operation and wouldn't look at me for hours. He had a curious habit when I was doing things he didn't like of acting as if I weren't there. He cringed at every blow of the hammer and clearly hated the smell of paint. Mostly he sat under the truck in the dry, the thumping of his rear hock on the ground as he scratched himself the only reminder he was still there

By the fourth day he'd had enough. Totally bored, he sneaked off when I wasn't looking. He'd done this several times recently and I wondered where he went, for neither the old bulldozer driver nor the cafe folk had seen him. By now Booto was deep into my affections and I found myself quite jealous when he deserted me for two days at a time. There were still moments now when the loneliness of the depths of winter, before he'd come into my life, returned.

Once the "new" patch-up truck was finished I thought of my trek in earnest. I quelled rising fears by deciding that as I had to go to Vancouver to buy a boat and equipment anyway, I'd find Ed and somehow persuade him to come with me. Surely he'd not refuse a chance to relive youthful adventures, for despite his age he was fit enough. Should I take a gun? I could handle one, having spent much of my youth with a fine old Sussex gamekeeper, and having been good enough to hit running rabbits through the head with a .22 rifle. I'd also been a fair marksman in the Guards. But now I felt sport hunting was a schoolboy pastime, and not in keeping with my need to fit in with the order of nature, not to intrude upon it. No, the hell with it, I had no gun and wasn't going to buy one.

On the drive down south Booto suddenly ran to the back of the truck and started whining and scratching at the door. Remembering his sneaking off, I stopped. He immediately ran up to a small cabin, the home of two elderly pensioners, who greeted

Booto affectionately, called him Prince, and told me they too had adopted him over the past few years and fed him whenever he turned up. I looked at Booto in surprise. This odd wild dog, now idiotically smiling at bringing some of his best pals together, apparently thought little of trotting the seven miles between our homes if he felt bored. I told the couple of my impending trip and they agreed to look after Booto if I didn't wish to take him with me. Then we headed for the ferry.

We spent three days in Vancouver but as the big, unwieldy truck was herded from lane to lane by the frenetic rush of city traffic, I was convinced yet again that modern city life had become, for me, a meaningless windmill. I drove around buying my supplies and looked for Ed at night, sleeping late in the truck by the cascading rainbow waters of Furry Creek up the Squamish Highway. My plan for my trek seemed simple: buy a boat, stock it with petrol and supplies, drive to a certain fishing village on the northeast coast of Vancouver Island, then hug the coast by boat until I could turn east, and helped by the prevailing westerlies, make it to an island where there was a government wharf and store. From there, with full tanks, I'd launch my assault on the fifty miles of inlet that remained. When I located a fine plywood boat and secondhand five-horse-power outboard for only $185, I decided to invest in a tough little rubber boat too. Not only could I tow the fuel cans and non-perishables in it but I'd have a spare boat if one got holed. I bought a light nylon pup tent and green shower suit, both of which would keep off rain and reduce my scent. Other items included two small camouflage nets, fishing line and treble hooks, a 2½ pound down sleeping bag, a light groundsheet, a pocketknife, and the lightest welded-frame back pack I could find. With my trusty pocket telescope and staple foods like lentils, dried peas, barley, dried meat, flour, and oatmeal, I worked out I could carry all I needed on my back for up to ten days in a pack weighing less than forty pounds.

In Vancouver, Booto surprised me yet again. He took the big city in his stride. Where he learned kerb drill, heaven knows, but he stopped dutifully at main roads and walked over pedestrian crossings, keeping to heel when I told him. If he wasn't sure of what to do he looked at me for guidance. He waited patiently, outside various stores, snoozed in the truck when I was in the bank, systematically ignored other dogs, and never barked once.

On the third night I finally located Ed at the beer parlour he'd once named. But after the first surprised greeting he said he would not come with me. "No, no, I'm too old now," he protested. "Good God, a man is safe enough alone in that country, if he doesn't do anything foolish."

Back in his small room in a lodging house not far from Stanley Park, Ed drew me a map of tidal flats and creeks where he thought bears could be found. He checked my supply list, added suggestions, then looked at Booto, who was lying supine at our feet, his eyes travelling from one to the other's face as we talked.

"What will you do with the dog?"

"I'm not sure. There's folks up the coast who'll take him, they've fed him before. But he's good in the woods." And I told Ed about the black bear incident.

Ed laughed. "Well, maybe he'd behave," he said. "He seems a smart animal. A black bear will usually run from a dog but a grizzly – the honly man I knew got mauled by a grizzly had his dog yappin' at his heels. But you can never tell with those bears. They're as different as people."

He thought a moment, then reached for the rough map he'd drawn, and inserted a dot. "Look, if you get to the end of the hinlet, visit this friend of mine, George Tihoni. I'm sure he's still there. Heck, I should've written to him before now! He's about, ho, five or six miles hup river, on the north bank."

He laughed suddenly at a memory. "What gun are you taking with you?" I said I wasn't, that I didn't own one.

"Can you handle a rifle?"

I told him of my former experience with guns. He reached down under his bed. "You'd better take this," he said with a strange smile, then determinedly thrust a stocky old World War I Mauser at me, and a box of fewer than a dozen shells. "We bought this old gun years ago at the cattle hauctions. Beautiful old thing – went through the First World War. Good gun, but you hold it real tight!"

I was astonished he possessed such a thing. "I'm not sure I want to take a gun," I said.

"You take it, professor. You may need it! But don't use it unless you really have to. And you haim for the brain if it's close and sideways, or else the heart – right behind the front shoulder. Nothing else will stop a grizzly. And if you see tracks in the meadows, keep close to trees!"

"I'm not much of a climber these days."

Ed laughed again and said, "Boy, hif a grizzly's comin' at you, you'll be up a tree like you were blasted up there! But be sure and take a piece of rope to throw round the trunk, to haul yourself up or tie on."

I took all the advice Ed had to offer and as I prepared to leave he scribbled a note. "Hif you get questioned, just say you're taking the gun to Tihoni, for me. Ho, one more thing."

"What's that?"

"Hif you find grizzly, you tell no one else."

I agreed, thanked him, and left. Too late to catch the ferry, I spent the third night in the truck. I couldn't make up my mind whether to take the rifle and Booto. I'd certainly feel safer with the gun.

Back at the cabin I spent a few days ironing out problems I was loath to wrestle with for the first time on the actual trek: breaking in the new back pack, practising with its full weight on rocky, treed slopes, sleeping in the pup tent, cooking the kind of food I'd use on small, open fires. At this time Booto again walked out on me and spent a couple of days and nights with other friends.

But on the day I left Booto watched me haul the plywood boat to the truck's roof with reproach in his eyes. He whined moodily when he saw my food, equipment, and rubber dinghy. Then he disappeared. Next day as I walked up the trail with final provisions, he still hadn't come back. I was sure he'd realized I was leaving and had decided to stay with one of his other friends. Wanting to make sure he was in good hands, I drove to the cafe but there was no one at home, and the retired couple hadn't seen him either. But they were sure he'd turn up there when he found I'd gone, and they promised to feed him until my return.

I drove away with a feeling of guilt, but he seemed to have made the decision himself. Then slowly my guilt was replaced with a slight resentment at his fickleness. Trying hard to allow this shallow anger to justify my guilt, I headed south to the ferry but then, in a bend of the road two miles past the logging trucks above our cabin, I saw Booto mincing along. He looked like he always did, trotting slightly sideways as if his back feet were about to overtake his front. He heard the truck coming and turned around, but in my anger – he was heading *away* from our cabin after all – I went straight past him. He started to run as I went around the bends and I saw him in the mirror, tearing after the truck as fast as he could go, his body leaning over sideways round the corners like a motorcycle rider, as he tried desperately to catch up with me. I trod down hard and went around a lot more bends until I'd lost him, but after about a mile I had to stop. It was no good. I just couldn't bear to leave him behind, thinking perhaps I'd left him forever. Possible dangers ahead or not, he'd been my only companion for months. And anyway, after thinking about what Ed had said, I'd decided to take the gun after all.

There was a sudden scuffling of stones by the truck door and there he was. Panting, exhausted, his ears were pricked forward, his eyes full of hurt and query. "You silly damn fool!" was all I could say before he leaped onto the seat, licking my face, I slammed the door, and we set off for the north of Vancouver Island and the wild inlet.

11 Black Bears and the Wild Inlet

*A*s we drove up from Nanaimo on Vancouver Island to the fishing village on the northeast coast, it rained steadily and heavily – and it rained all the following day too, so that I was unwilling to launch the boat. But when the third morning dawned in a dead calm, with a low cloud mass shrouding the distant mountain peaks in mist, I decided to set off. By noon the next day Booto and I had covered well over forty miles. The waters of the inlet were a jade green colour where the recent rains had melted some of the high snow and had washed mud and litter into the creeks and rivers. As we alternately rowed and putted eastward through the pea-soup sea, the mountains dwarfed us. Their almost sheer slopes, densely covered with spruce and fir, fell precipitously into the water and there were hardly any beaches on which to land. If a storm had hit us we would have been in real trouble. For we were now insignificant specks in a harsh and inhospitable landscape, and I had never felt so puny in my life.

A cove marked prominently on the map as a settlement almost halfway up the inlet was totally deserted, just a battered wooden pier and some ruined shacks showing the remains of an old logging camp. As dusk began to fall we had covered another fifteen miles and I noted a huge rock slide on the north bank as we rounded a right-hand bend formed by the promontory of a high conical mountain. Both signs coincided with the area where Ed's rough map indicated we might find bear. I pulled into a small bay below a cleft in the mountains, heaved the wooden boat over wet branches, carried the rubber dinghy up to the tree line, and set up camp by a small creek mouth.

His feet now back on terra firma, Booto recovered his spirits, and as I set up the pup tent, made a mattress of parallel rows of spruce branches, and cooked our bannocks and mush-stew supper, he sat watching me with a big, pink-tongued grin. I found it hard to sleep that night. I was acutely conscious that the nearest human was some forty miles away. This was the domain of the bear and the cougar, where *man* was the interloper, and I felt as much a greenhorn as when I'd first arrived in Canada. I woke up several times to hear curious bumping noises, but as Booto slept peacefully with his usual snores and whuffles, I finally concluded the noises came from the creek waters tumbling over rocks and not from big bears clumping around the tent after smelling our food, although I'd wrapped it all in plastic bags. My imagination would have to be severely controlled if I was going to complete this trek.

At dawn, leaving the boats under some bushes, upturned over a tin box containing a third of our food supply, we set off up to the mountain cleft. Although it was only some three thousand feet above, it lay well to the east, but by traversing the thickly wooded slopes sideways to reach it, I felt the steep inclines would be reduced to a manageable climb. It was still the toughest country I'd ever packed through. In places windfalls lay across each other in high, eight-foot barricades, their butts and tips often ending against sheer rock faces that made going around them impossible. They and the standing trees were covered in grey wefts of old man's beard and lush green carpet mosses that hid the holes between giant trunks and muffled all sounds so I could move quite silently despite my load. Frequently I had to remove my pack and haul it through later, for a stumble when moving forward with one's foot caught between the trunks would have easily resulted in a broken leg. How I envied Booto's ability to squeeze through narrow openings below as I laboured over the slippery tops.

It took the whole day to reach a small plateau between the peaks, and I dumped the pack in a spruce glad to make camp at the edge of the forest, then stole forward to take a look. Although dusk was falling, it was just light enough to see the downward slopes, where a number of small creeks were draining into what must be the start of the river below. As I walked back with water from one of them, I smelled the fresh sweet scent of the sword ferns I'd brushed against and it almost seemed a pity to spoil it with the smoke of a fire.

Next day we had barely covered a couple of miles when a gap in the trees revealed the opening of the valley a long way ahead. Lush green arms of meadows lined the mouths of creeks where they joined the broadening river, making the valley floor a giant fiddlehead fern. The morning mist still shrouded the cottonwoods, white birch, and clumps of willow in a silent white shawl. After another mile of gradual descent we had just paused for lunch, when I heard a faint noise ahead. It sounded just like a man with hobnail boots kicking at a rotten stump. I looked at Booto – standing still, legs braced and ears forward. Instructing him to stay quiet and behind me, I lowered the pack quietly, unhitched the rifle, and crept forward through a small thicket.

I found myself looking through some trees into a small clearing and at first I saw nothing unusual; then my eyes focused on a black stump on the far side, about forty yards away. Suddenly it moved, with a sort of hunching motion, then it moved again, sideways, thrusting a paw under a rotting prone log. I squinted through my field glass. It was a bear, a small black that couldn't have weighed more than ninety pounds or so.

I grabbed Booto's neck ruff to keep him silent but the bear was completely oblivious to our presence and was having a marvellous time. It ripped under the log with its left paw, shifted swiftly round to the side, made a snuffling snort, ripped a slab off the top with its right claws, darted its head down and tore away some pulp, then it scuffed madly at the earth like an irate boxer in a clinch. Suddenly it leaped back, ears flat, and flailed away with its right paw – whap, whap, whap. Whatever it was after, maybe a mouse, clearly got away, for after swiping at the earth for a couple of yards, the bear buried its nose under some tree roots, snorted twice, scattering leaves, then gave up. Its look of disappointment, despite my excitement, made me want to laugh.

Now the bear shambled back to the log and stared intently again. I wondered if it had found another mouse, but now its behaviour was different. It eagerly licked at the top of the log for a minute or so, then lay down in front, its almost tail-less backside to us and, resting quaintly on its left elbow, casually began placing its right paw under the log and bringing it back to lick off whatever was now on it. My first thought was that it might have found some honey, but in the earth? Now I saw that the light buff part of the log where it had torn off the slab was covered with small moving patches. Ants! Scratching out the mouse, the bear obviously had disturbed an ants' nest and was now more than happy with these easier pickings. Obviously their bites didn't bother it for it never once shook its paw or head. In fact, the bear looked completely at its ease, like some plump little black Pharaoh.

Booto stirred again at my side but a shake of the ruff kept him quiet. After a few minutes the bear ended its feast, stood up, licked its lips, and looked this way and that as if wondering where to go next, just like a mischievous child looking for new trouble but not sure where to find it. Then it ambled slowly to a tree, drew itself up the trunk, hooked in its claws, and bore downward like a cat stretching. The sight of those strong sharp claws sent a slight shiver through me and my elbow tightened involuntarily on the gun. Even a bear this size could rip a man badly. Now it yawned, then suddenly sat down on its haunches with a little thump and started swinging its head slowly from side to side as if thoroughly bored.

It was such a cute little beggar I could have watched longer, but Booto finally broke the cardinal rule and whined. I gripped his ruff again but it was too late. The bear's acute ears had heard the alien sound. It jumped up so fast it almost fell over backward and with only a swift glance in our direction, as if knowing its short sight would reveal little, it bolted into the dark safety of the trees. I told Booto off in no uncertain terms. I couldn't afford his making such a mistake again; a heavyweight black, a mother with cubs, or any grizzly was quite likely to come and investigate the sound. I wanted neither to have to use the rifle nor to have any close confrontations with bears that could be avoided. And I hoped Booto now had this firmly fixed inside his canine skull.

We went over to the log and the dark-brown wood ants were dashing hither and thither, some with bigger jaws appearing to be on guard, while the rest busily rebuilt the entrances to the nest. A yard away three of the bigger ants had found a large grey beetle grub, missed by the bear when it had torn the bark, and were promptly dispatching it, sinking their powerful mandibles into its soft body as it thrashed about unavailingly, trying to reach them with its own. I watched them a little longer and then walked back to my pack and a lunch of my cold pemmican.

Not till the early evening of the next day did we find any more bears, but discovering some unmistakable prints that seemed fairly fresh on a hard sandbank of a creek, I knew there were probably some still in the area. The hind tracks of bears are astonishingly like humans', broader across the toes but lacking the high instep and sometimes showing marks of the five claw tips. What puzzled me about one prominent track was that I could find no claw marks and the front marks were too indistinct – much smaller than the rear, they were deeper, as if someone had thrown jagged rocks into the sand. Then I worked it out. The bear had probably crossed the creek fast, had landed on her front feet, and her rear print, which was least blurred, had taken less weight than the other and, being on the downward slant of the firm sand, had left no claw marks. It is fun playing at wilderness sleuth, but once we reached the thick swamp grass over the creek, where an experienced hunter could have distinguished which new patches had been flattened by bears passing and which by other animals or by wind and rain, I felt a hopeless amateur.

We had come down into the river valley now, just before it opened out into boggy pasture. The cotton-wool clouds were crossing over our heads from the west, but the wind, perverted from its true course by the high mountains, was blowing up-valley into our faces. As the sun was sinking behind the hills and I was thinking of making camp, I decided to walk along the firmer edges of the forest in the shadows. It was a lucky decision, for if we'd gone along the east bank the sun would have lit our moving forms like lamps and we would not have seen the sight we now did.

Walking through a spruce and hemlock grove, I noticed there were clumps of willow and some alders ahead and just beyond them the sound of flowing water. Booto pricked up his ears as if he'd heard or sensed something I could not. Quietly urging him back, I threaded my way through the alders, keeping low, and as we came to a bluff of grey rocks I heard splashing sounds. I put my green net over my head, took one step onto a small ledge, and peeped between some shrubby plants. In the shallow ravine, merely forty yards below us, was a black bear with her two cubs. She was actually a beautiful cinnamon-brown colour, with darker patches where her winter coat was shedding, but while one of the little cubs was as light as herself, the other was dark brown and had orange tips to his ears.

The cubs were having a whale of a time, dashing in and out of the water from the bank, while their mother was trying to catch something. Crouching on the verge, she was fiddling with her paw in what looked like some weed. She didn't appear to be having any luck and whether in exasperation at this or at her two cubs fooling around a few yards away, she gave two sharp coughing grunts. Instantly the cubs stopped and ran to her, ears back like little dogs, as if afraid they'd be cuffed if they didn't hurry.

Booto must have seen them for the first time right then, for he stirred by my ankles. I quickly grabbed his muzzle as the mother bear put her paw in again and started delving even lower under the bank. To my surprise I now saw the river was teeming with fish, mere dark lines in the water, barely moving. They would be cut-throat trout, for this was a good gravelly spawning area, and at this time of year they would be near finished breeding, thus dopier and more tired, than usual.

Now the mother bear may have overbalanced or she may have thought, "To hell with it, I'll get right in!" for the next thing I knew she had landed in the river with a great splash. As she hit water there were flashes of silver as fish scattered in all directions. When the turbulence settled I felt she must be young, for she couldn't have scaled more than 180 pounds and she certainly didn't seem too good at angling. She stood still and square with the water flowing past, barely covering her belly, and the trout now swimming round her legs. As her cubs stood on the bank to watch, she tried standing on three legs and using her right front paw to hook a fish. But apart from flipping an occasional one up to the surface, she had no more luck than when groping down from the edge. After a while she changed her method. Instead of trying to flip one out, she moved to shallow water and delved around underwater with her paw, pinned something down in a rocky cleft, plunged in her head, grabbed it in her jaws, and then bounded dripping from the river and dropped the object on the bank. It wasn't a fish but a big frog. Immediately her cubs joined her and, small though they were, they snapped and snarled at each other, pawing at the dead frog. As far as I could see the mother bear only bit at the frog a couple of times, as if showing the cubs, then turned back to the river. At that moment a huge bald eagle came from over the forested mountain behind me in a shallow glide, flapped momentarily, hovered as if about to snatch the frog as the cubs scattered in terror, but then sailed on downstream, braked wildly, and dropped like a stone onto a shallow pebbly bed. I lay against the rock, riveted by this extraordinary sight, but more was to come. The mother bear was quick on the uptake. The moment she'd seen the eagle flying low near her cubs she had started to charge, then when the eagle landed twenty yards away on the riverbed, she just changed direction and continued after it. I now saw the eagle had hit into a fish and as the bear landed in the river and crunched toward it in an ungainly gallop, sending up sheets of spray, the eagle tried desperately to rise, literally bouncing on the struggling fish. It couldn't quite make it though, and when the bear got too close, the eagle relinquished its grip and soared into the air. The bear pulled up, seized the dazed fish in her mouth, and with a seeming leer of triumph, bore her prize back to the cubs. The eagle performed two power dives over the trotting bear, then sailed away in disgust. The bear took the fish some thirty yards into the lee of some trees up the far bank and, as far as I could see, shared it with her cubs.

Booto was now getting fidgety, and it was time to move on as dusk was falling, also I thought it might be a good idea to find out exactly what he would do. We seemed safe enough now – the mother bear was nearly eighty yards away across the small river, a black bear was hardly likely to leave her cubs *behind* to attack, and Booto was no fool – so I took the chance. Stepping out from the rock bluffs beneath the alders, I let him go.

He didn't bark, merely ran forward a few steps, then stood with braced legs looking at the bears. I moved further out into full view. But the bears just carried on eating. I stood there a few moments, heart beating fast, then gave a loud cough. She heard instantly, dropped what was left of the fish, reared on her hind legs, saw us, and made a short whoofing grunt. The two cubs shot up the same tree, one after the other, little balls of black fluff. I turned, trying to make it look as if I was just going about my business but still keeping an eye on the bear, and said softly, "Come on, Boot." The bear gave an odd snort and rapidly hauled herself up the trunk until she reached the first crotch, where she poked her nose at us with an anxious look. She showed not the slightest hint of belligerence. Booto gave a small whuff, indulged in a little sneeze, then turned to follow me. I had never seen a bear climb and if it was surprising to see how fast the cubs could climb at such a tender age, it was even more impressive to watch their mother claw her way up the trunk, like a giant moth-eaten squirrel.

I felt it better not to appear as if we were retreating, so we walked off at a sideways tangent, in about a mile semi-circle, before making camp in a glade less than two hundred yards from the river. I set up the tent beneath a large spruce, keeping well away from anything that looked like an animal trail. Although I felt the tent was useful for reducing our scent, I didn't want to risk some bad-tempered old bear stumbling upon it at night. Booto would almost certainly put up a fight and things could get really nasty.

Next morning, tired of cold pemmican, bacon and crushed hard boiled eggs, I decided to try for some trout. When I peeped over the edge of a pool below a riffle, I was astonished to see how many there were, but they were too far down to try tickling them by hand. I searched laboriously under stones and rocks for worms or grubs, then with a small chip of lead, clipped on two feet up from the baited hook, and a small stick for a float, I "long trotted" downstream, so the bait went ahead of the float. Within minutes, I caught two trout between one and two pounds each. The river had probably never been fished, and the trout would have gone for almost anything small that moved.

As I ate my delicious breakfast, sizzled in a trace of vegetable oil, I felt a slight sense of triumph. I was really travelling light and carried no utensils save one light pot divided into two adjustable compartments by a piece of aluminium, a stout plastic spoon, and my pocketknife. For frying I used tinfoil bent over a looped green birch twig – it held out against the flames long enough to cook fish or bacon or to boil water. My one luxury was an enamel mug, for I like my tea or coffee to taste good.

Those first three days were an exceptional prelude to our wanderings through that rugged terrain. We saw several more black bears, found tracks, droppings, and places where they had uprooted rocks and torn rotten stumps and logs apart for grubs and insects. And on each occasion we came across them, they took to flight once they became aware of us. They seemed quite unaggressive by nature but though a feeling of safety grew, I tried not to relax vigilance. Once after dawn we actually passed a bear without seeing it. Booto suddenly stopped, looked up into a tree, and there, sitting on a crotch, was a young bear the colour of jet. As I stared up, it made an oddly raucous, anxious sound in its throat, then flirted its loose top lip out at us, rather like a naughty schoolboy about to make one of those rude noises!

Although female black bears can be ready to breed at four, grizzlies are usually five years or older, but both meet mates in the most romantic time of year, the summer days of June. Yet, like seals, bats, and some of the weasel family, they have a great advantage over many animals, for the length of their pregnancy is controlled by a phenomenon known as delayed implantation. Put simply, this means the fertilized eggs don't begin to develop into babies until the most convenient time, which for she-bears is when they are in their winter dens.

After running with their mates from a few hours to a couple of days – grizzly bears are often ferocious at this brief time and may even charge other bears if they come too close – the dams have the rest of the summer and early fall to put on plenty of fat. As denning time approaches, around early November or even six weeks earlier at higher elevations or in the colder regions of the Yukon, the pregnant bears will, like all bears, break the rule of eating mostly at dusk and dawn and feed during the day too, thus increasing their vulnerability during the fall hunting season. Then, unlike the males, who often wait until the first snowfall before denning, she-bears will look for a warm site in a rocky cave, under a log or some windfalls, and line it with leaves, moss, grass, conifer boughs and needles or other plant debris before entering for the long sleep. Bears are not true hibernators – their body temperatures and metabolism drop only slightly and they still breathe between five and eight times a minute, and during warmer days in mild winters will even rouse to look for food or find a more comfortable den. In January or February they give birth – one or two cubs for a young mother, up to four for a bear in her prime.

Surely bear cubs represent one of evolution's finest successes, for they often weigh little more than half a pound at birth. They are the smallest babies, in relation to their mother's size, of any placental mammal so that they won't be too much of a strain on her system, for pregnant bears don't feed at this time. Even grizzly babies may weigh little more than a pound. Blind, toothless, and almost naked, they wail and squeak like little pigs, snuggling up to their mother for warmth while she licks them tenderly. They are said to hum like large bees when suckling her milk, and dens have actually been located by this odd noise.

One warm late March or April day, out they all come, and a few weeks later the shiny new fur of the well-fed cubs contrasts strangely with the tattered, woebegone look of the mother bear, who is now shedding her winter coat. The cubs are still tiny, weighing only around six or eight pounds – around eighteen pounds for grizzlies. Now the long process of learning to be a good bear begins. From now on they'll learn everything from their mother. At her gruff command they must immediately scoot up trees. If they disobey her they'll be cuffed, and if they wander too far they'll be carried back in her mouth by the scruff of the neck, like kittens. But the most important part of her teaching, though they're not fully weaned until seven or eight months, is how to find food.

Bears will eat almost anything organic and when the adults emerge from hibernation, their stomachs flat from lack of use, and start delicately nipping tender shoots of new grass, their appetites are fairly easily satisfied. They munch the heads of clover, dandelions, wild violets, young tree shoots – especially sweet maple; they bite roots and chew off the bark of some deciduous trees for the juicy sap pulp beneath. They scratch for bulbs, skunk cabbage roots, and wild rice, and dig and tear at old stumps for grubs, bugs, bumblebees, ants, grasshoppers, mice, frogs, and – if they can catch them or drive an osprey or eagle from its prey – fish. They adapt their menu to the food-of-the-month, prizing in summer the profusion of wild sarvis, salmon, and blue and red huckleberries. Once a bear finds a luxuriant berry patch it will stay perhaps a week, constantly standing on its hind legs raking down clusters of the fruit into its mouth with its claws. In the fall bears crunch up acorns, beechmast, chestnuts, hazelnuts, and the seeds of conifers. Although mostly vegetarian, they aren't averse to killing an occasional small mammal or eating carrion either. Grizzlies farther north even clean up wolf kills, sometimes driving the wild canines from their prey.

The young black bear males and unbred females have very lively natures and an insatiable curiosity unmatched by any animals except monkeys and maybe otters, and they deserve their name of clowns of the forests. Several times watching bears I was close to roaring aloud with laughter.

Early one morning as I was lying awake in the tent and mentally cursing that the fire had gone out despite my having banked it the night before, I saw Booto prick up his ears and heard an odd brushing sound. Holding him to keep him quiet, I peeped out. There, in a grassy open patch some sixty yards away, a young black bear, moth-eaten and moulting, had walked over to a thick low bush. Using its still leafy twigs like a brush, he was now busily marching backward and forward over the bush with an expression of ecstasy on his grinning face. After he'd had a good scratch, he stood with head lowered as if wondering what to do next. Spying a dead log, he shuffled slowly over to it with that curious, wobbly, baggy-trousered look black bears have, sniffed one end, then made two half-hearted digs at the base. Suddenly he pricked up his short ears, made a few quick and more purposeful stabs at the ground, jerked back his nose, then started whacking the grassy roots with his big right paw. At first I thought he was trying to scratch out a mouse nest but through my fieldglass I made out some tiny black-and-orange creatures lurching clumsily through the grass and moss. Bumblebees.

Having presumably stunned or flattened a few of the bees, he started picking them up in his mouth one at a time. He chewed each bee with a quick snap, his lips held back so I could see his white teeth flashing, shook his head violently, dropped the bee again, then lapped it up for the final swallow. After disposing of several this way, the supply apparently having run out, he again looked bored. He clambered up on the log, ambled the length of it, turned cautiously at the other end like a tightrope walker afraid of falling, then lay full length flat on the log and stretched out with a big yawn. If he'd been stung at all he hid it well.

After lying there a few moments, he started to let himself roll off the log. First he put a hind leg down, as if to check that the ground was still there, then he rolled off the log onto his back, completely relaxed for a second, suddenly powered the air with all four feet like a pair of upturned tandem cyclists, then wriggled violently from side to side to scratch his back. Having eliminated his back tickle successfully, he lay still a moment, then rolled over onto his feet, stood up quickly as if startled, and began sniffing the air. A slight wind was blowing from the southwest – between us, but I hoped not sufficiently in the bear's direction so that it carried our full scent. The next thing the curious animal was walking *toward* us. Ed had explained if ever a black bear was walking toward me and clearly not aware of my presence, I should expose myself naturally, the "minding my own business" act, rather than have it suddenly stumble upon me unaware. Scared now, holding onto Booto's collar, I stood up and started poking at the dead fire.

The bear stopped immediately in its tracks, reared up to get a better look as Booto started to growl, gave a loud huffing snort, and made off into the forest with great bounds. The sight of the fleeing bear was too much for Booto and tearing himself loose, he dashed a few yards in pursuit, giving some barks to send the bear on his way. Luckily the young bear was not bad-tempered and he was soon lost to view. But again I gave my headstrong companion a sharp dressing down.

Two days later, on a fine afternoon, I decided to walk along the meadows by the river. We had seen no bears for forty-eight hours, and the land was open and marshy in places, and I wondered if we'd reached the kind of terrain bears don't like. Suddenly, wading through the lush, high swamp grass, we came to a sandy stream bed in which were two large bear prints. They were broader than any I had so far seen, a good nine inches long, and were spaced some three feet apart, and there were other imprints in the sand almost two inches beyond the toes. As I realized these longer shallow claw marks were almost certainly made by a grizzly, I felt scared. It was really open country here, not a tree within four hundred yards, and if there was a grizzly snoozing in this thick, deep grass, I surely had no wish to wake it up. Turning west I headed back for the forest.

We had barely covered a hundred yards along the side of the stream when we came to several trails of flattened grass. I slowed down, eased well away from the stream and the tracks, lifted the rifle from my pack, and craned my neck to see over the grass ahead. A few yards farther and we came to a large patch where grass had been crushed and torn up in places and, at the edge of the neighbouring stream, mud and sand had been ripped up and scattered around. It seemed there had been a scuffle of some sort, but everything now looked still around us. Keeping well back, we walked on, and reaching the shelter of the trees, I climbed a cottonwood about twenty yards back from the meadow and, with Booto amicably lying down and yawning below, decided to keep watch.

It was hard sitting in that tree, for while the branch was broad, it grew up at a slight angle so that it was uncomfortable to lean against the trunk for long. And while I'd stuffed my spare sweater beneath me, no matter which way I shifted, one of my legs eventually went to sleep. To make things worse, the clouds suddenly rolled away to reveal a large patch of blue sky and the sun blazed on my head and back through a gap in the leaves. After an hour I was thinking of giving up and making camp – for I never left this chore until dusk – when I thought I'd relieve my cramped position for a while by standing up. I had no sooner worked myself up backward against the trunk and taken a look over the meadow when I noticed what looked like a piece of black carpet rippling along the tops of the waving grass down by the river.

As it came to a slight dip I saw it was a bear, not a grizzly because there was no shoulder hump, but a big black, and as it walked it kept turning its head backward on each side as if looking at its own back feet. What an odd way to walk, I thought. Maybe it had been crippled. But as the bear turned in our direction and began to head up the far side of the stream, the grass jumped and moved beside it and looking through my fieldglass I saw the cause of its concern – three cubs almost as black as the she-bear. I slid slowly down the tree trunk, took a quick look at Booto fast asleep under a bush, and lifted the fieldglass again.

Now the family was halfway up the stream. The mother, a heavy, powerful dam I reckoned to weigh around four hundred pounds, shuffled along slowly with her head low while one of the cubs scampering beside her kept darting across her bows. Suddenly she gave it a sharp clout, bowling it head over heels in the long grass, and I faintly heard its little high-pitched squeal, the sound reaching me as it picked itself up, shook its head, and then fell sharply into line behind one of the others.

When she reached the spot opposite the flattened area, the mother bear paused a moment, snapped like a dog at the flies bothering her, and without more ado rumbled into the shallow water like a furry tank. She pushed her head under, briefly gave it a good shake, then rolled over on her back. Two of the cubs jumped after her, one scrambled over her submerged neck and made it to the muddy flattened bank beyond, while the other made two attempts to board his mother's broad belly in the region of her teats and made it at the third try. Whether it tried to grab a little suck on his way over or dug its claws in too far, I couldn't see, but it too got a swift wet cuff that sent it up onto the mud bank, whereupon it was pounced on by the cub already there and together they rolled, playfully clawing, back into the water. The mother took no notice of the third cub, whose constantly opening mouth and flattened ears indicated that it didn't like water and that it was bawling its little head off. She just lay back, snoot pointing skyward, flipping pawfuls of water over her sore dugs. Finally the cub edged gingerly into the water, apparently still bawling, and finding it could swim, probably not for the first time, scudded like a beaver around mother's vast bulk and joined its brothers or sisters. The cubs loved that wet sandy mud; they crawled, rolled, slid down backward, then forward, wrestled, bit each other's necks, and when they got tired of that they hustled like animated mud lumps around their long-suffering mother. They were as playful as young otters but unlike those sleek swimmers, their mud-clotted fur stuck out at ungainly angles. Whether this was a bathtub used by many bears or their own private one I'd no way of knowing, but a bathtub it seemed to be. The mother bear wallowed about like a stranded whale, no doubt ridding herself of ticks or fleas. At times only her paws and part of her head showed above water, her buff chin and nose looking like a weird, conical floating bottle.

I watched them until my arms grew tired holding the light eyeglass. Finally the mother bear felt cool and clean enough to wallow out, stand on the bank, and shake herself like a great dog. Two cubs followed her out and stood there dripping wet, but the third attempted to emulate its mum – braced all four feet and tried to shake itself like she had, but all that moved was its head. His mother looked at it briefly as if to say, "Not so fast Charlie. I haven't taught you that yet," then shuffled off with the cubs trotting beside her, back the way they had come.

Of all animals in North America, the black bears must have the freest and most enjoyable family life. Their appetites are easy to satisfy, they wander over a fairly small wooded home range of some fifteen square miles, sleeping in temporary dens in thickets or in glades under shady trees like cedar or spruce, and apart from man their only enemy is the occasional cantankerous grizzly male, who has been known to kill small mothers and cubs if there are no trees handy in which they can take refuge – but such instances are extremely rare. Devoted mothers, black bears don't ovulate when feeding and running with their young the first year, so they breed at most only every second season. Should a romantic black male show interest in her the first summer with the cubs, she drives him off with considerable ferocity. Young mothers usually den up with their cubs again the first winter but older bears, who with greater experience have taught the cubs all they need to know, will turn them away when winter comes and den up alone. The cubs may then den together and stay together and hunt for food the following spring before striking out on their own. The cubs of young mothers running with her a second season are left to their own devices in June or July, when she comes into oestrus, and her new lover may drive them away.

The family situation is different with grizzlies, who are slower-growing and usually larger animals. Here mother and cubs always den up together at the end of their first season and frequently a second winter as well. Thus their breeding rate is slower. While grizzly mothers, especially when in their prime, can breed every second year, there are often gaps of three, four, and even five years between families. Contrary to popular belief, father, mother, and baby bears of both species do not run, hunt, and den up together at all. Male bears have an easy time of it. They meet their mates by scent and chance in the summer woods, may run together a few days – or only a few hours – make love, and their responsibility as fathers ends right there.

After coming down the tree, I decided to make camp early that night, about a quarter-mile up into the forested slopes. I thought it was unlikely, in view of the preponderance of black bears, that there were now grizzlies in the same region. The two species don't exactly believe in voluntary integration. Maybe the tracks I'd seen were of a transient one, heading for a favourite spring pasture at the lake's far end.

As I stirred supper in the pot, Booto sat looking at me patiently, then gave a huge yawn. Poor old Boot, I thought. How bored he must have been by this inactive day. His stoical acceptance of our trek, his interest in seeing bear but apparent lack of fear of them, was really impressing me now. Our trek had probably recalled earlier encounters with black bears, when our coast had been wilder than it was now, for after the first few days he'd been acting sensibly. Even his one dash after the young bear hadn't been foolhardy; he'd weighed the situation pretty well.

After the charm of the afternoon and our experiences so far, I felt surer that basically the black bear is a timid and inoffensive animal. I was beginning to feel, too, that the few who become potentially dangerous lose their fear of man by proximity to him around dumps are deviates actually created by man's constant incursions into their dwindling wild domains. I was in fact starting to relax my vigilance, a little, and late the following afternoon we had an experience I've no wish ever to repeat.

It had rained half the night and most of the morning, so we'd waited until the worst was over before setting off. After a mile the river swung eastward and the mountain slopes sheered down almost to its banks, cutting off the end of the valley. I decided to traverse the incline, then cut up into gentler hills on the other side of the bend. While we were at the river, the sun now out again, I washed some underclothing and tied it with my damp bag onto my pack to dry in the sunny breeze. As afternoon ended we were walking along a fairly high ridge where the dark spruce forest opened out a little, and through a gap I saw we'd drawn abreast of a lake but were about a mile above it. We were now within five miles of the next valley at the lake's end, and I was trying to decide how much farther to go before making camp, when the land started to dip and we came into a large, park-like clearing. By now I'd grown a little careless and had allowed Booto to run some thirty yards ahead. Suddenly he stopped, ears up and one foot in the air. A small cub was stumbling between scrubby manzanita and huckleberry bushes some fifteen yards to his left, and the line of its path lay between him and myself. There was a noise to my right and I looked over to see a large black bear at the edge of the trees. Immediately she gave two coughing grunts, sending the lone cub and another with her up the nearest firs, where they clawed their way into the foliage of high branches and started to cry out.

The mother showed no desire to tree herself but looked toward the dog and made a strange coughing snarl. Knowing we were in real danger now as Booto was between her and one of the treed cubs, my knees suddenly jelly, I quickly unhitched the rifle, muttered a silent prayer, flicked off the safety catch, and commanded Booto to "Come here" as softly yet firmly as I could. As Booto slowly obeyed, walking toward me with a stiff-legged, deliberate, and cautious gait, his ears down, the mother bear whined nervously as if she didn't know what to do, then she gave a vicious snort. As Booto reached me and I quickly held his ruff, the bear gave two low warning growls, pawed the ground, then seemed to change her mind and started walking to and fro, a few paces each way, with an oddly furrowed, anxious look on her face. At the same time she kept giving chuffing coughs and higher-pitched growls, gnashing her teeth and raising and lowering her top lips in ghastly smiles.

I was so terrified I was about to fire off a round in the hope of scaring her away, when the isolated cub on my left suddenly scrambled down the tree in a shower of bark dust, dropped with a heavy thud that made me think it must have killed itself, then got up and ran around behind its mother and on into the forest. Now the bear backed up, gave a final coughing growl, and walked off after her two youngsters with an odd, massive dignity.

I dared not move for a while, but, then, hearing the bears crashing through the forest, I wanted only to put distance between us, and we headed left on a diagonal path toward the lake while I cast nervous looks behind. We were once more in rocky windfall country, and we covered less than a mile before gathering darkness forced us to make camp. It had been a chastening experience but it taught me, finally, never to allow Booto to precede me by more than a yard or two through such wild terrain. I'd been extremely lucky.

That evening I felt more afraid than at any time on the trek, and I searched for a really safe camp site. Finally I found a mossy bed atop a rocky knoll that had three small firs growing around its edges. I set up the tent between the trees, still thinking of the run-in with the bear and knowing if Ed was right, I was nearing grizzly country. Now I recalled the big tracks again and realized if grizzlies were in the habit of wandering between these distant pastures, they would probably keep low along the river and lake shores – and I was now fairly close to the lake. Then I had the idea to rig myself an alarm system. Tying some fishing line to a can of stones, I ran it around the fir trunks some three feet above the ground, then brought the end back so I could tie it to my mug, which I also filled with stones. By placing my pack on a flat rock in the tent and putting can and mug on the pack, if anything hit the line hard during the night, one of them would fall onto the rock and wake me up, if Booto hadn't already awakened me. It wasn't likely, of course, but I felt safer.

As I stirred the pot, Booto stole quietly over, thrust his wet nose into my lap. As I stroked his head, I thought what an ideal companion he'd turned out to be. Had I been totally alone, I might well have turned back before this. The lake nestled at the foot of a large mountain, its snow-capped peaks rearing over eleven thousand feet into the sky. According to Ed, there should be grizzlies on the south-west aspect of its heavily timbered slopes, for they lay up in the woods between grazings on a huge acreage of lush swampy pastures that stretched partly along the far lake shore. The whole point of the expedition had been to see wild animals, particularly bears. I'd really had good fortune with the black bears, despite the afternoon encounter, and the sight of a grizzly would put the cap on the trek.

Up early, a touch of frost about, my clothes were as initially damp and clammy as usual, but I was soon back in the hard-breathing, perspiring state that besets the wilderness trekker. As we neared the lake, the rocks of the old snow slides grew bigger, and when these and tangled windfalls weren't the main hindrance, clumps of devil's-club bushes, sharing small flat shale areas near creeks with willow and alder, ripped at clothes and pack, slowing us even more. These thorns are well named, for they're barbed and hard to pull out, yet if left in the flesh they work inward and fester. After toiling through an alder thicket we came to the shores of the lake itself.

It was an idyllic scene and I gazed entranced. Early alpine flowers grew along the shores, not in profusion but shyly peeping out from behind rocks and old roots like fallen stars. In little bays the placid water was encouraging a new carpet of polished-green water-lily leaves, some spread out already while others, paler green and bunched like little hands, struggled to join them through the watery depths. Grey, jagged sentinels of dead fir and spruce sprang along the shores, holding out their spikes like hat racks, while away on our right a woodpecker drummed on a barkless birch and a robin sang his cheerful little rising and falling song. Nearby a red-winged blackbird chased his mate into a willow bower, fluttering his red and yellow wing patches at her briefly, before she flew on, leading him a flirtatious dance.

As we sat down resting quietly, the whole lake seemed to come alive in the warmth of the springtime sun. Ahead on a mudbank where the dormant bulbs of bog iris were thrusting up new green sword blades, pintail ducks walked with a strangely graceful gait. As I swung my fieldglass over the lake, scaup, scoter, and mallard ducks swam singly and in pairs while out near the centre a red-breasted merganser was working himself up in a spirited courtship to his drab mate. He arched his wings, bowed and gestured with his long-toothed bill, raised his spiky, dark-green double head crest, then pattered along the surface around her in a cloud of spray.

Stealing back into the trees, we worked our way toward the end of the lake. I had just glimpsed a river ahead and realized we would somehow have to ford it when a strange clattering noise came from the trees above. I looked up to see two animals dashing through the top branches, both too large to be squirrels, and as the front one soared through the air from one tree to another, I saw it was a pine marten. It landed badly, scrabbled on the twigs, then shot off again as its pursuer, streamlined but thick-legged and heavy as a fox, landed in the same spot, missed its footing, twisted catlike in the air, hit the branch below, then bounded to the trunk and tried to make up for lost ground as it chased the flying marten. As they shot from my view, sending bark dust and tiny twigs falling to earth, leaving branches swaying in their wake, I realized I had just seen the rare fisher in action, and I felt little sympathy for its intended prey. Pine martens are the squirrel killers of the treetops, so it seemed fair justice this one should now be tasting its own medicine, if only for a while – for if it managed to find a small hole the fisher couldn't enter, it would escape. Maybe my good luck hadn't run out after all. The fisher is rarely seen in North America and does not exist in Britain, yet next to the wolverine perhaps, it is the most interesting of the weasel family. Browny black and bushy-tailed, it is the group's light heavyweight and is the only animal that can prey successfully on the heavily armed porcupine and survive – it attacks the underparts after twisting the porky on its back, and if it does happen to swallow a quill, its digestive system is so tough it either turns back and digests the quill or heals around it. Hungry cougars in winter also will tackle porcupines but can die more easily from the poisonous quills.

We reached the lake's end by late afternoon but as the outlet river was too wide and deep to cross, we walked about a mile downstream and made camp in the forest just before it opened out into the next valley. I figured out the safest way of crossing the river next morning while I was cooking a brief breakfast. The river was some thirty feet wide but only three to four feet deep in places, yet the flow was discouragingly fast. There were no fallen trees across so I had to wade it. First I threw over heavy items to lighten the pack – bags of meal, mug, pot, and trousers and other clothes wrapped in stones – then my boots. I kept a pair of thick socks to protect my feet. Then with a short pole as a bracer and towing a desperately swimming Booto with the tree rope tied around him harness fashion, we struggled across without mishap.

The water was bitterly cold, so after drying off we put on a bit of speed and crossed the log tangles in the swampy area at the lake's foot as fast as we could to get warm again, the turned against a slight wind from the far end and headed back above the far side of the lake. By late afternoon I judged we were less than half a mile from where the forest opened out into the long, lush pastures ahead. Emerging quietly from the underbrush on a slight rise, we found ourselves above the edge of a large swampy area full of bog willow clumps and skunk cabbage. As I stood wondering if it would be too treacherous in places to cross directly, I suddenly spied a young black bear digging in the ground about 120 yards to the right. Telling Booto to sit quietly, and leaving my rifle below, I climbed up a large cedar with heavy foliage to get a better look. To my surprise, there was another black bear further on, also a young adult, and it too was raking sporadically at the lily roots. The two bears took no notice of each other, as if not from the same family. Each worked in an odd silence, as if deliberately ignoring the other's presence. After a while there was a faint scuffing sound and I saw another black bear, larger and lighter brown than the others, coming through some short spruce and tall hemlock trees.

As soon as it reached the boggy edge it stopped abruptly, lifted its head, and went through an odd pantomime of sniffing and peering around without giving a sign it had seen the other two. They, in turn, just carried on feeding, and while a slight change in their manner showed they knew the third had come, they made no distinct moves. This strange performance of deliberately ignoring each other reminded me of commuters sharing a suburban train to London – each is well aware of the others but not one speaks until something usually happens.

This was clearly a favourite feeding ground. Parts of the marsh looked as if some homesteader had raked it with a tractor and harrow, it had been so well worked over. Adjusting my position on the uncomfortable branch, I waited to see what might happen next. I looked down and found to my surprise that Booto had vanished. I looked around the tree but couldn't see him anywhere, when a sudden series of puffs and snorts made me look up. Every one of the bears was galloping out of the marsh as fast as it could go. One shot up a tree two hundred yards away while the others disappeared into the forest.

The sun was now sinking behind the mountains and a slight northwest wind was murmuring through the trees ahead to my left, where the three bears had fled, and I fancied I smelled some iodine traces in it. I waited a few moments but as nothing stirred I decided to get back down, go back on my tracks, and make camp. But before I had time to move a huge animal emerged silently, like some vast, silvery ghost, from the trees to the east, as if part of the mountain itself had suddenly shifted, sniffed the air briefly with a broad black muzzle, then carried on into the marsh with a dignified but shuffling gait. It seemed as big as a locomotive, like some huge, hairy, tuskless rhinoceros, with a back so broad behind the menacing hump on its shoulders it looked almost flat. This was the first time I'd ever seen a boar grizzly in the wilds and the sudden soundless approach of this behemoth was quite terrifying. I had been told that mature grizzlies can't climb trees, for their claws are long and shallow and lack the in-curving hooks by which the lighter black bears haul themselves up. But at the moment my tree seemed less than adequate.

In fearful fascination, I watched it move across the clearing, thanking heaven the wind was blowing toward me. Then it quickened its pace, breaking into a trotting lope reminiscent of the way a fighting bull moves when first released into the arena, except this animal seemed as heavy as three such bulls together. What was most frightening about its run was the feeling of enormous, rhythmic, yet contained, power. Only the great mountains, rocks, and giant trees of this wild fastness could have evolved such a creature.

It reached the trees to my left and began to prance along their bases like a wolf in a zoo park along the bars of its enclosure, seeming to get a stronger scent of the black bears. Suddenly it stopped, went up on its hind haunches, sniffing and peering into a tree, then it dropped down again, ran to the trunk, reared up it, and began to whine and growl. A shower of bark slivers and twigs came down as the black bear struggled to get higher up the tree. The furious grizzly gave two whacks against the trunk with a huge paw, dropped to the ground, and with a last frustrated disdainful look into the branches, shuffled off into the centre of the marsh to feed.

As I watched it dig for roots, the difference between the two species of bear was very obvious. It worked purposefully, not with the dilettante air of the black bears. With each stroke of its spade-like paws, it hurled up a shovelful of mud and stones. Through my glass its claws seemed about four inches long, shallow-curved like grey bananas, but ideal tools for digging. I judged it to weigh around eight hundred pounds. Other immediately apparent differences were the size of its massive head, with its short, round ears, and the strength of its jaws. Its muzzle wasn't short and tapering up from the lower jaw like the black bears' but long and square, like a box, and now and again as it chomped up the roots there were flashes of teeth that seemed as large as tusks.

By now, because of my awkward perch, my left foot had gone to sleep. But the thought of moving while that animal was within sight or scent of me, seemed ludicrous. The fear shown by such large creatures as the three black bears when this grizzly appeared had done nothing to allay my own terrors. I had no wish whatever to test the theories that grizzlies attack man only when they're wounded, surprised, cornered, or provoked. I felt certain this bad-tempered old bear would attack me on his first scent or sight. The feelings of confidence I'd built up over the past days through overcoming much of my fears of black bears, being 'at one with nature' and all such fanciful imagery, had all oozed away. I thus stayed in the tree, oblivious to the painful sensitivity now creeping back into my leg. Slowly, moving my head like a clockwork puppet, I looked down again for Booto, but there was still no sign of him.

The grizzly had now worked its way over some seventy yards of ground and had come slightly nearer my tree. After a few more minutes it suddenly stopped digging, looked up all alert, turned, and stared straight at me. Lifting its nose a little higher, it sniffed the air as a dog does in a garden when the kitchen window is opened. I froze, trying to appear part of the trunk and not to transmit fear. I told myself what a magnificent animal it was, tried to think good, positive things about it, to feel sympathy, appreciation, even friendliness. The bear walked some forty feet, full of distrust, coming nearer at an oblique angle, sniffing the wind trying to get the scent of this object it couldn't quite see. He stood on his hind haunches, looking like a giant black golliwog in the fading light. Poor-sighted as grizzlies are, he couldn't make out whether I was a hole, a broken branch, a glimpse of rock bluff, or what. Suddenly he dropped onto all fours, gallumped back to where he'd been feeding earlier, pawed briefly at the ground, then, to my relief, turned and headed out through the far end of the marsh and into the trees.

My first thought was to get down and retreat. Then I thought the beast might try to sneak around behind to satisfy his curiosity and I waited a few more minutes, straining my ears, but all I heard was the mournful call of a towhee bird. Hearing nothing more, I eased my cramped limbs down the cedar. I was trembling with fatigue and fear. I grabbed the rifle as if it were an old friend, checked the catch and shells I had left, and was just swinging up my pack when I heard a sudden rustle in the bushes nearby. I whirled around, desperately ready to use the gun – to see Booto. He had hidden among the leaves under a thick clump of bushes ever since the appearance of the grizzly and now was as glad to see me on the ground as I was to see him. He too was trembling and he licked my hand nervously. I suddenly noticed how thin he'd become. I looked at the distorted image of my own face in my knife blade and it was pale, pinched, my hair sticking out at all angles.

"Old Booto, mooto," I said, "it's time we got out of here and went home." And as his tail started to wag, I added, "But before we go we'll just fire off old thundergun here in case that old devil bear is sneaking around." I aimed the gun at a hollow tree and its deafening roar as the big bullet sliced out a great chunk gave a slight boost to my flagging morale. We retraced our steps into the forest for more than half a mile and, making sure there was no marsh nearby, I set up the tent between small trees so I could again arrange my primitive alarm system.

I found it hard to sleep that night, partly because the memory of the grizzly still haunted me, but also because I couldn't make up my mind how to tackle the long pastures ahead.

Next morning the valley was shrouded in mist. It lay in heavy layers, like huge skeins of wool with no one to spin them, as if they would stay there until God himself put down his hands. And way ahead, at the far end of the pastures, the mountains reared far more steeply up from the river bank than I'd realized from the opposite side of the lake, and the clouds were so low they formed a thick blanket down to around the seven-hundred-foot level. There was almost no wind, so there seemed little prospect of much improvement that day. I decided to turn back. It would have been foolish to tackle those high rocky passes in that mist and cloud, especially with a dwindling food supply, and most unwise to wander by the pastures in such conditions. I was tired and I'd been lucky, exceptionally lucky so far, but in this remote fastness fifty miles from the nearest outpost of civilization I wasn't going to push it.

We retraced our steps and after lunch once more forded the river where we had crossed before. Then we set off on the return journey, going back roughly along the route we had come. As we went I now had to admit a grudging respect for the grizzly hunter. Not that I approved of his murderous activity any more, but a man would need a lot of guts to stand up before such a big charging bear, take steady aim, and fire. I marvelled too at the courage of the old trappers, a dwindling breed, who spent entire winters in such terrain laying traplines for twenty miles at a time, sleeping out alone in the snow. Just packing out the 150-pound hide and head of a big bear over such rugged country would call for exceptional endurance.

On the way back we moved as fast as safety would allow and, perhaps because of this making a fair amount of noise, we saw only two black bears throughout the four days it took to reach the shores of the inlet. Both were moving swiftly and had clearly gained a whiff of our scent on the slight following wind. The tide was on the turn from high as we reached the boats just before noon, but I was relieved to find no bears had scented the wrapped food in the tin box, for we'd almost finished the supply in my pack. I hauled the wooden boat into the water before the tide went too low, shared a hasty lunch with Booto, then we set off, bucking a stiff southwesterly wind. Luckily we still had nine gallons of fuel left and the tide was with us, so we had more than enough to reach the government wharf on the island at the inlet's mouth. But as dark began to fall with the tide well down, I holed the wooden boat on a rocky reef. Soaked to the waist, ruthlessly dumping everything I could, and with Booto showing his contempt for my navigational abilities by shaking his wet shaggy coat all over me, we finally got both boats to shore and camped overnight.

Next day, towing the empty wooden boat behind, we made it to the wharf in the dangerously sagging rubber boat. There, as the southwesterly was increasing in force, a fishing-boat skipper took pity on our plight. In return for the wooden boat that he reckoned he could patch up without too much trouble, he shoved $30 into my hand and agreed to transport deflated dinghy, engine, Booto, and me back to the fishing village on Vancouver Island where we had left the truck. Two days later, after a night out in Vancouver with friends, which I very much needed, we were safely back at our cabin up the coast.

I spent the next few days in an oddly euphoric mood, and in a small way felt rather proud of myself for having overcome my fears during the first few nights of the trek, for having gone as far as I had, and for having seen so much. I felt I'd earned the right to be a part of the real wilderness and for this it had rewarded me. But it was also a curiously intimate experience. In Vancouver, I had let slip the fact that I'd been north and seen some black bears with cubs and someone in the group who worked for a TV company had immediately wanted to know where, so he could get a camera crew up there; I'd managed to fend him off until the conversation turned to something else. I found I was loath to talk about it, that I didn't want to share it, even verbally, with anyone else. I now understood precisely how Ed Louette had felt.

The summer months passed by as I fulfilled writing commissions, and spent time just fishing, relaxing in the sun, smoking oysters and fish, and patching up the cabin.

I now knew the female eagle's mate hadn't returned, for on the days I saw her flying over the bay she was always alone. One afternoon my hopes were raised when I saw a smaller eagle beating its way, outlined black against the sky, over the northern land spit, and before it passed from view, the female appeared over my trees and flew straight toward it. Instead of the joyous reunion I expected, she dived again and again on the intruder and drove it, wildly swerving, back the way it had come. As it flew over the cabin I saw it was a young bird, its mottled black-and-brown plumage lacking the white head and tail of the adult. Perhaps it was her own youngster from last year, returning as young eagles often do to its former home. Here seemed further proof the youngster was also a female, for sometimes a bereaved eagle will mate with her own son. Although it would have been too immature to breed in its first year, I felt the old bird might not have given it such a hostile reception had it been a young male.

The father eagle wasn't the only one who failed to return that summer, for neither had Ed Louette. Nor, to my disappointment, had he written. While I knew he never spent two summers in exactly the same spot, he had said he would be back on the coast somewhere.

By the middle of July my book had been rejected by four publishers and I decided to rewrite. But I went at it leisurely, only working on it and stories when it rained or was too dull to deepen my mahogany tan, pretend I was a seal, find new ways of cooking oysters, mussels, and clams, or find better holes for salmon on the far reef. Booto didn't take kindly to such enforced idleness, however. Just as he disliked the thud of an axe and the bang of a hammer, he despised the tap-tapping of my typewriter. He often disappeared for days, pursuing his love affairs or visiting the cafe folk up the coast. They had their children from Vancouver for the summer now, and he liked spending time on the beach with them.

But as the weeks passed I felt again the lure of that wild inlet. I knew I had merely scratched at the edge of the experience of that lonely, savage wilderness, and I felt vaguely, too, that my funk at the first sight of the grizzly was something that ought to be conquered. I remember asking a top Italian racing driver after the Mille Miglia in which he'd placed well, if he was not afraid when driving in what was then the world's most dangerous road race.

"Fear," he had said with a strange smile, "is *why* I drive. I need that fear sometimes in my life, to know that I am battling with danger, that only fast reflexes, good sight, and quick decisions save me from death. It is like a drug this fear, something I have come to need."

I now understood what the racing driver meant, though it wasn't a need for that kind of fear that attracted me to the deepest wilderness. It was more a feeling that out there in the wild I might yet find the answer to some deep unspoken question, perhaps gain an insight into *how* I ought to spend my future. There is something in the need to be constantly alert, to pit your wits against the elements, to be prepared for trouble when trekking through harsh remote country among bears that could kill you with ease, that makes life itself more poignant. You feel aware and alive to your own existence in a way you cannot find in a sedentary repetitious job. And studying wildlife in its natural setting in the past year had given me more pleasure and spiritual insights than anything else I'd ever known.

Once again I determined to locate Ed, and this time convince him he ought to make one more trek before old Father Time claimed him. I admired Ed and felt I could learn still more from him, particularly under such challenging conditions. I wrote to every address I could think of and was about to give up when at the end of August I finally had a reply from a small village on the west coast of Vancouver Island. An old friend of his had offered him free boat, board, and lodging in return for help in building a log-cabin annex.

Ed's letter opened with a few reflections on my bear experiences, then chided me for not contacting George "Pappy" Tihoni.

> You should have headed straight there as I told you. The best grizzly country starts with the big mountains where you stopped and the river and valley at the head of the inlet. Tihoni's cabin is about six miles up it on the north bank, as on my map. If he was there I know he would have gone with you. That gun you have is his gun. I figured he would be so glad to get it back he'd go anywhere with you! Looks like my little plan misfired. But if you're definitely going up again soon I'll write him so there'll be no slipups. He knows that land far better than I do. I can't come but I'll be back on your coast next spring.
>
> Yours,
>
> Edmund Louette
>
> P.S. *Don't* take the dog. Tihoni will say why.

It was early September before I heard again from Ed, saying Tihoni had agreed to meet me and he enclosed a page of Tihoni's letter: "I will take this guy on *your* word – and *if* I like him. But tell him – no guns, no cameras. I don't take out hunters anymore. Some flew into the valley this spring and I was sick. These men come only in fair weather, to kill. They *don't* pay the price, Ed. And you also tell him no words. He must swear never to reveal the exact location of this place or even my real name in talk or writing. So you tell him – these are my conditions."

Tihoni sounded like a man I could respect, and I would meet his conditions. I would change his name when I referred to him and I would not identify specifically the places we would trek. I got ready to go. Booto had spent most of the previous week with his friends down the coast and when the day of my leaving dawned bright and clear, seeming like a good omen after two days of heavy rain, I drove him back there. Reckoning it might help establish my claim to him, I bought ten dollars' worth of his favourite dog food and, laughing away the couple's protests that they'd be happy to feed him themselves, I put the food on their veranda and promised to pick him up in about a month. Then I drove down to the ferry for Vancouver.

Next day I exchanged my inflatable boat for a sturdier, ten-foot rubber one with reinforced rowlocks, took an evening ferry to Vancouver Island, and headed north for my trip to the wild inlet.

12 Tihoni the Indian

*Be*cause I now had only one boat, I could not carry much fuel and so I rowed most of the way with the ingoing tides. Progress was slow and heavy rain made my second day miserable. But by adapting an ancient Viking idea I passed the night comfortably enough. On their long voyages, the Vikings turned their boats upside down at night and sheltered beneath them. So I hauled the rubber boat onto the tiny gravel beach where I'd landed for my spring trek and tied it upside down from the wind, bridging it across some rocks and bushes. Then, erecting my pup tent beneath it, and with the rain hammering along its inflated keel, I cooked my meal and slept, remaining reasonably dry.

In the morning I hid two cans of fuel in the bushes for the return trip and rechecked my stores – two dozen cold hard-fried eggs, plastic bags of lentils, split peas, flour and oat meal, dried soups, milk, and vegetables, salt, sugar, baking powder, tea, coffee, cheese, raisins, corn oil, and bacon, plus a plastic bag holding five pounds of dried strip beef and venison that I'd immersed in brine and semi-smoked so it would keep longer – some forty-eight pounds in all. I felt Pappy Tihoni would be pleased by my contribution, especially with the three flat half-bottles of rye I hoped would help lubricate our first meeting. I slipped one into my jacket pocket, lashed everything else tight into my two packs, and strapped the rifle to one of them. Then I covered the last eighteen miles to the inlet's head.

As I approached I had to check my map, for I was confronted by three river mouths. The lie of the mountains indicated the central river must be my true way. Even so, it constantly diverged around fir and spruce-covered islands and I had to make split-second decisions as to which was the correct course. The water was lower than I'd anticipated and its pace in the narrower currents was fast. I had to use the engine, constantly slowing and speeding to avoid going aground, and my backside was soon soaked. After some five or six miles the ravine sides became steeper and behind the foot slopes the lofty mountains began to rear higher into the sky, the bare slide of talus contrasting starkly with the dense underjacket and thick forests of spruce, hemlock, cedar, and fir that clothed the less steep hills. Three times I came to shale reefs and had to carry the engine and tank a few hundred yards, return for the supplies and rifle, then carry the boat on my back. I re-learned the wilderness lesson – never hurry. Better to camp early than tire oneself out. There is room enough, and time enough.

As I stumbled along with the boat, pausing for rests, I felt no fear of bears. There wasn't a bear in the world that wouldn't have taken instant flight at such an odd apparition. It was while I did my first portage I realized I wasn't the only one trying to reach the higher river and its pools. Fall runs of echo and humpback salmon were going up to their spawning grounds, and occasionally their backs hit with little dull thuds against the bottom of my boat.

As the river narrowed between the converging side hills, large bedrock boulders divided its flow and I soon learned to hurry into their lee and hold the boat steady in the foaming water for a few moments while deciding which side to tackle. By the time I'd covered an estimated seven or eight miles, I'd seen no sign of Tihoni's cabin, which Ed had said was some six miles up. Scolding myself for not having asked him to draw a scale map, I felt I'd missed the place. I throttled the engine down while debating whether to go ashore and walk back, when without warning it cut out. Four quick pulls refused to start it although the tank was half full. There was no alternative but to drift down river until I could manoeuvre to a bank. Not until then did I realize how strong the current really was. The only way I could control direction at all was to let the boat go backward while I heaved with rapid strokes on one oar or the other.

With increasing fright I saw great jagged rocks flash by as I sought to steer between them and half-submerged trees in the small whirlpools. For about five minutes the dinghy shot and whirled about alarmingly as I tried to stave off disaster, then I saw the fork around the rocks where I'd made my third portage. The left fork went over some sharp rocks while the right flashed through a twenty-foot gorge in some deep, turbulent rapids. My only hope was to dash through there and try to reach the quieter water beyond. I managed to straighten the boat up but when I was halfway through, the dinghy twisted violently, capsized sideways, and I was thrown out. A whirlpool at the far end sucked me down about twelve feet until my ears popped and when I came up I saw a trapped tree with other logs against it moving up and down in the swirl. Gasping in the icy water, hampered by my heavy wool lumberjacket, I instinctively struck out against the current for the log, came up beneath it, and felt the way to the surface blocked by other logs. I was nearly exhausted from frantic rowing and the brief swim upstream and felt I would drown.

Desperately I threw myself backward, praying for enough strength to come at the log again. As I surfaced, gulping in air, I heard a voice shouting, "Don't go against the river, go *with* it. Swim *across* – here!" A huge man had leaped into the river from the north bank on a bend below me and had somehow grabbed my boat and packs as they hit into the bend on their way down river. With a last strength born of terror, muttering prayers, I managed to swim, working my way obliquely across and with the current to where the man was clutching my dinghy with one hand and a tree on the bank with his other. As I drifted past I clutched the side of the dinghy so hard my fingers met in the rubber.

As I hung there with both hands, gasping for breath and terrified, my eyes popping, the man smiled grimly, then with great presence of mind and humour, said, "Tomkies, not Mackenzie, I presume?" This was my introduction to Pappy Tihoni.

He heaved both boat and me ashore with one powerful sweep and said, "The first rule on falling from a rubber boat is never lose hold of it!" I managed a weak smile as, white with shock, I sank down on the bank and watched him haul up the water-logged engine, which was tied to the boat by cord, and then the tank, which was still miraculously connected to the engine by its hose.

"How on earth were you *here*?" I asked, staring at him in amazement.

"Oh, I heard your engine popping away half a mile back," he said laconically. "Figured it might be you." Then he undid the rifle from the wet pack, shook the water from it, handling it fondly, and as he shook hands, said, "Hell, I'd pull ye out all over again to get this old beauty back! Are you okay? Come on, let's clean her up and dry off in the cabin. An' you can tell me how that old buzzard Ed is gettin' along."

I stood up shivering, felt the heaviness in my pocket, reached down and, with a faintly theatrical gesture, whipped the top off the unbroken bottle of rye and handed it to him. Pappy took a long swig, shot me a quizzical look, and as I followed suit, said, "Reckon you'll do."

That night as we draped my sodden clothes and packs before his red-hot pot-bellied stove and I sat hunched in one of his outsize jackets, I learned a little about Pappy. He resembled a grizzly bear with his square head, almost romantically heroic with its thick, aquiline nose, set upon massive shoulders and his natural dignity. At sixty-four he weighed around 208 pounds, and as he stirred the perpetually simmering pot of black tea, into which he'd dropped a few pine needles for extra flavour, the muscles from years of hand logging swung in layers from his arms. His paternal grandfather's parents had been Highlanders from Argyll who had emigrated to the Yukon, where they had worked in gold and copper mines. Pappy had been born on a sledge while his family was going south, and somewhere along the line Indian blood had been mixed into his strain, making him three-quarters Scots, one-quarter Indian, and one hundred percent Canadian. Pappy had a deep respect for and an affinity with the Indian way of life, and in recent years had adopted the name Tihoni.

When he'd been little more than a boy, he'd volunteered for service in World War I. Injured by shrapnel, he'd been washed up from a bombed hospital ship onto Brighton beach with a fractured skull. In the hospital they'd patched him up as best they could and sent him home. Still confused when he had arrived back in Edmonton, Alberta, he was unable to adjust to the death of his mother, and one day he had set off to walk nearly seven hundred miles through the Rocky Mountains to get to Prince Rupert and the coast he had loved as a child. He'd lived on berries, roots, fungi, and grasses and had caught deer by hiding wire snares at head height between leaves and piled brush along their forest trails, working windward and then scaring them into a run. He'd caught mule deer and even a young elk bull by its antlers. After several months he'd reached the outskirts of Prince Rupert, a wild semi-madman, and had smashed the window of a butcher's shop to get a haunch of meat before the Mounties managed to subdue and arrest him. Newspapers printed stories of these extraordinary exploits and he was still known among those old enough to remember as the Wild Man of the North.

He seemed a curious mixture. Although he sometimes spoke in the slang of the Canadian bush with a trace of Scots, he often injected long obscure words into his conversation, attractively mispronounced, and it was clear they'd come from years of lonely reading. He said: "I always reckoned I was a lucky son of a gun. The Highland blood gets me up these damn mountains. The Indian gives me ... heck, love I guess. Sure, love and a sort of reverence for this land, for the animals, birds, trees, rivers." He paused, handing me a brimming cup of his spicy tea. "When we European hordes brought our so-called civilization over here, lured the Indians with whisky, mirrors, knick-knacks, and guns in return for millions of furs, we called 'em savages. Guess they were some ways, but by God they know how to live in this land without wreckin' it, without killing everything in sight. And I tell you this, that kind of instinct and feeling for the land the Indians were born with has to be taught again or modern society will destroy everythin' natural that's left."

"Taught how, as a basic attitude, you mean?"

Pappy filled a huge curved pipe with tobacco, blew two clouds of dense smoke, and sat back with the air of a born wilderness philosopher: "Sure, the Indian fitted in with the landscape. Modern man overbreeds, expands his frontiers, takes it over, and changes it. Mining, logging, fishing, dredging, farming – in every way he eats up the last wild places and takes, putting almost nothing back. But don't get me wrong. I'm not saying 'Give the land back to the Indians' or that we should go back to their old ways. That's impossible. The Indian's as spoilt as the rest of us now, likes his TV set, washing machine, high wages, fast cars."

"But what we *should* do is go back into the past and learn again the best qualities of the Indian way of life, then shove those qualities and values back into society some way. By education, I guess. Hell knows, modern society is going off the rails anyway. One thing it needs is a good stiff injection of primitive values!"

As he talked I had the impression Pappy was deliberately acquainting me with his views and sounding out mine, perhaps to condition me for the adventures ahead. When he saw I was ready to listen without interruption, he set two large, thick metal crocks to warm on the stove and sat back again. Then he described the unspoiled Indian social life: how they cared for and respected the aged, revered their wisdom and council, how they seldom punished children but brought them up by careful instruction and most of all by good example – encouraging them as hunters by holding small feasts when the young son brought home his first squirrel or grouse, teaching them to be modest, charitable to others, never to scoff at the deformed, to respect their elders. A good hunter, luckier than his fellows, always threw a feast and invited the others, and the talk was mainly by the chiefs, the hunters, and the elderly, while women and children remained attentively silent – yet always came first when times were hard. He explained how matters of war, religion, and barter never intruded at social occasions, being reserved for special meetings where all oratory was carefully prepared in advance.

He then likened the Indians' religious concepts to ours, showing that in spite of necromancy, superstition, and witchcraft, they bore much in common with the white man's belief in the Judeo-Christian God. He retold the story of Tarenyawago (Hiawatha), a direct emissary of the Great Spirit who came to earth performing miracles and teaching the Indian nations art, wisdom, and knowledge, and the maxims of the Great Spirit – and how closely allied it seemed to him to be to the basic story of Christ, even to the ascent into heaven. The Indians held similar beliefs in evil antagonistic powers (the Devil), and to them the entire animal world was invested with good and merciful or evil and malevolent deities, representing the two main forces.

"In many ways the general religious ideas of the unspoiled Indian were superior to ours," Pappy reasoned. "While Christianity mostly dismissed the animal world, theirs were far more closely linked with natural forces and the world they lived in." He spoke of their instinctive poetic soul that invested every animal, tree, waterfall, mountain, lake, and river with mystic sensitivity, each under the guardianship of a good or evil deity. The very words they created – like Ticonderoga (place of the inflowing waters), Saratoga (place of the bursting out of waters), Ohio (beautiful river), even Canada itself, reflected nature in a poetic language that today has been sadly neglected.

"Another astonishing thing was that their populations were stable, even declining in some places, so they never drove any of the animals they hunted toward extinction," Pappy added. "Not like the white man who can't control his numbers, who nearly wiped out the useful beaver –"

"And the sea otter, buffalo, plains wolf, and –"

"Sure, and the lovely passenger pigeon and many others. Today even the eagles and bears are in trouble," Pappy agreed, smiling as if satisfied I was at least near his wavelength. "But we'll get to that. I've just one more point about the Indians."

Finally he told me how they brought hunting to its golden age. They held the animals in reverence, never killing for sport or enjoyment but purely for sustenance, using every portion of meat, bone, and gut and wasting nothing.

"What few skills I possess in these woods in tracking animals," he finished, "were all learned from the old Indian ways. I guess I was lucky, meetin' some of the last old teachers."

Pappy Tihoni was far different from the hermit trapper I had expected to meet. His years of isolation, quiet study, and contemplation, matched with a few city years plus many wilderness experiences, had produced his unusually whole, almost universal view of life. He'd remained simple in expression and often earthy in language, and instantly commanded my respect.

As appetizing, gamey smells emanated from the two crocks, he checked my stores and smiled at my homemade pemmican and attempts to smoke meat. "If you want to make real good deer jerky," he said, "you cut it into strips about half an inch thick, boil it in salty water for six minutes or so, tie cord or deer sinew round it, dip it in thick brine, then smoke it in alder chips till it's got a skin on. It'll keep a couple of years."

He lifted a crock off the stove and ladled generous helpings into two bowls and handed me one. "We'd better eat this up," he said, watching my face as I ate. It was delicious, gamey but rather sweet.

"My own pemmican," he said with a touch of pride. "Mostly moose with a dash of venison. What I do is cut the meat into strips, dry it in the oven – or sun if there is any – then I beat it into a dry paste. Then with boiled fat from the meat and the bone marrow, strain the mixture, pound in about ten percent dried cranberries or blues, and a few nuts. If you like it sweet, add honey or sugar, a few raisins. Chopped onions give it flavour too. And a dash of salt, of course. If you want to keep it awhile, make sure the fat covers it to keep out the air. You sew it in deerskin bags and put it in a cold place. You could do it with beef, caribou, any meat, but buffalo is best! Heck, a man could live healthy on nothin' else!"

"You got salt with you?" he asked suddenly.

"Sure, about half a pound."

"Not enough," said Pappy, putting two small packs of salt in a huge canvas bag. "You'll see why," he said, smiling at my puzzled frown.

When we'd finished the moose dish, he took our bowls and swilled them in his sink, put them back on the table, then ladled out the second crock. From it came an aroma as fine as any bouillabaisse I'd eaten on the French Riviera.

"My *fish* pemmican." He beamed. "You can make it with trout, salmon, almost any fish. Similar ingredients, but I throw in plenty of onions, grated carrots, and barley or lentils. You can spice it up a bit with swamp lily roots or the inner bark of poplar if you like."

When I'd eaten my fill and paid my compliments, Pappy put some water on for coffee and we got to talking about the wilds. He surprised me with his knowledge of North American animals, of which his natural favourite was the grizzly. He knew the Latin names of many of the seventy-eight species and subspecies, but dismissed the early complicated classifications as the work of 'over-zealous acadeemics'. He felt there were at most three main types – the giant Guyas or Middendorfis of Alaska and its islands, the coastal mountains, and the rare plains or Barren Ground bears.

"The grizzly wasn't officially seen by white men until the early 1800s, about the time my great-grandpaw was born. And when the Lewis-Clark expedition first ran across him on the Missouri-Yellowstone rivers in Montana they were terrified. For years the grizzly was the ferocious tyrant of the woods, a symbol of terror and romantic adventure." He reached up, took two tattered volumes from his rough board shelves, and handed one to me. "No wonder George Ord, who first named the grizzly, called him *Ursus horribilis* – horrible bear!"

I read the passage Pappy's finger indicated. Ord, in the second of Guthrie's geographies in 1815, had written, "This animal is the monarch of the country which he inhabits. The African lion or the tiger of Bengal is not more terrible or fierce. He is the enemy of man and literally thirsts for human blood … He resists with amazing strength and attacks without hesitation and tears to pieces the largest buffalo … He does not climb trees which enabled hunters when attacked to make their escape …"

Pappy handed me the second book. "For nearly fifty years these early notes by Lewis and Clark were the only real information man had about the grizzly," he said. "Here's another bit."

122

The Lewis-Clark notes described their meeting in 1804 with a grizzly:

"As we fired it did not attempt to attack but fled with a most tremendous roar and such was his extraordinary tenacity of life that although five balls had passed through his lungs, and he had five other wounds, he swam more than half across the river to a sand bar and survived twenty minutes. He weighed between five and six hundred pounds at least, measured at least 6 feet 7½ inches from the nose to the extremity of the hind feet, 5 feet 10½ inches around the breast, 3 feet 11 inches around the neck and 1 foot 11 inches around the middle of the foreleg, and its talons, five on each foot, were 4 inches in length ..."

He finished brewing the coffee as the fading fall light shrouded the cabin in gloom, tipped a big slug of rye into the cups, and handed me one. "You know, there've been more lies told about the poor old grizzly than any animal we have. You can understand it, specially around this area where we got the biggest grizzlies in the world. Most of the big Boone and Crocketts come from between here and Alaska. Mind you, I'm sure the grizzly those days was a fiercer animal. But after years of bein' shot, civilization destroyin' its lands, fear of man has been bred right into its instincts. In my years here I've only once been chased by a grizzly - had to shoot it unfortunately. An' sometimes they stamp about and snarl, mostly warnin' you not to do anything stupid."

I told him of the big grizzly I'd seen farther down the inlet in the spring.

"Sounds like Fat Albert," he said and chuckled. "I reckon grizzlies range up to eighty miles, especially when looking for mates. I know him well. He wouldn't have hurt you. He's a comical, amiable old fellow. Too fat to get nasty. I found him rootin' round the cabin one morning, lookin' for garbage I hadn't burnt. Had to cut that out – a friendly grizzly can tear down your cabin trying to find food. I opened the door, yelled real loud, and he ran off into the forest up back of here."

I asked Pappy why he lived here all alone.

"Simple enough. Ever since I was a kid and read all those old adventure tales about the explorers and trappers I wanted to live in remote bits of the Cariboo and Chilcotin country. But I married, had some kids. We worked the log camps all round here. Finally Louise, my wife, got tired movin' around, so we went down to what's now West Vancouver – real primitive in those days. We made ourselves a wooden house and I started a tree business of my own. Well, the kids grew up and left. Then Louise died. One day I thought, 'What the hell am I hangin' round here for, gettin' mopy an' all.' I'd never forgotten this place – this is where Ed and I ended up after our little walk through the mountains from Bella Coola.

"He told me about that trek."

Pappy laughed. "That guy! Ed's a wanderer. At first he was going to live here, too. You know, two beat-up old guys gettin' back to boyhood, the hell with the world! But he gets itchy feet, never likes spending two summers in the same place. After we put up this cabin a few years back he took off – takin' my good gun for protection. Haven't seen him from that day to this."

I told him Ed had asked me to apologize for his not returning the gun.

"Hell, I wasn't bothered. I got a smaller one. Anyway, apart from a deer or two I don't kill anymore. I only shot … Ah, a man grows up! I figured after all the work Ed did on this cabin, he was entitled to the gun if he wanted it. Just take a look around. I doubt there's a man alive who can work logs like Ed.

I walked around the two-room cabin, unable to feel the faintest draft between the cedar logs in spite of the cool fall winds. The whole place reflected Pappy's existence – a life honed down to essentials. The big pot-bellied stove sat on a flat rock in the room's centre, throwing out its heat all around. An iron plate on top was his cooker. Inside the stove, a small iron box with a door gave him a tiny oven – far better than my biscuit-tin effort. Above it wire racks held layers of berries drying on paper and deer sinews hung from the roof, ready for splitting with a razor into threads. Now Pappy was walking around the room, lighting what seemed to be candles in small iron cups to augment his oil lamp. But they were black and ragged-looking.

"They're eulachons, what we call 'candlefish'," Pappy explained. "They come up the inlet in millions, same as herring, and you catch 'em in a fine net, even scoop 'em out with a pan!"

"And you light them?" I asked, incredulous.

"Sure, they're full of oil, you know. I boil 'em three or four times, skim off most of the oil by pouring in cold water, then put the oil in a jar or cedar dish. It's better than cod liver oil and tastier. You just dip your food in it now and again. You can either eat the fish that's left or use 'em for garden fertilizer. For candles, just shove a wick or pipe cleaner up through them. But I don't burn 'em too often – the oil's too good to waste that way."

Every corner of the room had its own function. One had a rough wood table for eating and reading, with bookshelves above. Another was his "kitchen", with dishes, cutlery, mugs, food boxes, and a washbowl fed by a gravity pipe from the creek. (Like Ed, Tihoni had a brine tank for keeping trout and salmon fresh.) A third corner housed a bed and a clothes cupboard made of hand-hewn boards. Above the bed dozens of musty old volumes, mostly classic literature, lay in friendly attitudes against each other on three rough shelves. In the other room, a wooden bunk with a headboard made from gnarled, twisted branches huddled against the wall away from a tangle of axes, sledges, toolboxes, brooms, shovels, hoes, and other outdoor bric-a-brac that threatened to engulf it. Some of the gardening implements were made from the antlers of mountain caribou and blacktail deer.

As I browsed around, admiring and learning, Pappy's voice came through the door. "I often told Ed he was crazy. He spends his life building beautiful things for other folks, movin' on and never taking a cent for his work. Know what he says? 'When I build for pleasure I remain my own man.' You were lucky meetin' him."

"I know it," I said. "He helped me build my place too."

"He's a real strange guy. Never got married, you know. He had a girl once. Met her at Ocean Falls when I was courtin' Louise. Beautiful lass, younger'n him. She loved him all right but ... you know how it is with really good-lookin' women – she wanted more, the big city life. Her beauty took her away, went off to some place called Hollywood and got into the movies. Never did hear how she made out. Haven't seen a movie in twenty years. Poor Ed was real shook up. Never looked at another woman. Hell, he must've told you about all that. How about you? You been married?"

At this revelation of a love affair Ed had never once mentioned, at this odd reminder in this wild, remote place of my own former life and of how much the same thing had happened to me, I found myself telling Tihoni more about my life than I would otherwise have done.

We talked on into the evening and at a suitable point I asked him why he hadn't wanted me to bring Booto along.

"Sorry about that," he said, "Mebbe he's a good animal from what you say, but it's like with bears – you never know what a dog will do under stress. I knew a man who reckoned he had a real courageous dog, would face anything. One day they're in the hills and see a grizzly ahead on the trail. The bear turns off, quite amiable, but the dog barks and chases, after it. You can guess – back comes the dog, tail between its legs, with the grizzly now real angry. The guy got mauled as he was gettin' up a tree, lucky not to lose his life.

"You really got to be sure of a dog to take it in this country with so many grizzlies. The only guy I know got killed by a grizzly was through his dog barking at it. It's a risk I'd rather not take."

After handing me a second mug of coffee, Pappy went outside and returned with an armful of leafy spruce sprays and a small tin bath that he set on the stove and half-filled with pails of water.

"Give me your spare jacket, sweater, trousers, and empty pack," he said.

"Okay, but why?"

Pappy stuffed the spruce twigs into the water and followed suit with his own pack and similar spare clothing. "You know how keen bears' noses are? Well, I boil everything I use for actually tracking them in spruce first. Helps destroy the man scent. We'll dip our boots in for a minute or so too."

As I pushed my gear in with his and helped stoke the fire, Pappy went into the smaller room and lit another stove made from an oil barrel, but smaller than mine, whose chimney went out through the wall.

"This is for my smokehouse," he explained. "I keep the heat in the cabin, but the smoke goes into a big wooden box outside where I put the fish and meat."

"That's a hell of a good idea," I said.

"Sure. Tonight it'll not only keep you warm and smoke your meat right but will dry your clothes out by morning! If you wake up, an' you're bound to in a strange place, just keep it stoked and get back to bed!"

It was after midnight when we prepared to turn in and Pappy said he was as keen to start up country as I was. "I haven't been up in the real grizzly and cougar country for a while myself," he said. "It'll be good to have company. So if it's okay with you we'll leave early. The caribou should be headin' through the high plateaux to the valley before too long, so with any luck we'll catch 'em too, maybe see a wolf or two."

He held out what looked like two scraps of birchbark with marks on them, "Ever seen anything like these?"

I took them from him. On one scrap of bark had been drawn or burned with charcoal the image of a bear on its back, eyes closed, with a long tail growing over and down to its mouth. On the other was a moose, with a line drawn from its mouth to its heart, in which were also embedded two arrows. I'd never seen anything like them and was mystified.

"They're Indian pictographs," Pappy said. "Represent the art of the Meda. Before they went hunting, the warriors drew these and made their magic incantations upon them. 'I shoot your heart, wary moose. I hit your heart.' You see, they believed this could put the animals under enchantment."

"Do you believe it too?"

"My friend," replied Pappy gravely, "have you ever bitten the Communion wafer, sipped the wine, prayed before the icon of the Man on the Cross? Were you God the Creator, the Great Spirit who created all living things, would you see any great difference?"

I felt justly rebuked, and then asked how far we'd have to go before we were likely to meet grizzlies.

"There's a good bear fishin' ground about sixteen miles up river. We'll head there first. When they're runnin' good you can almost walk across on the backs of those darn sockeye!"

"Will we take the rubber boat and tent?"

"Hell, no. If we took any boat we'd take my canoe, much easier to work in the rapids, paddling, poling, or haulin'. But there's nearly ten miles of box canyon a few miles up. And we certainly won't need your tent."

"But I thought it would keep off rain, lessen our scent –"

"Listen," said Pappy. "I spruce-boil what we'll wear when we're actually tracking bear. At night you can wear the trekkin' set an' smell as much as you like. Your scent and your fire are the best things goin' for you. If a grizzly stumbled over your tent 'cos it hadn't scented you, and you moved, you'd be a goner, a fine little punchbag!"

I wasn't sure he was right here, so I mentioned the fishing-line alarm system I'd used on my spring trek and said I'd heard grizzlies were sometimes attracted to a campfire.

Pappy laughed good-naturedly. "Yeah, I've heard those ideas often enough. Some guys use cowbells – what guy in his right mind is going to overload his pack with half a dozen cowbells! And as for fires – that's garbage; dump bears you're talkin' about – grizzlies that associate fires with dumps and permanent camp sites where there's always human food to get at. The bears out here wouldn't go near a man's fire or human scent."

He paused, reflecting. "Nope, we won't take a boat, either. Too much hassle packin' the damn thing. We ain't aimin' to bring back game or trophies. It's real tough country up there." He slapped his huge thigh suddenly. "We'll just use the transport God gave us. Think yours will hold out?"

"Well, I am twenty years younger," I said jokingly, instantly regretting what might appear impertinence.

Pappy Tihoni paused at the door, his eyes twinkling in their large deep sockets. "That may not turn out to your advantage," he said.

13 Among the Grizzlies

*N*ot until the afternoon of the second day did we find our first grizzly tracks. We had been skirting the ravine, giving the river a wide berth and staying on its shadowy south side; the sun's light upon the far bank would partly blind any animal that might be watching. We were also trying to stop our scent from reaching any bears that could be lying up in the bankside trees before we returned to the river for a salmon supper, as well as avoiding the dense tangles of the devil's-club in the few flat areas of shale and marsh.

As Pappy had predicted, it had been really tough going. Packing our heavy loads along the steep canyon sides had been hell, a hard test for a man's feet and knees, for there had been no relief for over ten miles from the precipitous inclines. And the small spruces were massed so thickly that at times we literally had to force our way between them. Now, on shallower slopes as we headed toward the start of a long valley filled with willow, swamp birch, alder, and cottonwoods, heavy draperies of curving green moss covered the large rocks and decaying windfalls, obscuring the crevices that could break a man's ankle or back should he slip.

Pappy went ahead, moving for all his bulk and age like some silent, and stealthy gorilla, and I soon realized his slow pace was the right one. The rifle strapped across the top of his pack looked like a matchstick on his broad shoulders. He spoke little and only then in whispers, occasionally showing slight irritability if I didn't at once catch onto his meanings.

We found the first tracks, some nine and one-half inches long, in a small marshy area. They were the marks of a big grizzly. Pappy refuted the idea they might be Fat Albert's. "He has a claw missing from his rear left foot," he said. "This devil's bigger, maybe around a thousand pounds."

"It sure has big feet."

"Not just size," said Pappy. "Look how deep."

He bent down for closer examination. "I don't know if I can track this bear," he said, "but it's not too old. He's a good five miles, mebbe a day up on us. Want to try?" I nodded and we set off. The trail led down and across the river at a narrow part. We chose the darkest shallow point. With the machete Pappy cut two stout poles, handed me one, then, using his as a brace, began to wade across the rapid current. Without the poles we would both have been swept off our feet.

On the far side we removed our boots, squeezed our trousers and socks as dry as we could, then Pappy scooped water over where we'd sat down. "Always cover your rest places with water when you can," he explained. "Bears often turn back. They can smell you hours after you've passed." For this reason too, he occasionally broke off twigs we'd touched and threw them into the water.

For about half a mile we stumbled through the trees on the grizzly's trail, working our way up the lower mountain slopes. Pappy told me not to step on the few tracks in case we wanted to double-check them. He found traces where I would have seen nothing – an upturned pebble, a snapped twig, berry bushes that had been raked down and whose sappy twigs showed they'd recently been denuded of remaining fruit, scrapings under logs and small holes where the bear had looked for grubs or mice. When the trail seemed to peter out completely on the higher, rockier land, Pappy suddenly sat down.

"Now, what do we know for sure?" I'd heard Ed say that.

"Maybe it's turned off?"

"Could be," said Pappy thoughtfully. "Well ...I reckon it's a male. Broad tracks, toes spaced out. Middle-aged too, the claw marks aren't as sharp as a young bear's." Like some detective of the wilds, Pappy now put together the evidence, drawing inferences that never would have occurred to me. The grizzly had slowed down after crossing the river, deciding to look for food as he went, because his stride had lessened. He had moved yesterday afternoon or early this morning, by day anyhow, for if he'd walked at night he probably would have brushed against bushes, leaving hair on twigs, and we'd seen none. He had some definite place in mind because, although feeding sporadically, he was travelling fairly straight, not meandering about aimlessly. But he wasn't in any hurry. Nor had he been suddenly frightened or he'd have left droppings.

"Let's backtrack him and double check," said Pappy. Not knowing exactly how far he was ahead, Pappy insisted we tread lightly. "Grizzlies often press their noses into the ground to feel if there's anything heavy approaching 'em, just like elk do," he said. We were lucky it was a dry day, with humidity low, for scent carries farther on moist, warm days.

It was when Pappy paused, trying to work out wind currents, that I tried to make my own contribution. Picking up a dry leaf, I wrapped it around a stone and threw it up into the air, a trick I'd learned when stalking deer in Britain and had used on my own spring trek. As the leaf drifted down, it seemed to indicate the breeze was now more northeasterly, coming down from the mountains.

To my chagrin, Pappy was merely amused. "That might work back in jolly old England or bonnie wee Scotland." He grinned. "But out in these mountains it tells us nothing. Too many eddies and crossdrafts in these crannies and valleys. Better to look ahead, see how the lowest clouds are movin', the way the vegetation's blowin', the flight of birds, even the way the hair on the bear's back is blowin' if you're close enough."

After two more difficult miles of losing the tracks, re-checking, and finding them again, Pappy stopped, "Hell, he's closer than I thought and gettin' suspicious," he whispered. The trail, lower now, suddenly took off at a right-angled, northwesterly tangent. Pappy turned off at a sharper angle downwind, keeping leeward of the track. Then warning me to keep an eye on any bushes or thickets at the edge of open spaces where the bear might just be lying, he made a tight semi-circle until we came back on the bear's track. He paused and said, "Just as I thought. The old bear is checking his back trail." He chuckled. "We got a real smart son of a bitch here." He bent down, picked up some white-tipped hairs from the rocks. "See? He made this detour to the left, then sat down sniffin' the air and lookin' back and all around to make sure he wasn't being followed. Grizzlies often do this. But when they lie down to rest they usually look downwind, like deer, so while they can see trouble in front, the wind brings any dangerous scent from behind to their noses. Real cunning devils!"

He looked down toward the east. "Yep, I reckon he went down that way to rejoin his original track lower down and carry on. Okay, we'll just have to try to outmanoeuvre him." We headed northeast for a while, east, then southeast, making a long circular detour back down toward the river, hoping to pick up the grizzly's trail there. But we couldn't find it.

At first Pappy was annoyed, feeling we'd overestimated the bear's speed and that it was now behind us, "We've lost him if that's so," he said. "He'll have our scent now for sure." He sat down for a while to think and I was grateful for the rest. At that moment, though, two whisky-jacks found us and began fluttering through the branches above our heads and squawking harshly. Immediately Pappy picked up stones and hurled them at the fluffy grey jays to drive them off. "Hate to do it, but we've got no chance if they stay with us," he said. "Some damn hunters must've fed 'em sometime so they reckon we may be good for a meal! Ravens follow hunters sometimes too, for pickin's. A grizzly can read all these signs of danger, even a squirrel chirpin' at you from a tree."

Pappy thought hard a moment. "There's just a hope the old devil's going up the other side of the river," he said finally. "Let's check." Once more we plunged across the river and there, sure enough, in the swampy parts on the far side we picked up the grizzly's sign again. Pappy looked at the leaves of trees, first at their tops then the lower branches, then at the way bush tops were moving closer to the ground. The ground wind was now coming more from the east.

"Let's try some straight trailing," he said. For two more miles we moved directly along the river bank, but then the big bear's tracks turned to the right, heading south of the river into the treed, shallow slopes. Pappy thought this was a bad sign. After a quarter-mile more, it seemed clear the tracks were doubling up and back in a half-circle.

Suddenly Pappy cursed under his breath and sat down heavily on a large rock. "My friend, we have just been outwitted by a very smart old grizzly." I said I didn't understand, and he pointed downhill to where some moss-covered shale and windfalls lay against two granite boulders, forming a natural sheltered observation point. "Take a look down there." As I moved he added, "And if there's any new shit there, feel if it's warm."

I half-slid down to the rocky arbour and there were the signs Pappy had expected – white-tipped hairs, huge claw marks on the bark of a dead fir, droppings that looked as if they'd been deposited by an elephant. Overcoming my initial repugnance, I plunged two fingers in – they were still warm. A huge print beside the rocks was slowly filling with watery ooze. From above the rocks I could see the river along which we'd just walked.

"Dammit," said Pappy, when I wearily climbed back to where he was sitting and told him my findings. "That old devil not only knew we were followin' but sneaked back to watch us go by!"

As we sat there, defeated, we heard a faint splashing sound from below. "There he goes!" hissed Pappy, pointing down. Below us a huge grizzly had leaped into the river, heaving its vast body across the current in a series of surging powerful bounds. In a moment, as it reached the opposite bank and shook the water from its coat in a cascading rainbow spray, Pappy had the big rifle to his shoulder. But as the grizzly cast us a brief look, almost of reproach it seemed, before vanishing into the trees, Pappy let down the gun with a chuckle.

"Just practisin', keepin' it fluid!" He indicated the catch still back. Then he removed his pack, stretched, and as he lay back in the last of the evening sun, he sighed and said, "Well, at least we *saw* him. That's all we wanted, right? Some guys – big, intrepid, fair-weather hunters smellin' of smoke, soap and fear – come up here and spend a couple of weeks staggerin' around and never even *see* a bear. The pricks!"

After a long silence, he propped himself up on one elbow. "You know, I only shot two grizzlies in my whole life. The first was just after I got here. Fool I was – just wanted to bag myself a grizzly. One day I was sittin' up by a big cedar tree after a long walk when I heard the scuff-scuffing sound some big grizzlies make when they're walkin' over needles. I looked up and there was this big bear walkin' along, quite casual, about twenty yards away. How it hadn't scented me I don't know. I quietly upped the rifle, aimed at the heart – you always hit a bear in the heart or brain but the brain shot's hard if it's comin' head on 'cos of the big bone above its nose and the thick bits above its eyes – anyway, I fired. The bear did a sort of somersault, landing facing me, and charged.

"I leaped up, tryin' to dodge behind the tree, fired again in a hurry but only hit its left shoulder. It fell again, tearin' up great clods of earth in a circle, and growling horribly. How it did it I'll never know, but it got on its feet again and started comin' on three legs, but not directly at me. I fired again, hit its right shoulder, and down it went ..."

"Hell!" Pappy pounded a huge fist into his palm. "It was terrible. It just lay there quiverin', jerkin', and moaning something awful. I put another bullet through its head and that did it. But I was scared to go near. I walked around that clearing for about half an hour. Then I finally went up to it, and do you know what I found?"

"What?"

"It was blind. Blind! An old sow, must've been around thirty years old, and one eye had gone completely. The socket was all healed up. And the other had a blue film all over it. Her hide was all scarred where she'd either blundered against sharp rocks or other bears'd attacked her. Yet the strange thing was she was in good condition, plenty of fat. She must have been smellin' out roots and berries, or carrion, bits of fish other bears had left. She hadn't even seen me." Pappy looked into the distance, his face oddly tortured.

"I killed another, a young male two years back. I'd no damn choice. A freak thing, a chance in ten thousand. I came through this thick tangle of trees and there was this great cliff, like a corner." He indicated with his hands as he spoke, showing how the steep rock faces had run into each other at an angle. "Well, there, right in the corner, was this young grizzly. What could I do? I couldn't run – he'd have charged me for sure. There wasn't a tree branch below twenty feet. I couldn't keep goin' toward him – there was nowhere for him to go. You don't know but a grizzly has great dignity. If he can get away without losing his self-respect he'll usually go, but if he can't, you're in real trouble. Well, I thought fast, I had to let him off the hook. So pretendin' not to see him, I turned off to the side and kept walkin', still keepin' my eye on him, thinking he'd slip away through the trees on my left, But hell, this was a real stupid young buck about two years old. He didn't go. As I walked, tryin' to look like I was mindin' my own business, he started whining and snarlin' and stampin' about. So then I kept still and tried to talk him out of it – you can do that sometimes. I looked him straight in the eye and tried to reason with him, tellin' him in a firm, calm voice to go away. But not this one. He charged. Once a grizzly does decide to go for you, nothing will stop him. I had no choice. I shot him twice."

"You know, a man can walk through all the wild forests of this continent and see a lot of animals, yet none will go out of its way to attack unless provoked in some way. I believe that. Well, a rabid wolf might or a starvin' cougar in winter might go for a child, but it's very rare. And with grizzlies … oh, there's all kinds of yarns – the Barren Ground or Rocky Mountain types are fiercer than our forest bears. But I'm sure there's a definite reason why some bears attack – like it's defendin' a cache of food you don't know about, protectin' cubs you've not seen."

He sat up straight, ticking points off on his fingers. "The only times grizzlies will attack, I mean to kill, not just bluff charges like blacks, are when they feel threatened, or cornered, are suddenly surprised by a guy they've not smelled or seen coming, or've been maddened by wounds. And I tell you this – if you ever get caught in the open and have to shoot, dive a few yards aside into the bushes, for sure as hell if it's not a fatal hit the bear will remember where the sound came from, maybe see the smoke, and charge there. Then, of course, there's the main reason – a mother with cubs. Ninety-nine times out of a hundred these are the only reasons. Their anger is defensive or protective, seldom offensive."

He grinned then. "Mind, you can never tell what any individual bear will do. Came across a mother grizzly once who was so scared she just took off and left her bawling cubs behind. They're as different as people – some brave, some cowards, some stupid, While others are so damn wise and shrewd a man couldn't get near 'em no matter what he did. A grizzly can smell you ten yards away no matter *which* way the wind's goin'. And apart from that they're very curious.

"Often folks think they're about to be attacked when the bear, not sure what they are, comes closer. They love to check up on anything new on their patch. An' they love playin' around, 'specially when young, like black bears. Oh, I tell you, you can keep your darn tigers, lions, and elephants. I came here wantin' to shoot grizzlies, sure, but not anymore. Today I'd rather shoot the goddam hunters."

We ate some of Pappy's oatcakes with my cold fried eggs and cheese between and then lay in silence for half an hour, letting the blood restore some energy into our tired limbs. I removed my boots and found to my annoyance a small blister forming on the edge of one of my big toes. Pappy reached into his pack, pulled out a small soft pliable piece of buckskin. "Don't burst it. Put that in your boot," he said. "It's a sure cure, been dressed down with the buck's brains. You'll find the blister's gone by tomorrow." (It was.)

"You know the best sock of all? A fresh rabbit skin! I used 'em on my trek through the Rockies. Skin the rabbit, mould the wet skin, fur side out, round the foot, and shove it back in your boot. They last a week but are better than any woollen sock." As the sun faded behind a cleft in the mountains and the air grew colder, Pappy said the bear fishing ground was still some four miles farther upstream.

"We'll make camp soon so we'll be there before dawn," he said, slinging on his pack and heading back down to the river. My legs and shoulders were stiff but if his were he gave little sign. Tracking animals under the old laws, he said, brought a man nearer to the animal state himself. Normal fatigue and pain could be worked through until they capitulated to the will, were healed *en passant* by inner belief and the natural rhythms of the trek. I was astonished at his resource and energy, as if he drew a mystic strength from the very earth. Before long Pappy would qualify for an old-age pension, yet although at times he breathed heavily, the aquiline nostrils dilating just like an old bear's, this harsh pure terrain had bred a power and endurance into his huge thighs that more than made up for his lack of youth. I never met a man who resembled more the animals he both loved and respected.

"You know something?" he said as he stopped after a while and indicated more tracks. "Our old grizzly pal is heading for the fishing grounds too. What's more, it looks like he's going to have company." He pointed south over some swamp grass ahead, sweeping his arm back to the river. "See, other bears came along here before. His tracks join theirs right here."

I could only see what looked like the occasional blurred print of one smaller bear.

"That means nothing," said Pappy. "There could have been two or three bears using this trail this afternoon. Maybe a couple of two-year-olds. They often walk in each other's tracks."

"Why do they do that?"

"I'm not sure," he admitted. "Maybe to confuse interlopers like us – *if* they know we're here. Maybe it's just an instinct they have. They're the kings of this country – don't have a natural enemy."

As we walked along the river bank and came to an eddy caused by some jammed logs, Pappy sneaked up and peered over, "Hmm, we'll take a fish or two ourselves," he said, extracting a three-pronged fish spear with barbs on the inside of its two outer prongs from his pack. "Cut me a willow pole, will you, about seven foot. Oh, and soak some of that barley mixture of yours in a can." I cut and handed him the pole, and as I scooped up water downstream of the jammed logs, he bound his spear to it with some of his nylon fishing line.

"One of civilization's greatest boons – nylon line," he said with a laugh. "Holds tighter than any sinew!" He crouched on the logs and, after several deep jabs, impaled a salmon of about five pounds. In a trice he'd whacked it on the head, gutted it, and chopped it into steaks with the machete. As I poured the excess water from my can of barley and lentils and replaced the lid, Pappy wrapped the fish pieces in a plastic bag, handed them to me to put in my pack with the can, then set off upstream again.

After another half mile, he filled his lidded pan with water, then struck off at right angles to the southeast. "No sense camping near the trail," he said before I could suggest it. "There wouldn't be a bear anywhere near the fishin' ground by morning." We forced our way through the dense bush and thick spruce forest for almost another mile before we cut leafy cedar boughs for our lean-to camp. Within an hour we had made our camp fire, feasted royally on pemmican hors d'oeuvres and the salmon steaks simmered in rice and my broth mixture, and were in our bags.

In the morning we had found a good position from which to observe the fishing ground. We lay hidden under the bright green leaves of kinnikinnick brush among small alder and by a thicket of willow, on the leeward side and some ninety yards from the ground. Our faces were covered with the small camouflage nets – one of the few items I'd brought of which Pappy totally approved. The lowering clouds, which had increased the dark eeriness of the pre-dawn light on our awakening, still held off with their rain. Pappy whispered that this was lucky – heavy rain could cause sudden spates that increased the height of the water, gave the crowded salmon more room, and so made it harder for the grizzlies to fish.

From the shallow riffles in the river below us came a constant chattering, splashing noise as the salmon tried to batter their way through these natural ladders into the deeper pools above. The larger fish sent up a fine spray of water as they bored their way through the rocky shallows, their humpbacks often half out of the foaming flow. Occasionally a weaker male got only halfway, turned on its side showing its brown and yellow flanks, its upper jaw hook giving it a grisly leer, as it was swept back into the pool from which it came. For many fish this pool would be the end of their long valiant haul from the ocean to reach their spawning grounds in the gravelly pools above. They lay on the bottom, some of them barely moving, like tatterdemalion scarecrows, their tails and fins worn almost bare from their battles through the rocky beds below. These, the weaker, were the fish the bears caught, and in the first heavy spate, many would be washed away downstream.

Pappy spoke little, only whispering occasionally when he knew the sounds from the river were drowning his voice. He explained this fishing ground was the best place to be, both for us and any grizzlies, because farther up, the river first drove through a box-like canyon of high steep cliffs, then opened out into a valley with treacherous bogs and marshes that made access without a boat almost impossible.

Above us now an eagle and some ravens were gathering, circling in the wind, with the ravens below talking to each other in their strangely guttural voices. At times the splashings and bird cries ceased and an ominous silence prevailed, heavy with the prescience of death. It was not a place where a man would like to be alone.

Suddenly as we lay there resting, the ravens above began a loud squawking commotion and the metallic *kri-kri-kri* of the eagle sounded from higher up. Pappy cautiously raised his head. "We're in luck," he murmured. I too looked up carefully. Two young grizzlies were shuffling slowly along the opposite bank. Both were in superb condition, their fur sleek and shiny with what appeared to be a grey wash on their humped backs and flanks. They had light-coloured ruffs around the backs and sides of their heads, giving them the odd, golliwog appearance I'd noticed before. "Three-year-olds, what we used to call grey backs," muttered Pappy. "Must be from the same litter." They appeared to be in no hurry, walking along with a rolling gait, their heads held low, swinging from side to side ponderously as though they were thinking out some problem.

As we watched the first came to a huge dead fir that lay partly submerged across the creek bed, the stumps of its branches embedded among black boulders that jutted above the riffles. It sniffed the air, slowly negotiated itself over the tangled roots on the bank, and cautiously crept out, as if testing whether the log would take its weight. Although it must have come deliberately to fish, it acted as if it had only just seen the salmon. Its short ears pricked forward and its head darted from side to side as it followed the flashing movements of the fish below. Then, with stealthy movements, it flattened itself slightly and, followed by the other grizzly, moved out to the end of the trunk. Once there, it hooked the claws of its left forepaw into the log to give itself anchor, then thrust its right paw into the water, stirring among the crowded salmon like a cat trying to hook a goldfish in its bowl. After a few convulsive darts it hooked a salmon to the surface but then didn't seem to know what to do with it. This happened several times, the big fish wriggling free at the last moment.

Then the grizzly tried a different tactic. It hooked its claws under another fish and with a quick jerk flipped it out of the water. As the salmon shot up into the air, the bear flailed at it with its paw, then watched with an oddly silly expression on its face as the salmon dropped heavily onto the shallow riffles some fifteen feet upstream. Instantly ravens fell from the sky like sooty black bats, pecking at the eyes of the stunned fish.

The quieter bear on the far end of the log was having better luck. It had hooked under a fish of some six pounds and was holding it against the rough edge of the log with its claws. Twice it lowered its head to grab the salmon in its jaws but seemed unable to make it without losing its balance. Eventually it scraped the fish up the side of the log, seized it in its teeth, and with a slight growl and its ears back, backed off the log, then loped into a marshy area of the bank with the fish's tail slapping weakly at its face, dropped it, and began to eat.

There was a sudden flurry in the water below. The first grizzly had turned around on the log, had hooked under a smaller fish, and with a deft flip had sent it sailing through a shower of spray to land some twenty feet back in the brush at the river's edge. As the salmon tried to wriggle its way back to the water, the bear ran to it, held it down with both paws and began chomping it up, raking skin and scaly flesh from the bones with its teeth.

While the two bears were eating, there was a slight disturbance among a patch of willows and alders across the creek to our right, and a large bear, lighter coloured than the first two, emerged and began sauntering toward the fishing ground, with a much smaller bear scuffing by her side. The cub couldn't have weighed more than seventy pounds and its head was occasionally hidden by the long grass. When its mother paused for a moment, sniffing the wind and gazing about her, the youngster put his front paws on her shoulders and also peered ahead with an oddly wise-owlish look. The two bears who were already eating gave little sign they'd seen the newcomers but quietly picked up their fish and discreetly retreated about thirty yards away, where they continued their meal.

"This should be real interesting," whispered Pappy.

Without appearing even to glance at the two young bears, the mother continued toward us and the far bank, occasionally giving little grunts and whines as if she were talking to her cub. She reached the river's edge where the cub sat down obediently and watched intently with little round black eyes as its mother waded quietly into the shallow water just below the first riffles. There she stood stock still, up to her chest in water, looking straight down into it. For a full minute she remained like this, still as a statue, then after a sudden flurry with her paw she plunged her head below the surface and emerged with a large fish in her jaws. With three slow bounds she galloped up onto the bank, shook herself vigorously, then took the fish onto a flat grassy patch, followed by her cub. As she seemed about to tear the fish into smaller pieces to give to the cub, she suddenly stopped, alert, made an odd coughing blast, snatched the fish in her jaws and bounded toward the forest edge, closely followed by her scampering youngster. In the same instant the two other bears, who had seemed to be on their way back to the river, also turned tail and loped away. As the ravens swooped down onto the remains of the fish they'd left, a deep-throated roar and a crashing in the brush to our right made them fly up again, squawking with terror. It seemed simultaneous – as the fleeing rumps of the other bears disappeared into the forest to our left, a huge black boar grizzly burst into the marshy clearing, covered the entire forty yards with some half-dozen long bounds, huffing loudly with each leap, and just as it seemed about to pursue the others, it brought itself up short with a great tearing of earth clods, like some runaway bulldozer suddenly applying its brakes.

"Holy crow!" I heard Pappy mutter beside me as he reached instinctively for the rifle. "Look at that mean old son of a bitch move!"

I stared at this animal with the same fearful awe I'd felt for the big male I'd seen in the spring. This old boar was even bigger, must have weighed over a thousand pounds, its forelegs like thick, bristly tree trunks, its back behind the hump muscles wider than a Percheron stallion's. It was impossible to believe such an animal had entered the world smaller than a squirrel. Now it cantered ponderously around the edge of the clearing as if making sure it had driven all the other bears from its own private reserve. My heart pounded at the thought there was nothing between us and this monstrous animal but thin air. "For God's sake," I heard myself whisper, "keep the gun ready." Pappy only hissed at me to keep my head down and stay quiet.

Through the brush tangle I saw the grizzly had settled down to a slow majestic walk and was heading back to the river. For all its immense size and ponderous gait, it gave the impression its reflexes and powerful muscles were always under control, that not for a second was it off guard. Now that it was nearer, its fur seemed blackish-brown, with some fifth of its hairs tipped with silver. But the short hair around its huge square muzzle and ears was a light buff grey. With its small eyes glinting black like coals in the early morning sun, this mask of grey gave the grizzly a ferocious look.

It paused as it reached the half-submerged log, sniffing the scent of the two earlier bears. Then, apparently thinking better of fishing from the log, it moved slowly to the shallow water running down the rocky bed of the riffles and crouched there as deathly still as a heron. It almost seemed to fade into the background like some ancient slab of granite.

The sky had gone dark and suddenly the surface of the pools in the river was wrinkled and a tinkling musical noise sounded all around us. It was raining. The grizzly remained motionless except for the occasional flick of an ear. A medium-sized salmon suddenly shot from the pool and landed five feet up the riffle, gave a tentative wriggle or two, then was washed back again. The grizzly appeared to take no notice. Another half minute ticked by, then the head of a large salmon with a pronounced upper jaw hook appeared momentarily above the surface as if actually taking a look at the obstacle ahead. There was a pause as it disappeared again, then with a surge it was out of the pool, sending up a shower of spray as it tried to drive against the shallow, onrushing water of the riffle. The grizzly bunched its muscles slightly, waited till the fish was almost halfway through, then made a quick surging dash, pinned the fish down with the first stab of its great paw, snatched it up in its jaws, then casually wandered back across the riffle and up onto the far bank. Instead of eating the big salmon there, it continued on to a large cedar. There it dropped the fish in some long grasses and started on its way back. Halfway across the clearing it paused and looked gloweringly at the ravens, who had now been joined by the eagle as they hopped and picked at the remains of the fish the other bears had left. Suddenly it made a quick dash at the birds. The eagle flapped away with a piece of fish in its talons, while the ravens and two crows hurtled into the air in consternation. One of the crows swooped down again as if dive-bombing the bear, which stood up on its haunches, batting away with its claws.

Pappy chuckled quietly beside me. "Oh, you mean old bastard! He's sure showing 'em who's boss."

"Why didn't he eat the fish?" I asked in a whisper.

"He's real cunning," replied Pappy. "He knows the rain will soon swell the river. He's just catching 'em and caching 'em till later."

He was right. For the next half hour the bear concentrated on catching fish. He seemed to feel they could see him so he occasionally changed his position, sidling into the water from behind rocks and old tree stumps. He worked with as much economy of movement as his bulk made possible. After catching three more fish, each of which he carried flapping to the cedar, the grizzly settled down to his first meal. Even at that distance we saw occasional flashes of huge canine teeth that must have been over two inches long. After eating two fish, he carefully piled the other fish together and started to dig.

Anyone who doubts the grizzly is the most powerful creature alive in all the Americas should have seen that animal at work. It tore into the rocky ground with the apparent ease of a bulldozer. Using its long, shallow-curving claws like small spades, it ripped through root tangles, hurled a rock weighing two or three hundred pounds aside, buried the fish, raked the earth, roots, and leaves back over its cache, the whole operation taking a mere few minutes. Then, with a last look backward and a few sniffs at the air, it sauntered off into the forest.

For the first time I became aware that my back was soaked from the heavy drips of rain that had fallen on us from the trees above.

"Satisfied?" asked Pappy, stealthily punching me on the shoulder. I told him if I'd seen nothing else during my years in Canada, the last four hours would have made it all worthwhile.

"Well, the show's over," he said. "That old bear will be lyin' up now till evening. So will all the others. No self-respecting bear is about between nine and three in the afternoon. Let's go and dry off."

We stood up, stretching our wet cramped limbs. I kept glancing to where the grizzly had disappeared. Pappy grinned. "We're okay," he said, guessing my thoughts. "We're darn lucky the wind hasn't changed, I can tell you. I reckon if that mean old boar had gotten wind of us we may have had to down him. Now, you want to try to find some cougar?"

He made it sound as if we were tourists in a zoo. I said I did, if he didn't mind going on. He pointed up to a valley between the distant mountains. "You see that last line of cedars on the right below those high bluffs? We go up through there, down the other side, then head around again to the river valley. There's a big lake in there and it's real good cougar country. We'll start up there in the morning."

We retraced our steps to our last camp site. Blasé though it may seem, we were a little tired of salmon and on the way back Pappy shot a small coast deer that ran, then stopped and looked back, as deer often do. As we butchered it on the spot, I remarked this was something I could never do without a feeling of distaste.

Pappy laughed and said, "Yeah, we should all be vegetarians! But hell, a man couldn't live in these forests without meat once in a while. There's a protein in it comes right from the very land we tread with these animals, maybe things scientists haven't yet measured." He cut layers of fat from under the breast skin and took some from the inner back.

Back at the lean-to we piled rocks in a square and made a roaring fire, helped by the resin-solid centre spear from a broken-off fir stump. For future use we boiled the shoulders in brine, then hung them from a pole frame to smoke awhile. For our meal Pappy roasted a haunch on the red-hot windward side of the fire, basting it with the fatty portions he'd scraped off and had sizzled first in the flames. Then he cut the ribs into four sections, wove sticks through them, and stuck them in the ground, so they too would roast, but slowly. "Turn 'em round occasionally," he instructed. "We can chew 'em as we travel. I want to get through fast and that way we don't need to stop for lunch!" We sat in our spare underwear, slapping at the perpetual mosquitoes and flies, our wet clothes steaming from the ends of the pole frame.

Pappy Tihoni, in his simple way, was both ecologist and ethologist. He firmly believed in the power of wilderness life, with its necessity for self-mastery and discipline, to build character. His dislike of sentimentalists and anthropomorphists was matched by his distrust of hunters. He'd discovered that over sixteen million hunting licences were issued each year in North America and had been both astonished and annoyed, not only by the incredible amount of potential wilderness death thus legally sanctioned but also by the sheer incompetence of many "hunters" he'd met.

"There's just no excuse for killing rare animals like cougars, eagles, wolverines, fishers, or grizzlies now," Pappy commented, turning over the roasting haunch. "Sure, some grizzlies eat meat. But it's rare for them to kill healthy animals, 'specially farm stock. But if you do get one that's turned killer, you shoot it and that's the end of the problem. It's not like 'flu, it's not a – what's that word – a contagious habit. Heck, a grizzly's teeth are better for crunching grass and roots than tearing meat. I reckon one man eats more meat in a year than ten grizzlies around this coastal region."

I agreed. "But I'd find that small comfort if a bear like the one we saw today ever went for me.

Pappy paused a while before replying, as if working out exactly what he wanted to say. "Listen," he then said gravely. "If ever a grizzly does go for you, stand your ground. Don't run – ever."

"I'd try and get up a tree. That's what Ed said."

Pappy laughed. "Ed's great at building and trekking. But leave the grizzlies to me! If you're near a climbable tree, and if the grizzly's a fair distance away, by all means get up it. But remember two things – a fit grizzly in its prime can run as fast as a horse for fifty yards, can cover a hundred in six seconds. And a small or medium one can climb, at least to the lower branches. Even a big one can swipe out at you up to ten feet or so. So put not all thy faith in trees, laddie!"

"No, my first rule when I come across a grizzly some way off and it rears up, as they often do to take a good look at you, is to stand still and try to look like the scenery. If you're among straight trunks, stand straight and tall. If you're near tangled roots, stand crooked with your arms bent like they are. If you're among rocks or stumps, stand and look square. If it comes toward you, curious, stay dead still. If it keeps coming, talk to it, calmly, firmly, tell it to turn off, go away. The human voice scares nearly all bears. Then if you have to, retreat slowly, backward, still talking. Don't make any fast movement. If that doesn't work you either shoot it or drop down fast behind a log or bush, play dead, and hope for the best. Always remember if it charges, deep down it's scared and it might just go over you and keep on going."

"The most it will do is bite you all over, then leave. But if you move, resist, try and fight back, it'll smash your skull with a blow or rake your ribs clean out. Mind you, I knew one guy who saved his life – his terror made him desperate – by running full out at the bear, yellin' and wavin' his arms. But I don't recommend that too much!"

"Mostly, grizzlies are pretty tolerant and don't look for trouble. More'n I can say for human hunters, who want to blow out his brains at first sight. The old grizzly can teach man a few things, let me tell you."

I asked him why he thought the old boar had rushed out of the forest the way it had.

He grinned. "Reckon there were two reasons, One, it felt like you might if you got back to your cabin one day and found some kids breakin' into your food store and helpin' themselves. Also, big old males are often downright nasty and cantankerous. They seem to hate all cubs. If he hadn't been goin' fishing he may have gone after that one. And when its mother went to protect it, he'd have gone for her too. Often a big sow fights so ferociously for her cub she can drive a male off, but against a boar that size she'd have had little chance."

Pappy cut out a chunk of the delicious-smelling venison. After a few mouthfuls he looked at me and said, "We'd better turn in early. I reckon it'll take us a couple of days to get up these little hills and down into that cougar country. It's real nice up there, alpine flowers and all. And there's a big lake with a slough in the valley there that is plumb full of muskrats. If we don't find cougar there, I'll …"

"You'll what?"

"I'll burn down the old cabin and go back to live in the towns," he said, winking, as if it was the worst thing that could happen to a man.

14 Days with Bighorn, Muskrats, Caribou and Cougars

*I*t took us all next day to reach the lower bluffs near the belt of cedars. At times the forest was almost impenetrable, the trees seemed to gang up together to impede us, thrusting branches into each other as if clutching hands like policemen holding back a crowd, and ever since early morning a steady drizzle had made every trunk and rock surface slippery and dangerous. As we paused looking for the best way around high barriers, I saw the river far below us, winding in and out of the jagged hills like an unending silver millipede. After the first few hours of climb-walking a numbing fatigue set in, but at least our exertions kept us warm. We were still slightly below the pass when we camped the first night and built a big fire to dry out our clothes.

By noon the following day we were through the pass, but strong winds cleared the mists from above to show another, higher pass through the peaks a long way off. Pappy said we should now head east.

"Maybe we should have brought a compass," I said, as we were now out of sight of the main river and previous landmarks.

"Oh, I used one years back, but not now. You can usually tell north easy enough," said Pappy.

"Moss on the north side of trees?"

"That's only okay on vertical trunks," said Pappy. "It's not always reliable. But there's other ways – less branches grow on the north usually, unless the prevailin' winds are from the south or west. Bark's usually smoother on the north side, growth rings on old stumps are thicker too. In sheltered places frost lasts longer on the north side – the sun melts east, south, and west first. An' snow usually piles up on the northeast side of rocks 'n trees too, but again you have to watch the prevailin' winds – while they pile up drifts in a blizzard, they also melt it quicker after."

As we set off toward the new high pass, I doubted if I'd have gone much farther if alone. I'd have tackled the obstacles with mounting nervous irritation and soon have become exhausted and discouraged, But Pappy worked with the small machete and moved at a casual pace, tackling each problem as it came, regarding five miles a day as fair going. "Don't look at the peaks thinking we'll never get there," he advised. "We're in no hurry."

Often he stopped to point out new wilderness phenomena, or just to talk about odd items that had nothing to do with our trek. Once when we came to a hay meadow, a rarity at over three thousand feet, he stooped, picked handfuls of grass, rubbed it in his hands, and smeared it over his face, clothes, and hands. "It's a kind of buffalo grass," he said. "Unusual to find it around here. Many Indians in the old days believed it made 'em invisible to animals. True or not, it sure cuts down your scent, so get some of it on you."

Toward the end of the second day, as we reached the gentler slopes leading to the first alpine plateaux, we came to a huge rocky slide and to talus areas, the edges of which were covered with several kinds of bushes and thick brush. Because of the frequent avalanches in winter and early spring, some of the brush seemed to have bent down toward us vindictively, turning twigs into prongs. We took turns hacking through the worst parts with the machete.

With the wind now veering through the high snowy peaks, it was much colder. At dawn I huddled deeper into my eiderdown bag, glad I'd spent the extra dollars for the best, treasuring the last few warm moments especially when it was my turn to rise, light a fire with the dry tinder we'd plucked from the dead lower branches of conifers the night before, and brew the sweet tea – the one luxury we both liked.

On the third afternoon the brush thinned out and we came to broad, park-like areas studded with small lodgepole pines. Here there were precipitous square bluffs with rocks polished smooth by wind and rain. In crevices and in the more fertile stretches of the peaty plateaux a few alpine flowers were still blooming. Pappy identified arnica, yellow mimulus, and willowherb. There seemed to be creeks every half mile, some of them dropping down in beautiful and spectacular waterfalls framed by ferns and bright red and pink flowers. Above us the clouds draped white necklaces across the bare mountain walls, cutting off the tips of the last zones of firs. In patches between the cloud traceries we saw the permanent snow line.

As we walked along Pappy suddenly stopped, examined the ground, then looked up at the crags around us. At first I thought he'd found some cougar tracks but as I followed his pointing finger to the high bluffs, I saw some large brown-and-grey animals with white underparts, long legs, and huge curving horns looking down nervously as if ready to flee.

"Bighorn sheep," he said with surprise. "Well, I'm derned. Didn't know there were any bighorn around here. They're gettin' real scarce now. Come on, let's try some fun. Did you know sheep can fly?"

He ducked down behind a small outcrop, took off his pack and rifle, told me to do the same, and then started stalking upward toward them, keeping low along creek beds and in gullies until we'd covered over half a mile. Not once did he try and check that the sheep were still there. Finally he crawled behind a large rock on a high promontory with a big grin on his face. "Okay," he whispered. "Let's jump 'em. Now!"

We both jumped out, showing ourselves. Three of the more curious ewes with shorter pointed horns had remained near where we'd first seen them. As soon as they saw us they shot away, leaping down the almost sheer face of the rocks with incredible agility. At times their feet just touched down, as if to maintain balance only, as they hurtled forward at a breakneck speed, their hair rippling in the wind of their rapid descent. Within seconds they had covered about a quarter-mile of almost perpendicular rock face, that no man could have negotiated without climbing irons, and disappeared.

"Now," said Pappy, "you *know* that sheep can fly, and none fly better than the bighorn." We went down and he pointed to the tracks they'd left. They looked like large slots of deer but were broader, less pointed, more concave. Pappy explained the bighorn were a coveted prize of the hunter, mainly for the huge horn trophies of the rams, and where once there had been a million or more in North America, he doubted if today more than 20,000 had survived with fewer than 3,000 left in British Columbia.

This little herd was a real find because it was probably pure. In many herds domestic sheep had escaped, gone wild and interbred with the bighorn, so the pure strain had been greatly reduced. Some provincial governments were now air-lifting small herds to new places and dropping them winter feed from helicopters, and at the same time restricting domestic sheep more on the winter ranges. It was a hopeful development.

Pappy admired the bighorn because of their rugged independence. They live the true spartan life, their kingdom on barren peaks at the very roof of the world. They disdain the easier life in the lowlands, can scratch away snow with their forefeet to get at food, and if winters are really severe, can subsist on browsing scrub bushes or even balsam and fir.

Pappy chuckled. "They are the original battering rams, you know, have even been known to kill old wolves. Some of those rams grow to over five feet long and when guarding their small harems they fight worse than elk. I only saw one ram fight but that was enough. They square up like ancient jousting knights, charge at each other, and the shock vibrates through the hills. They stagger about as if drunk but keep goin' at each other till one of 'em drops. Sure wouldn't like one of 'em to go for me!"

Occasionally now we came across tracks of black bears, a fox or two, and once what Pappy thought to be a bobcat, unusually high for this time of year. But it wasn't until we were heading down the far side of the mountains that we found the first four-inch pug marks of a cougar. We had now swung around from the high passes and were above the large slough before the lake in the long valley when he stopped and indicated with triumph the round tracks in the mud by a creek.

Several creeks fed into the slough, which spread out to a large lake some four miles long. The placid surface was alive with ducks and waterfowl. Along its banks the conifers gave way to clumps of alder, golden birch, and willow trees. As we stood in the forest gazing in silent rapture, we heard the sound of flashing pinions above us. A flock of huge, rare trumpeter swans had circled the lake and were homing their long necks onto its far end. Angelic white, their wings beat against the air with a strange whistling sound as they vanished below the tops of the trees ahead. The needles beneath our feet were yielding, like a cushion, and our nostrils were caressed by the gentle scent of resin, pine, and earth. Yet for all the beauty, there was nothing here of the romantic alpine idyll. Rather, this place seemed beyond time. Here were species pursuing their urge for life along a thousand separate courses, not subservient or inferior to man but fashioned and complete in a world of their own. The lake was semi-glacial, almost as old as the Palaeozoic rock on which it lay. It had been here before man was known, and when he was gone again, as far as this place was concerned, nothing would have happened. "God's country," said Pappy under his breath.

As we reached the edges of the slough and made our way toward the banks of the lake itself, the air seemed warmer. Pappy said the place was a rare phenomenon because of its height above sea level. "As far as I can make out, this is the only natural valley between the mountains from the north for at least forty miles," he explained. "It supports many birds and animals and with any luck the caribou should be heading down any time now. " As he spoke there was a splashing sound fifty yards offshore. Some small trout were leaping frenziedly out of the water. There was a quick flurry and we caught a glimpse of a large, grey dappled fish with a cruel, beaky mouth as it broke water and disappeared again.

"Grey trout," said Pappy, instantly identifying the thick torpedo body of Canada's largest and most predatory lake trout. "They get real mean this time of year, slashin' at every fish in sight, even their own kind, tryin' to put on fat for the winter. They go up to sixty pounds, you know, and that beauty must've bin half of that. He pointed to some flat grassy land that extended far beyond the willows and white-trunked aspens on the far shore. "Speakin' of winter," he said, "that's what brings the caribou here, those hay meadows. It's rare pasture and there's not much around this region. And, thank God, there's too much muskeg and swamp for domestic cattle or sheep!"

As we neared the lake itself I noticed some V-shaped ripples in the water that were being made by the heads of swimming animals. At first I thought they were otters or beavers, but they were the muskrats Pappy had mentioned. "Otters usually swim in a sort of zigzag as they're on the lookout for fish. But muskrats an' beavers go straight for where they're heading," he said. "Beavers have broader noses too, so they make a wider V." As we walked along the marshy banks, a slight mist rising among the reeds, we found some muskrat lodges. Two or three feet high and about three feet across, they were made of chewed plants, mostly broad-leaved cattail or bullrush, and were built on old fallen logs, banks of mud, or in clumps of weed, using the stems like stilts. We soon had to look carefully where we were treading because there were holes in the bank where the muskrats had also made dens by burrowing into the earth. At times they had so undermined the bank that it wouldn't bear a human's one-footed weight.

"They seem to prefer these bank dens in summer," Pappy whispered, "but as it gets colder, like now, they move into the houses farther out. Maybe 'cos their enemies are gettin' hungrier! That swamp out there is deep and cougars, lynx, and foxes that dig after them don't like gettin' bogged down. The muskrats seem to know that."

We sat down in a thicket and stayed quiet for a few minutes. As we watched, a muskrat came swimming along, whiskers high above the ripples, and in its mouth it carried a thick piece of freshly cut root. It paddled up to a house, climbed out of the water, and vanished into one of the two entrance holes. "They often store bulbs and roots in there," Pappy said. "They can go in the top or through little underwater tunnels." He picked up some small stones but missed with the first one, which landed with a plop in the water. His second hit the house. Instantly the muskrat came out, looked around, and voiced its anger by making a little chattering sound at us with bared teeth, slapped its flat scaly tail, then disappeared with a noisy plop into the water. Pappy grinned. "They're quite fierce little devils," he said. "Sometimes when you're in a canoe, especially when they're breeding, they'll come up beside you and attack your paddle. Yet otters and even minks can kill 'em, by waitin' for 'em to come out. Otters sometimes take over their homes for their own families. Mind you, they have a job catchin' 'em. Muskrats swim real fast and their tails bein' flat up and down, not like a beaver's, are like rudders."

The muskrat community extended thirty yards along the edge of the lake, and as we were nearing its end Pappy stopped, pointing to the tracks of a small cougar. Then he started examining the alders on the bank and peering at the bog willows that grew in the marshy part. Eventually he indicated two torn shelters in the weeds of a mud bank far out. They looked as if a miniature tornado had hit them, with dents in the muddy debris a few yards from each muskrat home. Pappy pulled me closer to the trees. "See the rips in the bark – how they go right out! The damn cougar clawed its way through the trees, keepin' itself out of the bog. Could've been last night." He pointed to the dents by the lodges. "See those marks – that's where the old cat flailed out at the poor little devils as they tried to escape."

"Yes, I heard cougars hate getting their feet wet," I said.

He laughed as we struck off at a tangent to make early camp away from the lakeshore, walked through the birches into the higher, dry, more open forest of spruce and pine. "Oh, the cats don't mind water but they don't like deep mud too much. No, I reckon it went through the trees because it's quieter than splashin' through the bog, wouldn't scare the rats away. It's hard to say. Muskrats would be easier prey at night, I guess. Either way, it wouldn't dirty up its nice clean coat."

As we cut wood for our fire Pappy explained that in the winter muskrats were much safer from cougar or lynx attacks. When the lake froze over they would build a third kind of house – 'push-ups'. These were made on the actual surface of the ice, usually from the roots and stems of water plants, and became tiny frozen igloos. The muskrats would swim along until they found a pocket of air trapped below thinner ice, then using the air like a swimmer uses an oxygen tank, would gnaw through the ice and build the push-up. Or else build it just before the final freeze. The relative warmth of the vegetation, with its later insulation of snow, plus the constant comings and goings of the animals, usually stopped the water freezing again under the little house. These push-ups weren't strictly homes but temporary feeding places where the muskrats could eat in fair safety away from their lodges and to where they could flee underwater from danger.

"Cougars don't much like going out on the ice, too exposed for their sneaky natures, I reckon," said Pappy. "Of course, foxes and coyotes will at night but as the

145

only entrance is under the ice, the muskrats often have time to get away when the diggin' starts."

I said they seemed as smart as beavers.

"Smarter! " exclaimed Pappy. "You know, the old trappers believed the muskrats acted as sentries for beaver. They felt if ever a muskrat saw them and they let it go, it right away swam off and told the beavers. Seems one reason beavers tolerate 'em in the same area.

He lit his pipe, making a wry face at the emptiness of his tobacco pouch. "Next time we see any kinnikinnick we'll strip off some leaves. Mixed with baccy, it ain't too bad," he said. By now the stocks in our back packs were getting low. We had less than four pounds of combined flour, rice, barley, lentils, and dried peas between us. Luxuries like sugar, cheese, hard-fried eggs, and dried foods had now run out. While we were less than forty miles from home – a reasonable two-day journey in flat country – it would take us a hard four or five days in that rugged terrain.

Next day we breakfasted on boiled rice and a seven-pound lake trout. Pappy caught the fish by a unique method; like most lessons he'd learned from the wilderness, it was completely unorthodox but interesting. First he caught two small rainbows by using a grouse feather as a wet fly, sending it out with a tiny lead shot as weight. He then rigged the trout onto his heavy line with two small treble hooks, so that, when tugged, the fish darted and tumbled as if wounded. Three feet up the line he fastened a small lead weight and close to this he loop-knotted a piece of smooth light wood in which he had slotted a broad shaving. At first I thought he'd hurl the ensemble as far as he could into the water, in which case I reasoned the wood float would either become untied or hold the bait too high. But no. Walking to the end of a small bushy promontory, he checked the wind, then gently swung the float out to land with a faint splash in the water. With the wood shaving as a miniature sail, the wind slowly carried the bait about forty yards, then with a series of gentle tugs Pappy freed the line from its loop knot on the float and as the rainbow sank toward the lake floor he brought it back slowly with a jerking movement. Three such casts produced our breakfast. Later his length of fishing line came in handy again for snaring the high fronds of berry bushes that still contained a few fruits beyond the reach of bears.

That morning we noticed that after a couple of miles the banks of the lake petered out. Facing us was a series of huge rocky escarpments that abutted onto the shore line. At first we thought of tying a couple of logs together with liane creepers and poling around the cliffs, but we soon discarded the idea. Not only would the logs be hard to cut and get into the water, but we'd be seen and heard by every creature on the far shore. Instead, we decided to climb the escarpment some four hundred yards back from the shore. As we walked across the hilly tops of these cliffs, we came across two enormous, freshly dug holes, each about eight feet long and five feet deep. They looked as if they'd been dug by a heavy bulldozer. Huge rocks weighing up to five hundred pounds had been ripped up and torn aside, and tattered tree roots projected from the sides, waving slightly in the cold breeze.

Pappy was surprised. "That's a big grizzly's work," he said. "After a bit of tender meat." He walked around the perimeter of one of the holes peering intently at the ground. Then he pointed to a small patch of blood, which conveyed nothing to me. "Yep, I thought so," he said. "He was after marmots' nests. Looks like one of the poor little devils almost got away but the bear got him right there." He said we'd better keep our eyes skinned as a bear with such carnivorous tastes in the area could be more aggressive toward humans, but we saw no more signs of the bear that day.

By late afternoon we had reached the far end of the lake. We negotiated the rocky beds of the river and were clambering down through some tree arbours toward the grassland when I noticed some curved white objects lying in the grasses under some stunted birch. As we walked over an astonishing sight greeted us. Two skeletons lay side by side, locked in an eternal combat. The larger one, Pappy said, was of a mountain caribou, while the smaller, more streamlined one was that of a cougar. The caribou's head was twisted to one side and one of its semi-palmate antlers was embedded in the cougar's rib cage, its tip just a fraction away from the spinal column. Pappy lifted the cougar's skull. Some of the teeth were worn down almost to the sockets, two were broken, and the canines were brown and blunt. There was a deep fracture above the cougar's right eye socket.

"Must've been a hell of a battle," Pappy surmised as he let the cougar's skull fall back to the ground. "This old cat must've stalked the caribou till it got in here, then it climbed onto that rock up there and came at it from above. They sometimes do that when things are right. They hold the nose with a forepaw and bite down through the neck at the base of the skull. This one must've been real hungry to tackle a caribou this size." He bent down to examine the caribou's head. "Yep, it was an old bull too. Two old guys fightin' it out to the end. Hard to say which died first. The cat probably raked its throat out but the bull must've smashed the cat against the rock and fractured its skull. Reckon its horns must've gone clean through the lungs, maybe hit the heart too." For a few more moments we looked down at the remains of the two animals, an inevitable result of the relentless laws of evolution and survival.

The grasslands extended farther than was apparent from the other side of the lake. They opened out from its birch and willowed banks in a broad wedge, vanishing into the lower slopes of twin mountain ranges, flanking the river. For the first quarter-mile the ground was marshy and filled with countless hummocks of grass that twisted the feet, aggravating half-healed blisters. Some of them sprouted tiny gnarled bushes. Farther on, up the drier, shallow slopes, chunks of rocky bluffs broke up the grass meadows in places and dotted here and there were shrubs of mountain ash, sitka willow, and sage, with straggling birch and aspen and patches of lodgepole pines. Higher still, hilly timberland with spaced-out cottonwoods blended into the spruce and fir forests of the mountains. This was first-class cougar country, Pappy said.

As we walked back through the birch glades near the lake to make camp beyond the leeward edge of the grassland, several caribou antlers lay out in the pasture. Pappy turned off and went to inspect them. "Some have been through already," he said, picking up the remains of thick antlers. "See that? There's blood on this one."

"Why? They've just been shed?"

"Naw. These are last year's, surprisin' there's anything left. For some reason caribou chew on old antlers, along with mice and porcupines. Look at these, down to the brow patch! Some folks say they chew 'em to get calcium. I reckon it's for that and to keep their teeth strong. Gums too, by the look of it!"

We hid ourselves in the scrubby bush at the edge of the pasture, hoping some caribou might come down from the treed slopes to graze on the far side. Pappy explained that in caribou both sexes were antlered, though the females' were smaller and lacked the big forward pointing "shovels". The bulls cast theirs after the rut, around late November and December, while the cows kept theirs until late spring. Although we waited until the light faded we saw no caribou. We made camp half a mile away in the lakeside trees.

Next morning Pappy looked for signs of the wind currents in the valley. The wind had veered slightly southward, so to make sure it would be blowing toward us directly from the pasture when we settled down to keep watch, we hiked almost a mile parallel to the leeward edge, keeping well out of sight of the grassland. Around midday we cut in again, crept stealthily until we were almost within sight of it again, then crawled the last hundred yards until we reached a shallow mossy depression a short distance away from a rocky outcrop. There was still no sign of any deer or caribou, so we made ourselves comfortable and lay down to wait. It was cold lying there and we were grateful when the sun came out from behind the high clouds and warmed us briefly. But it wasn't until early evening that our patience was rewarded. "There they are," whispered Pappy, touching my arm.

Just under a mile away we saw the brown forms of grazing caribou, looking exactly like reindeer, their close relations. As far as we could estimate, it was a small herd of about twenty-five animals with two smaller groups behind, each seeming to be attended by a large bull. They were hard to see against the greens and browns of the pasture and the hills but the bulls were distinct by their greater size, heavier antlers, and thick, grey-golden manes and chest hair that contrasted with the brown-black of their thick barrel bodies. At first I thought the bulls were on guard because they were more conspicuous, but it was soon clear the adult cows with calves or yearlings were leading the foraging for grass, sedges, and mosses and browsing on the willow and birch bushes. The bulls were grazing placidly at the rear and the big cows, I noticed, seemed to raise their heads, scenting the wind, more often than the bulls.

"Well, that's just fine," said Pappy with a satisfied air. "They're hungry so they'll still be around tomorrow. They're gettin' the last of the grazing, puttin' on fat before winter snow sends 'em into the woods for the lichens. Come on, time to make camp." Then to my surprise he stood up and started walking away to the treed slopes behind. As I followed I asked if it wasn't dangerous to walk – the caribou would surely see us. Why, then, had we bothered to crawl in so laboriously earlier?

"Because they could have already been there," he explained patiently. "No, it's not dangerous. If we were on snow they could see us two miles off but against this dark background they'd need to be as close as half a mile. Of course, if the wind was wrong and the air more humid they'd have got our scent long back. We wouldn't have even seen 'em." I looked back. The caribou were still grazing, walking about with heads carried low.

As we cooked our meagre supper of rice, lentils, and trout remains and Pappy browned some bannocks in his little aluminium pan, I looked at his grizzled white head bent low over the fire and thought what an extraordinary character he was. This was a man who knew the wilds, the oceans, rivers, trees, and mountains not merely in mind, but as though they were part of his soul. Alone, I knew I would have seen little of what we had witnessed. It was more than timing, almost as if he released some mystic power that disarmed wild creatures of suspicion. It was altogether uncanny. I felt an enormous gratitude that this man should actually bother to take me out and reveal his secrets. For a moment I wanted to express it but Tihoni forestalled any such display of emotion by suddenly flinging a big bannock at me. "Catch that," he said, laughing. "It'll put some fat across your gut. As we'll be lyin' out in the cold most of tomorrow, you'll need it."

When we talked later I asked him what he thought of the theories that grizzlies and other animals had a sixth sense, and that that sense made them more scared when humans in their territories carried guns.

"I don't know," he replied honestly. "I've heard scores of ideas – that they sense a hunter's intent, his excitement, even his fear, just as we can sometimes sense there's someone watchin' us when there's apparently no one about. Or that they smell the metal, the oil on the gun, all that sort of thing. Sure, a glint of sunlight on metal would be foreign enough to scare animals in the woods – if they saw it. But bears don't see that good anyway. I know one thing. I see more bear and deer now when I walk about not meanin' 'em harm than I did when I was young and lookin' for something to shoot. But then I go slower now, with more care. I guess I learnt a few things. " He laughed then. "When you're a young man, you know, you're *doing*. When you're old, you're *talkin'*."

"I can think of a few exceptions," I said.

He laughed again, then explained he hadn't waited to shoot a young caribou buck because he wanted us to spend all next day watching the big deer. One shot would have sent them fleeing from the area for at least a couple of days and might have sent them swimming across the lake. "Caribou swim far more readily than other deer," he said. "As you saw by their tracks, they've much broader feet for their size even than moose, and in winter the outside of the cloven hoof grows longer, so they're ideal for snow walkin' or for scoopin' snow away from buried lichens. They splay out too so they can run over snow, where much smaller deer push their feet through and cut their knees against the crust. That means they're good for swimmin' as well. Heck, a caribou can swim up to six miles an hour. I've had a hard time tryin' to catch up to 'em in my canoe! Also, they have dense fur with hollow hairs and a thick coating of fat that acts like a built-in life jacket."

He reckoned the animals we'd seen were mountain caribou, distinct from the more migratory Barren Ground caribou of the northern tundras, and had probably headed west from the Tweedsmuir Park area. "I love to see 'em," he said enthusiastically, as he lit his pipe to help keep away the few biting flies. "Since the buffalo herds were pretty well killed off, those northern caribou goin' up to their summer ranges in spring are the last great animal sight left in our country. One day, if we got any sense, we'll look after our caribou the way they do the reindeer in northern Europe. The Lapps almost worship 'em, reckonin' they can't make it without the deer. Anyway, we'll let 'em graze first, then take out a weak buck if we can see one.

Next day we awoke in the pre-dawn twilight and crept back to the shallow depression where we'd spent the previous afternoon. We moved like snakes, with aching, trembling slowness, our heads covered with the camouflage nets and grass to break up the outline. The caribou were already grazing, almost directly in front of us, the nearest cows less than four hundred yards away. The mature bulls were now vaguely circling around the groups yet avoiding each other. It was almost time for the rut, Pappy reckoned in a whisper. Sometimes then bulls spar and fight for small harems of five to a dozen cows, but we were not treated to any such spectacle. During the winter, caribou seem to band together more, perhaps to deter predators, and the bulls forget their rutting squabbles and tolerate each other. The herd was larger than we'd thought, numbering some fifty animals, and it extended some three-quarters of a mile ahead and to our right. It seemed now some of the younger bulls were occupying the rear.

For an hour we watched them gradually grazing their way to the lake which Pappy said they probably would swim. Then as I was resting my head down on my hands, easing my aching neck, I felt him tug my arm. "Wolf!" he hissed. Slowly I looked up through the grasses and at first I saw nothing. Then, after straining my eyes, I saw three wolves gliding along through the birch glades on the far side of the pasture. They slunk along at a furtive trot like silver-brown ghosts in that early light, their thick wavy fur blending perfectly into the background. Their behaviour seemed quite unaggressive and the caribou cows nearest them, apart from momentarily looking up and moving a few steps away from their direction, just carried on. Two of the bulls, without showing the slightest signs of panic and seemingly by instinct, slowly stationed themselves between the cows and where the wolves had vanished into the trees. At any moment I expected to see the wolves re-emerge and make a dash at the herd, or single out one caribou, but absolutely nothing happened and we didn't see them again.

In a barely audible whisper Pappy said at this time of year a herd this size would have little fear of three coastal forest wolves, unless they showed signs of a concerted attack which, at the time of day and with the watchful mature bulls on the lakeside, was unlikely. He said wolves mostly went for females and sick, old, crippled, or very young caribou who were straggling on the herd's edges. They either ran it in circular relays, while the rest of the pack cut the corners, or tried to surprise it under close conditions for swift attack, and in snow they used the deer's own hard-packed trails.

"I believe that *shock* has as much to do with the victim's death as actual wounds," he opined. "A wolf hits for the throat of a runnin' caribou and its sudden dragging weight often bowls it right over. Wolves are a bit like weasels. Once they get onto one deer, they stay on it. She can go back right through the herd but they'll stick to just her, ignorin' all the others."

In many ways, predators like wolves and cougars have an overall usefulness to caribou and deer herds. By culling out the less-fit specimens and by keeping the herds constantly on the move in their winter ranges, the predators keep good browse and pasture from being overcrowded or overeaten.

"Do you think wolves affect their numbers much?" I asked him.

He grimaced. "For thousands of years there were a darn sight more caribou *and* wolves here before the white man came," was his reply.

During the noonday hours most of the caribou lay down, chewing the cud, and with nothing to do we dozed in the pale sun. By late afternoon they were back on their feet and three-quarters of the loosely grouped herd had passed us and were grazing on the pasture nearer the lake. Some of the cows were so close we could distinctly hear the cropping sound their flat teeth made on the herbage, and the odd clicking sound of their foot tendons as they put their weight on their hoofs – a noise that is said to alert the calf that its mother is moving. We even could hear occasional digestive rumbles.

After another hour my legs were numb from being so long in the same position, my neck and shoulders were aching from the effort of holding my head still and I was about to disturb Pappy and urge him to think of our supper when a sudden disturbance in the grass behind the rocky outcrop to our right made me reach for his arm. He raised his head slowly and we saw the flattened form of a cougar sneaking along between the rocks – its underbelly brushing the earth, its jaws slightly apart in a ghastly grin. In the late sun, its amber eyes reduced to slits, it glared balefully at a young buck grazing a few yards from the rocks and moved forward in little trembling crouches. At the end of each stealthy run it gathered itself for the next, its leg joints protruding above each corner of its tawny body like the round wheel covers of an old-fashioned racing car. When it neared the end of the natural rock and grass cover it stopped, sinews and muscles bunching for its final leaping charge.

Everything happened at once. A moment before the mountain lion charged, the nearest caribou became aware of it, jumped into the air in confusion, looked at each other for a lead, then hoisted their tails and bolted at a high trot. As the cougar streaked with bouncing, tail-high bounds, the buck shot away in a semi-circle and thus the big cat missed with its first lunge at the throat. The other caribou seemed to take little notice of the sudden movements of the few near us, but suddenly the alarm became general and the whole herd began to run in a circle as if to get to leeward and confirm by scent what their eyes had told them. The nearest bull lowered its antlers but it seemed more a symbolic or instinctive movement for it did not move to intercept the cougar. The running cougar ignored it completely, and in two more bounds almost caught up to the fleeing buck, then swiped at its hindquarters, knocking it momentarily sideways and raking great welts of blood with its claws. I heard Pappy say calmly, "There goes our goddam supper. Sorry, friend." In a trice he was up on one knee, took aim, fired, and brought down the buck. In the same split second the cougar bounded onto the fallen body, then heard the rifle's crack, leaped off again and, with flattened ears, shot behind a rocky outcrop and disappeared. The last thing we saw was the upraised tails of the caribou herd as they fled at great speed to the lake.

"What an incredible sight!" cried Pappy, whacking me hard on the back. "I doubt there've been more'n a dozen men in the whole history of the world who've seen a cougar attack. Holy crow! What luck!"

I was so excited I could hardly speak. The speed of these sudden primitive movements after the hours of quiet stillness was frightening. I felt my heart thudding under my ribs and as we walked out to the body of the young buck my legs trembled slightly. To our nostrils floated an odd, pungent, musky odour that the caribou had released from their rear glands to help spread the alarm. The buck was quite dead. The bullet from Pappy's superb shot had hit behind its right lower ribs, passed through its lungs and heart and out of the left shoulder. The animal was bigger than I'd thought, weighing around 180 pounds. Pappy pointed to the long slashes caused by the cougar's claws on its flanks and hindquarters.

"It must've been a real young lion," he said, "to tackle an animal nearly twice its size in near daylight." He pulled out his knife and smiled at my nervous looks at the rocks. "Don't worry. It won't be back, not after that shot, not before nightfall anyway." He plunged his knife into the buck's neck, slashed the carotids to let the blood and left it there. "Ah well," he added, "even if it had got away I doubt it would have lived. These wounds would weaken it, go poisonous, make it easy prey for other cougars or wolves. Besides our need is greater than theirs right now. Let's go get our packs and let it bleed awhile. When you're hungry you don't care much for hangin' meat, but I sure hate messy butchering!"

We walked back for our packs then returned, lifted the buck's rear quarters onto a rock to help the blood flow, then sat by some bushes. Pappy's knife projected from the buck's neck like some territorial marker establishing his claim. While waiting for the blood to let fully we talked more about the caribou. I was surprised how close they'd come to us.

"Are you? Heck, I was up here three years back and fell asleep watchin' 'em. When I woke they were almost bitin' at my boots. They could obviously scent me but it wasn't till I moved they ran off. Even then they stopped to look back – that's always been the deer's undoing, especially with the Indian hunters, for they often did it within arrow range. Did you notice how they started circlin' before they took off? I reckon that helps 'em smell their own alarm scent as well as see what scared 'em."

Pappy was disappointed we had not seen any moose around the lake, especially as they had recently been growing in numbers. "You haven't lived till you've seen a big bull moose on the rampage," said Pappy, grinning. "They go up to eighteen hundred pounds in Alaska, over nine feet long, and can stand eight feet high at the shoulder. Most of the year they're pretty timid but when the bulls are ready to mate in the fall, they reckon they're the gods of the forests. They charge through, flattening small alders and willows like bulldozers, as if they weren't even there. They have only one cow at a time but mate with several, and if a rival appears – look out! I saw this once. The old bull went berserk, battered his antlers against rocks, tramped on trees, and charged with a run that shook the earth. They hit so hard the smaller one was knocked into the lake, and he sure didn't come back, just swam off to find a cow of his own. If you're up a good tree and have found some antlers – elks', or caribou's will do, too – you can have some fun if there's one around. Just clatter them against the branches an' he'll soon come a-runnin'."

He grinned at the recollection. "When I was up here three years back I saw this old fellow standin' up to his shoulders in the swamp back there, wavin' his antlers about and splashing his head in the water, havin' a rare old time. I kept well out of the way. There's an old joke about moose, you know; they stand for hours in swamps not to escape flies but to hide their awful knobbly knees because they're ashamed of 'em!" He shook his head. "No, the moose is real smart. He can dodge all the summer flies while gettin' underwater roots this way, but the caribou can't. When the flies are thick, deer are often exhausted because of the movements they have to make to keep 'em off. Or they stand on windy hills without feedin' for hours. But the moose is like a hippopotamus. He eats water plants and I've seen 'em submerge completely, tryin' to get the juicy roots on the bottom. They can stay under nearly a minute. I tell you, a man can get a hell of a shock walking out of the trees by a quiet lake when suddenly a huge moose emerges from the water like some prehistoric monster."

The light was now fading fast and Pappy partly skinned, then butchered the caribou buck with the machete. "I wish those wolves had chased it around the pasture a few times," he said, "instead of the cougar's sudden attack."

"Why?"

Pappy cupped his hand over the machete. "Caribou meat is always better if it's run awhile. It's an athlete, you see. But a moose is better shot without bein' run as it's a lazier animal." We wrapped the heart, liver, shoulders, and part of the ribs in the last of our plastic bags to stop the blood seeping over our packs too much, then carried the big haunches in our hands to the lakeshore where we were going to camp for the last night. Before leaving, Pappy cut off a long length of hide. "It's the only leather I know that shrinks when wet," he explained. "It's ideal for snow shoes and bindin' canoes."

Although we were so loaded we had to stop every three hundred yards to ease our aching arms, we both felt bad about the meat and hide still left on the carcass. But dragging it to the trees and laying it as bait along what might be a puma's regular beat had little point. We weren't trappers and had no trap. We had already been treated to the rare sight of a cougar in action and if it or another came to the carcass at night we wouldn't see it anyway.

I tried to work out how this situation applied to the theory of territoriality accepted by many naturalists. I asked Pappy what he thought.

He just smiled. "Oh, I don't go along with all that territorial stuff too much," he said. "I've known two mother cougars with kits stay in a smaller area than the accepted one of fourteen square miles for a whole summer and fall. If there's plenty of deer around they hardly move at all. And males – heck, they wander for miles lookin' for girls in heat, can cover thirty miles in a single night. Cougars breed at any time of year, you know, and the big lads have mostly two things on their mind – food and sex!

"Strange critturs, cougars," he went on. "When the kits leave their mother at around two, the young males seem to have the hardest time at hunting – they and old cougars are the ones that'll take sheep and calves most of the time. I reckon the one we saw was a young male and he could be miles off by now." We decided to leave the carcass and see next morning if the cougar was still around, if it had at least ended up with a consolation prize.

Ravenous though we were, Pappy insisted that tonight we'd have the best meal of the whole trek. First he took his extra bag of salt, sliced a haunch into three heavy strips, and put them to soak in a brine solution so thick an egg would probably have bounced right out of it. "Takes out some of the gamy tang." he explained. Following his instructions, I built our biggest fire so far between three upended rocks, while he fetched a thin slab of rock and some mud from the lakeside. Then with smaller stones and the mud he made an 'oven' on the slab and set the whole heavy object across the rocks around the fire. This took almost an hour. As we appeased our hunger slightly with bannocks, he took the meat from the brine, set slices of liver between the strips, sprinkling it all with herbs, then with slices of two onions he'd kept in his pack and a liberal dressing of oil and fat, he wrapped the whole delicious package in tinfoil and set it in his oven.

As it cooked, the smudge from the fire thankfully helping to keep away the mosquitoes and black flies that still seemed to be hatching, we made a birch-pole frame and hung most of the remaining salt-dipped meat from it to smoke a bit, as well as the piece of hide that Pappy had scraped.

I learned more about the mountain lion as we waited. Pappy was sure mother cougars actually train their young to hunt and kill, though he'd never seen it himself. At first she leaves the cubs behind to go and make a kill, but at six weeks when the cubs weigh only about nine pounds, they can follow their mother on short forays. At four months they're running with their mother while she's hunting, and after she's produced the kill they all eat at leisure, laying up around the carcass until it's all gone. Often cubs run with their mother until two years old – when a male cub can be almost as big as she is. Pappy thought this habit made some naturalists believe that male and female cougars run and hunt together with her previous year's cubs.

"It might happen with a young male," he said. "But I reckon it's rare. When a new male arrives on the scene in her breeding period, he drives the kits away from his girl friend. And she knows it's right. The kits should now be able to take care of themselves, so she lets them go. Often this is the toughest part of a cougar's life. Suddenly it's alone and if it hasn't learned to hunt right, it can die. It'll keep goin' on marmots, grouse, snowshoe hares, mice, and frogs for a while, but it needs deer meat when it's bigger. That young one we saw today can't have been more'n two years old. It stalked the buck okay, but when it came to killin' – well, it made mistakes. Too many mistakes like that in winter, when there ain't too many small animals about, and it would die."

Young cougar skeletons have been found at the bottom of cliffs and it is believed they could have been driven off the edge by pairs of golden eagles. As we'd seen from the skeletons we'd found three days earlier, even big cougars – especially when old, with their teeth worn down or afflicted with arthritis – could be killed by their larger prey. A big cougar in its prime – heaviest recorded was a 276-pound male in Arizona – can kill a 600-pound moose or elk, but such killings are rare. The average weight of an adult cougar is around 125 pounds and, like wolves, it often has to content itself with killing young, wounded, crippled, sick, or very old moose and caribou, though it can kill almost any deer if stalking conditions are good. Cougars, like birds of prey, can adapt to a feast-or-starve pattern better than any other North American predator, are happy on six or seven pounds of meat a day but can eat up to thirty pounds at one feed when they are really hungry and food is scarce. A cougar kills some 2,700 pounds of large prey animals a year, but while females with cubs eat almost all their prey, transient males will leave up to thirty per cent – the skull, bones, feet, spine, and part of the hide. But this, again, provides food for other scavengers.

The odd thing about cougars and several other predatory animals is that they appear to regulate their own numbers. No matter how many deer there are in an area, the lion population doesn't seem to increase greatly. Male lions have sometimes been known to eat a couple of kits yet leave a third or fourth to live. During the winter, male and female cougars tend to keep to specific areas, especially where deer are abundant, but while females will often share the ground, grown males are more territorial. After breeding, when their spouses seem to lose all interest in them, they keep to themselves, as the grizzly does. The male then roams and hunts alone, marking ground by claw marks on trees and by making scratch piles of earth and urinating and defecating on them. Often these piles are used to inform females of their presence. Males have a healthy respect for each other, and while fights do occur, they are not common and seldom to the death. Pappy's respect for cougars almost matched his reverence for grizzlies.

He mixed the last of his carefully hoarded pipe tobacco with some kinnikinnick dried out in his pocket and on the stones of our fire, and we sat back, fat cats ourselves after that dinner. Letting the fire smoke drift over us to keep off the ubiquitous flies, we mused on into the night.

Next morning we returned to the caribou carcass to see what had happened. It lay where we had left it, and it had been partly chewed. But whether by foxes, coyotes, wolves, or the cougar, we had no way of knowing. The thick lichens and grasses made too dense a carpet to reveal any tracks. Cougars are not usually attracted to carrion apart from their own kills, and Pappy thought if the cougar had been back we'd have found deer-hair cuttings. "They often trim the hide a bit before eating," he said. "They cut the hair off neat as if with a barber's clippers."

Now it was time to return home. After Pappy had checked his bearings from various mountain landmarks, we set off on the long trek back. Laden as we were with the meat, going down the far side of the mountains from the lake was even more difficult than coming up. The strain on the knees was tremendous and I followed Pappy's advice that if I felt my footing go, I should land on my pack. "The meat can take it better than you can," he said. "We'll cut the rocks out of it later!"

We now both looked like wild men – our beards were over an inch long, we had lost a good deal of weight, our clothing was tattered and frayed. But as we traversed those mountains and rocks and clambered over the windfalls, tramping one of the loneliest places left on earth, I felt an extraordinary vigour, a bodily health I hadn't known since forced route marches in the Coldstream Guards at the age of nineteen.

We were walking along a corniced ridge next day, having emerged from the aromatic air and dappled sunspots of a hemlock and fir forest, and found the clouds were clearing almost completely, allowing the sun to gleam awake the supernal view. Without speaking, we both sat down as of one accord, gazing in awe at the immense snow-clad peaks around us embalmed in their eternal silence. Over their tips the last of the cloud shadows rippled like dark-grey flatfish along the corrugated bed of the ocean. Above us, the biting fall wind flumed the snow from a mountain crest in feathery trails across the cobalt sky. From a high crag two eagles launched, spiralling effortlessly upward in the warm air currents, the rightful monarchs of a world of island-studded lakes, rushing streams and waterfalls, plunging gorges and shimmering forests of spruce and birch and fir and pine. As we lay back to rest and watch them I felt an enormous exhilaration and well-being. It was more than mere euphoria, more of an absolute certainty that I was now feeling entirely *myself*. And that this is how we all ought to feel all our lives. It seemed ironic, almost tragic, that most of us never reach this peak in a lifetime, this natural harmony of mind, body, and spirit. It came to me then that, with animals, only the weak, immature or unhealthy man is vicious for no reason. Hating himself and unable to admit it, he seeks to revenge himself upon others.

By now we could have been excused for thinking our wilderness adventures were at an end. Somehow one never invests the return journey with the eager expectancy of the forward one, but my feeling we could now coast home without further incident proved wrong. Toward evening we came out on a marshy ravine a few miles above the river that would guide us home, when Pappy stopped and pointed. Out there in the soft mud between willows and alders on the banks of a broad creek was a large area that had been threshed flat. It looked as if a couple of elephants had engaged in battle. Small bushes were snapped off or torn up by the roots and their cores were still white and pithy, showing the disturbance had been recent. At first I thought a couple of grizzlies might have been rolling in the shallows to get rid of flies or ticks, but Pappy didn't think so, and he quickly unstrapped his rifle.

"There's been a big grizzly here all right," he said. "Look." And he pointed to rear-foot tracks seven inches wide and ten inches long. The first tracks went in the direction of a rocky hill some two hundred yards from the creek, but each track was preceded by a deep gouge mark. As we followed them and the flattened area that ran alongside them, the tracks changed direction completely on reaching the incline. They went into the centre of the flattened area but were partly obliterated.

"It was draggin' something real heavy," said Pappy, holding the gun in both hands, his eyes darting warily into the trees on each side. "Look, the bear towed whatever it was draggin' sideways but as it reached the hill, it went square and started haulin' backward. Keep your eyes skinned, laddie, and keep behind me."

We had gone only a few more yards up the slope when we found the remains of a huge leg. The thigh bone was crushed and what little flesh remained smelled faintly of recent decay.

"Goddam," whispered Pappy. "He was haulin' a whole damn moose by the look of it. He must've found it dead, maybe after another bull had killed it. He got as far as this, then stopped for a quick feed. Look at that leg, will you?" The powerful jaws of the grizzly, trying to get at the succulent marrow, had chomped the great bone up like spaghetti.

I followed Pappy along the short, steep rocky escarpment with foreboding. It was so steep in places we had to grab hold of bushes to stop ourselves falling back, and yet snapped and scraped bushes and overturned rocks showed the grizzly had somehow heaved the moose carcass as well as its own bulk up the same steep cliff. Such fantastic strength was hard to conceive. Certain the bear was probably asleep somewhere in the vicinity, I wanted to leave as quickly and quietly as possible. But Pappy put his head over the top slowly, then motioned for me to join him. Our eyes focused on a large pile of brush, roots, leaves, clods of earth, and broken spars in a small hollow, from the left of which protruded half a massive set of palmate antlers. Between the debris we could just make out the moose's eye, ringed with tawny brown fur and closed, as if in peaceful sleep.

"Let's get out of here," I whispered. I had a distinct feeling we'd taken enough risks and were now pushing our luck too far. After a quick look round, Pappy turned to me, his blue eyes holding an amused twinkle. How he looked at that moment is a memory I shall always treasure – he stood there silhouetted against the treed skyline of that remote fastness, his huge horny hands gripped the old rifle, his great chest heaving slightly, his nostrils dilating like some old wilderness war horse – staunch, secure, powerful, and loving. "You're right," he said softly. "We don't want to have to kill that old bear, do we?"

We reached his canoe two mornings later and I spent two more nights with him before saying farewell. In that time he shared more of his extraordinary wilderness lore, laughingly turned away my expressions of gratitude, but once again made me promise never to reveal his true name or the exact place of our adventures. Some hunters had already flown into his remote valley, he said. In no way did he want to hasten its destruction. Again I agreed.

As we stood above my boat in the river, neither of us knew how to say goodbye. Suddenly a gnarled hand shot out. "We'll meet again," he said, and we both turned away.

Blessed with calm weather, I negotiated the river waters and the inlet without mishap and returned home. At the retired couple's cabin, Booto just stood there, stared, turned away as if he didn't believe it, then looked back again. Then he ran around in wild circles, yiping, and leaped up to lick my face.

15 Time to Move On

*A*s the last months of my Canadian years passed by, a strange sense of anti-climax seemed to pervade my life, as if in some mysterious way I had served my time in my remote cliff-top retreat and ought now to move on. Even the magnificent view, constantly familiar, seemed only to remind me that nothing really lay ahead but a repetition of the past few years – and perhaps that would no longer be enough to justify being constantly alone, apart from my fellow man.

My re-written book had been rejected yet again and for days I drifted, lost in indecision. I was tired, dispirited, and low in funds. Even Booto now seemed bored with my company, for he was spending more time with the cafe folk and the retired couple than he was with me. Then two events occurred that helped change my future life. They followed close upon each other – a storm and an extraordinary summer day.

One morning I woke late in semi-darkness. Mosquitoes hummed in the cabin's oppressive air and, while the world outside was silent and still beneath the lowering clouds, there was a wild blue look on the horizon to the northwest. I busied myself with chores, split and gathered in some dry wood, then feeling in great need of some good talk, I went with Booto to seek out Ed Louette, who had been renting a tiny trailer in a bay near the fishing village. But the meeting with Ed turned out to be a sad farewell. He was leaving for Vancouver in two days and he told me he would not be returning to the coast next year. As he had always refused any payment for his help on the cabin, I gave him my best piece of clothing, a suede jacket he'd once admired and which fitted him well. He said it would be ideal for his long winter walks round Vancouver's Stanley Park.

But when I said I was now toying with the idea of going to live near Pappy Tihoni – if he would accept me – Ed told me I was too late. A new logging company had taken over the head of the inlet and was driving a road through near the cabin, and some American hunters had discovered the area and were coming up regularly in the open seasons. Tihoni himself was now in Vancouver, visiting two of his married children, before deciding what *he* would do next.

This news made me sadder still. Before I left, Ed insisted on giving me his treasured old leatherbound carpentry books as a goodbye present. "Hi'm retired," he said with a sad smile. "You're the carpenter now." I stayed far longer than I'd intended and I drove away feeling very lonely – my little world was beginning to crash around me. I knew, too, I would miss this proud, lonely, lovely old man. Heggs, honions, and hoysters – dear old Ed.

I got back to my land in pitch darkness and it was only by holding onto Booto's tail that I could find my way down the trail. As we neared the shore the trees were roaring in a high wind, swaying and creaking and clashing their branches together like gnarled old giants in some wild bacchanalia, and I heard the seas pounding on the shore. As we emerged from the trees into the half light of the cliff top, huge waves were smashing into the bottom of the log staircase, and the big log wharf was breaking up. The bow of the new wooden boat I had recently part-exchanged for my rubber one had been smashed repeatedly into the rocky cliff and it was completely beyond repair. But I forced my way down the staircase, thinking I could at least rescue the engine.

At the bottom of the steps I counted – three big waves and two smaller ones. It seemed to be a constant pattern. I leaped into the sea near the boat on the first smaller wave. There was a pause, a heaving swell, then a resounding crash as a huge wave picked up boat, engine, and one wharf log and threw them against my right leg, which was partly trapped against the log staircase. It seemed almost an act of deliberate malevolence. Clearly I could not rescue the engine and to stay down there was madness.

I crawled back up the steps, helplessly watching the huge waves thundering in and pounding the boat to fragments. The engine was shaken off and pulled out to sea by the undertow and I could hear it banging over the rocks. The wind increased in force and I saw that the big curving fir to which the cabin was braced was bending alarmingly in the storm. It seemed I was now losing everything, and I suddenly felt I didn't really care any more. The tempest seemed to beat all resistance out of me, as if in some strange way I was being *told* to go. And as this feeling grew stronger, I became full of overwhelming doubts. I felt my book had now been rejected for the *last* time and that after more than three years' work, I had totally failed. My efforts to write something fine now appeared mere vanity, and I nothing more than a paltry hermit whose work was solely an extension of his own lonely ego. There, in the battering wind, with the black, malignant sea crashing and the big fir creaking in the gale, it suddenly seemed I had no real future, nowhere to go, and that perhaps to die there where I had known a few moments of paradise was feasible enough. It was an awful, morbid, foolish, and self-indulgent night. And yet after the storm blew itself out, after snatching a few hours fitful sleep, I knew only that I was glad to be still alive.

Surviving a severe storm alone in the wilds comes as a violent catharsis, shaking one to a new awareness, The very next morning heralded the start of a short Indian summer, as if some great and good spirit had laid a healing balm across the earth and ocean. They were strange days that came now, golden, restful days in which I felt I would think no more but merely empty my mind and give myself up to nature.

There are rare moments in the wilderness when one's feelings are like none you have ever known before – they seem new and original – as if one had shed one's old self and grown a new one. The behaviour patterns built up over years of civilised living, and all the adjustments one has had to make from the innocent integrity of childhood to cope, survive, and succeed, have all been cut away. It is as if one has broken through some opaque spiritual barrier.

One afternoon I was swimming in the warm, gleaming sea of my bay, with all conscious thought processes suspended. I was just gliding along the crystal-smooth surface when quite suddenly I felt I no longer had a separate identity. My feeling of self, of being separated from the whole, had now become a delusion of the past. I looked at the island rocks shimmering in the heat and I was their granite hardness, at the treetops being stirred by gentle breezes and I could feel the winds sifting through my own body, at the slowly unfolding shapes of the tangleweed below me whose movements in the water also seemed to be my own. I felt strangely at one with them all and with all life, that, indeed, I was at one with all things everywhere. And I felt, too, a strange power that I could do anything I wished in the water. I began to swim without effort, to travel through the water with the minimum of movement and for a great distance with complete case. It was as if I had actually become a fish or a seal, completely at one with a cherishing sea, able to progress by merely willing it. The experience was too profound to doubt.

During this strange interlude I saw a line of wild guillemots swimming ahead near some drifting kelp, and I found I could move toward them without a ripple; from quite a distance away I submerged quietly, sliding under the weed, and came up beneath them, seizing the nearest by a bright red leg. The moment I did, it flapped and squawked, and as I let it go and the birds took off, their wings whirring like little black clockwork toys, my normal consciousness returned and the spell was broken. I was instantly aware again of only my *self* and as I was now over a mile from the beach, I felt a panicky awareness of danger, and my return swim entailed much effort.

Since then there have been similar experiences of intensified perception, exhilaration, of lost and ancient senses, of exaltation even, but such words are inadequate and cannot really convey the truth of the experiences. A feeling of being totally *alive* perhaps. Like so many of us, I often go through life without really living, like a deaf, blind, thoughtless being intent only upon my personal problems, without ever really being *there*. But during these strange, all too few moments, it has seemed as if, alone with nature for long periods, I have become blessed with occasional glimpses of a true cosmic harmony.

For years I had sought a basic code by which I might try to live, although in the cities it had become buried. But now, in tranquil moments alone and after all the experiences in the wild, this desire suddenly returned with redoubled force. Amid the rocky arbours, the dark temples below the cedar trees, I found myself staring at the ancient granite as if buried in this aged landscape I might find an answer. Every religion or philosophy I had studied seemed only to provide hints that when organized, structured, and tailored for large masses of people often became reduced to a ritualized system of dogmatic assertions.

Although I'd never been a complete atheist, I had hidden for years behind the skirts of agnosticism, asserting that for man complete knowledge of an infinite, omniscient God was impossible. But during the years in the wild, especially when trekking through mountainous bear country far from man, I had several times felt there were mysterious forces at work, both malign and benign. Often, when first seeing an animal that could kill me, I had muttered a silent prayer, hoping as I wished no ill to the creature, that I would thus be in tune with the benign forces. And when you come near to losing your life in rough seas, and for long periods are exposed to both elemental winter dangers and the glories of beatific summer days, observing all the while the pageantry of natural life, it seems impossible any longer not to believe in a creator of some kind beyond all. Yet today we are no nearer to understanding God than were the ancients, for man's finite mind will never satisfactorily define the Infinite. We may feel, sense, have faith, but we continue to stagger blindly. The primitive native beliefs that Tihoni had expounded so clearly – of many gods for the seas, rivers, forests, and mountains, all linked to the Great Spirit, may seem simplistic or mere superstition to most of us. But surely our concepts of a personalised and selective God whose will manifests itself in the destinies of chosen people, who watches the individual lives of billions at the same time, who punishes and rewards according to the degree of obedience, who dismisses the animal creation, even demands animal sacrifices, is no better? For months I had tried to understand this creative benign force I had often sensed, a force that lay far beyond mere goodness itself, and to strip away the heavenly props and petty dogmas of traditional organized religions.

On the afternoon that I returned from my strange swim I found my mind struggling again with these ideas, when I felt a sudden terror that in trying to delve too deeply into meanings I was approaching some spiritual abyss from which, if I glimpsed truth, I would not return. Presumptuous though this feeling was, it was extraordinarily real. I felt exhausted and went to lie between the moss-covered rocks that formed an armchair on the cliff overlooking the sun-burnished ocean. I fell asleep but after a while I woke again because some words were flooding my mind. Later I tried to write them down:

Only love emancipates man from his animal nature, so man's highest belief must surely be in God as original Love. Love at its finest concept, the root of all harmony, the height of all being, the Love that is Creation itself. There can be no higher concept of God, and we can perceive no more than this. Human love – the love of father, mother, friend, child, or love between man and woman - are only small subdivisions. That was all. A fragment of an idea. But for a while longer I found myself thinking in ways I could not remember before.

Is not our ability to love spiritually our *only* God-like attribute? So surely only when we live lives that contribute to cosmic order and harmony, thus overcoming the insensitivities of raw nature, and of our own natures, are we expressing in the universe consciousness of that ideal we call God? If, in the ultimate sense, God exists far beyond the finite understanding of man, then living Love in this way is the only possible path to complete understanding, the only reconcilable bridge, the only certain way to align with the harmony of original Creation. It suddenly seemed clear to me that as we are the earth's dominant species, our responsibility lies not only to ourselves but to all other life on this planet, and this responsibility is not only inherent but utterly inescapable. Only through a regard for all life, by aligning spiritually with the harmonious forces in nature and from a height of feeling, transfiguring the inharmonious or callous in loving creation, can we be at one with the source of true creativity and so be akin to what we call God.

I lay for a long time turning these ideas over and over in my mind. I thought then they would henceforth change my life, that wherever I went or whatever I did, I had found a code for living that made sense to me. I did not realize that afternoon that I would fail, as I have failed many times, through all-too-human weakness, to live up to them. But it seemed I had at least been given a hint, a key to a better life and I found myself looking at the world around me with new eyes.

A large blue beetle hummed in the air beside me, then fell with a thud into the grass. It closed its wing covers and desperately struggled to find a stem strong enough to support its weight, to fly free once more and fulfil its short destiny.

High above me a skein of geese were heading south, the strongest in front breaking the resistance of the wind for the weaker that followed. Away to the west two doves were flying into the limitless horizon, like two tiny souls emblazoned on the sky as they migrated to their new and blessed home.

I sat silent between the rocks in the rippling gold and blue of the sunset, feeling the wilderness had not only taught me many lessons but provided a meaning. Here the bodily rhythms had become one with the eternal rhythms of the sea, the sky, and the wind. Mere reason alone had died and become reborn. I looked at my little cabin, at the logs I had laboured to haul up the log staircase, at the sea that had provided most of my food for more than three years, at the northern land spit over which the eagles always flew, at the islands where the killer whales had once surrounded my boat. I thought of Tihoni again, and the days with the black bears, the caribou, and the grizzlies. I looked at Booto, panting contentedly in the late sunshine, and I suddenly felt an enormous gratitude. Canada had been good to me, good for me. It had shaken me from my city rut and had shown me a finer and fuller life. Here on this lonely cliff, five thousand miles from all I had previously known, my mind had been freed, I felt as if a new self had been formed. In the last moments of that golden dying day I felt strangely outside of time and space, suspended in a celestial limbo, shorn at last of doubt. I had lived close to nature, seen both its beauty and its callousness, and had been shown a path, a way that led beyond hope or fear, success or failure.

I knew now the time had come to move on. I did not know when or where I would go, only that my life, minor and of little account though it was, would be bound up somehow in the future between man and the last wild places. Oh, there was time enough to think about the future, time enough to decide.

16 Epilogue

The story, the Canadian wilderness adventure, ends here.

For those readers who might like to indulge in some 'wilderness philosophy', I have included the following Epilogue. It was written thirty years ago but perhaps the message bears repeating. Apart from bringing actual statistics up to date, it remains as I wrote it so long ago.

Mike Tomkies, 2001

I spent many hours during those first wilderness years thinking about man and the whole natural world, not only in the ecological sense but from a more mystic and whole view toward all life.

In the past we have tended to look at animals through an arrogant screen of our own superiority. We patronize them for their ignorance, their savagery, and their lower existence, but we are wrong. Mammals, birds, insects, and fish exist in a far older and more perfect world than ours, by senses we have long lost or never developed. They live by rhythms to which we are no longer attuned, by voices we can never hear. And the loss of any single species is immeasurable, for it often affects man in ways he seldom comprehends.

Since the time of Christ man has directly or indirectly exterminated hundreds of species, three-quarters of them in the last century. Today nearly a thousand other varieties are endangered, all important in differing ways to the intricately balanced webs of life.

Sentiment apart, the preservation of animals has long been essential to man's own well-being. Indeed, could we have survived to reach our present dominance had we not been able to domesticate horses for transport; oxen for ploughs and for meat, hides, and milk; sheep for meat and wool, poultry for food and eggs, as well as goats, pigs, carrier pigeons, and dogs to help us guard, hunt, and track? Many of the world's routes for roads and railways were not discovered by man at all but follow the original trails of animals. In America the Indians followed the animals and the traders followed the Indians, their posts now the sites of major towns along these natural trails. From animals man first learned the art of camouflage. The French claim the shape and flight of the dragonfly inspired them to pioneer the aeroplane. Studies of whales and dolphins not only helped man form the streamlined hulls of boats and submarines but have increased his understanding of blood circulatory systems. Louis Pasteur's life-saving theories of vaccines and inoculation could not have been achieved without the help of animals.

Living in the wilderness taught me not only love for the animal world but above all, respect. Do eagles fly as they do merely to find food, to go from place to place? Anyone who has watched their incredible courtship display, or has seen ravens tumbling head over heels in spring for the sheer joy of it, or has seen otters at play on a mud or snow slide, has observed the complicated behaviour of apes like chimps, or has watched a grizzly revelling in the warm waters of a natural spring must doubt all simplistic concepts of animals. Many have a distinct sense of fun. How does the wolf know he can tire the faster caribou (which can outrun a racehorse) by running it in circular relays? Wolves are not the born killers of legend but seem to tend the herds they run with, culling out the sick, wounded, old, and less-aware young. How does an eagle work out that if he flies low along the water or ground for half a mile he will be out of sight behind the rock over which he finally pounces on the unsuspecting rat, hare, or bird? How do young geese, who migrate later, know how to join their parents thousands of miles to the south? How do grouse, ducks, and plovers know that by feigning injury and dragging a wing along the ground, they can lure predators away from their young? How does the worker bee know by performing different dance patterns before the hive it can convey exact information about nectar supplies to its fellows? The animal world is full of countless such examples from which man can learn.

It is an extraordinary fact that cougars and some other predatory animals without natural enemies seem to know they have to regulate their own numbers, so they can have the right-sized areas they need to survive and prosper – an "instinct" that appears to have little to do with the amount of available food. Small deer have been increasing in British Columbia in recent years because man's opening up of the dense forests has created clearings in which more feed plants can grow. But cougar numbers have not risen. Yet will man ever achieve an instinct that will prevent him from overbreeding in the interests of his own species, as well as of the rest of the natural world?

Today mankind bestrides the earth, the most dominant and successful species the world has ever known. The astounding capacities of his intellect and the complex civilizations he has created, in which individuals and smaller groups have specialized functions, have helped him overcome the raw forces of nature.

While our demands on the earth's space, forests, seas, animals, land, and ores were small in relation to our planet's natural resources, we were in fair shape. But as we spread to every continent and our populations accelerated, we plundered and exploited as if nature were an enemy, to be subdued and beaten back. Now, short-term satisfaction seems merely a prelude to a long-term disaster.

Today, we have a surfeit of admonitions from environmentalists ramming home the facts about pollution of air, earth and water, the worsening erosion of the last wildernesses by damming rivers and lakes, blasting, mining, felling forests, spreading pesticides, building more roads, and drilling for oil. But admonitions alone are insufficient. Practical solutions will not improve until man learns to conquer his greatest problem – overpopulation. In less than 200 years the world population has leaped from one thousand million to six thousand million. The birth rate is dropping slightly in many so-called developed nations, but it is still increasing world-wide at the rate of more than 500 million every five years; such an increase, set against declining reserves of energy and minerals, and when world food reserves can be wiped out by vagaries of weather, seems catastrophic.

Population control is not a matter merely for government – the democratic politician needs mass votes, the dictator needs mass support to survive for long. It is ultimately a matter of individual responsibility. Each of us needs to know that those who deliberately have a large family are not exercising "freedom," but are globally irresponsible, are in fact unloving towards their own kind. And in the developed world we must learn to make do with *less* luxury – one city American uses twenty times the energy and materials of a Tanzanian native – and less so-called freedom. There is always revolt from restrictions of any kind. But it is easy to see that unrestricted freedom means later chaos. Without personal inspiration to self-discipline the future of the human race on this earth seems black indeed.

To those who say "Why bother about wilderness anyway?" I point first to its vital *economic* value – these regions are the finest recycling plants of our earth, neutralizing our wastes, regulating climate, filtering our water, producing oxygen, and, when managed well, providing an abundance of timber. But far more than such pragmatic considerations are the *intangible* values – to the millions who in their free time flock away from the cities to the beaches, lakes, rivers, fields and mountains, seeking, often unconsciously, time to be alone, to be at peace, to contemplate, to develop awareness of the fullness of life and of one's own self, to feel free amid wild nature, and to be inspired by its wondrous powers. And for the few who journey through their wildernesses alone, they have found there is no finer teacher of self-knowledge and self-discipline than harsh nature itself, for without such discipline they will not survive.

Every time I enter one of the last wild places of this earth, I feel I am walking into a vast hallowed cathedral. I enter timelessness, mystery, the unknown, where one feels nothing has been spoiled since the world began. In the wilderness lies one of the last and finest sources of spiritual inspiration; for great natural beauty is a powerful creative force for thought. In solitude, even temporary, there often comes a surging re-awakening of ideals that remain submerged during the distractions of everyday life. In the old still silences, intuition, perception, and all the spiritual qualities that distinguish man, that make him able to see himself and the universe in perspective, are enhanced. So many of us need such spiritual insights, the thrill that seeing animals in the wild gives our souls, and also the exhilarations of pure exercise in remote mountainous or forested wilderness. Just to know rare or beautiful creatures are still *there* is vitally important too, for the numbers of us who want to visit the wilds are rapidly increasing. And of these millions, however surprising it may initially seem, hunters are *not* the most dominant. In the United States alone the number of nature walkers, bird watchers, and wildlife photographers are three times higher than the number of hunters. Even so I feel strongly that wildlife authorities must increase their efforts to assess animal populations more exactly, and that to be fair to the rest of us the right to hunt be limited only to highly skilled marksmen (rigorously tested) aiming only at species who are not in the slightest way endangered, or culling those who are outgrowing their environment. To cut the excess of hunters yet still gain the same revenue (much of which goes on protection), wildlife authorities should charge a great deal more for hunting licences and also far higher trophy fees for each game animal killed.

Yet while hunting is certainly a considerable threat to the higher game animals and while it should be more rigorously restricted, it is not the main problem. The erosion of undisturbed habitat by all civilization's interests is far worse for wildlife.

Pollution, a polite word for poison, may be so laboured a subject that to many it has become a bore. But let none of us be misled. Despite all the belated efforts of anti-litter, clean-water, fresh-air, anti-ocean-dumping, and recycling groups in the most enlightened areas, global pollution is getting worse.*

The crucial question now is how much longer will there be any wildernesses left? Or animals left? If it is true that man must learn to control his exploding birth rate, reverse the tide of environmental pollution and possible genocide, then surely he must also set aside pure wilderness areas. These must not be only parks where unrestricted numbers can find recreation in boats, helicopters, trail bikes, or on horseback, but real refuges where dwindling animals like the grizzly, cougar, and bighorn can roam unmolested by vehicles, camp sites, low-flying aircraft, power boats, and hunters. And perhaps only those who are prepared to travel on foot or by canoe should be allowed access.

The primitive Indian concept was largely right. Our natural world and wildlife heritage does not belong to us – we belong to it. A new attitude to these last vital, illuminating, and enriching parts of our earth is needed and must be backed by law. That over a thousand species are now seriously endangered is to man's eternal shame. Some wildlife observers believe that in a mere century there will be very few wild animals, apart from those kept in zoos, left on earth at all.

And yet, apart from the aesthetic loss, the pleasure of seeing them or at least knowing they exist, there is far more at stake; the loss or near extinction of almost any single species weakens a link in the vital, intricate food webs on which the whole

---

* And recently, 'global warming' has come to haunt us – where our harmful emissions are alleged to be making holes in the ozone layers, causing melting icecaps and an increase in storms, floods and droughts in unexpected places. Maybe the jury is still out on this; there have always been long-term climate changes – look at the Ice Age 11,000 years ago, and its retreat ... four hundred years ago there were highly productive vineyards in Yorkshire ... England's greatest storm, which killed 8,000 people, occurred in November, 1703. However, we clearly need more renewable energy sources – solar panels and heating, wave power, wind power, and if investment was done on a *large* scale, costs would come right down and we'd be ready when fossil fuels at last run out.

tapestry of life depends, each one, in large degree or small, having an effect on all-important plant life. It would do us good to remember that man, who is capable of destroying most forms of life, is from the whole ecological point of view the least important species alive. If man were suddenly to vanish, almost every other form of life would fare better than it does now. But if all plants – the only living things capable of converting the energy of the sun – were to perish, so would all animal life, including man.

But we must not look at nature today with the dreamy naïvety of the romantic poets. There is no constancy or harmony in nature itself, only intricately varying balances in which each species struggles to survive against others. Death in the wild is usually savage and cruel. The mere balance of numbers is not the true harmony of which I still believe man is yet capable, for nature takes no account of the *individual* life. The question must surely be: can man, who has so far only used the world for his own selfish interest, finally fulfil the role for which his invention and foresight have at least made him capable? Can he become man the preserver instead of man the destroyer?

Eleven civilizations have already foundered when they cut their roots to the land and later affluence bred decadence. Today our arrogantly wasteful march through our natural heritage must be reversed, for the day will come – if we don't tread softly – when man can no longer control his environment, his way of life or his future, when he will become extinct as other dominant species before him. When man treats the earth with greed and insensitivity, he wrecks a creation more miraculous and intricate than anything he has yet invented or ever will. Clearly, we can survive in health and happiness only if we live in harmony with the natural world and learn to value it for its own sake.

Videos from Mike Tomkies

EAGLE MOUNTAIN YEAR (£25)

This 125-minute VHS tape tells the story of a magical Highland mountain through all four seasons. There are golden eagles at the nest, their glorious courtship 'air dances', and a female eagle hauling a deer carcass uphill on her own. Rare black-throated divers are seen diving, courting and, for the first time on film, at their nest. Pine martens are shown hunting, at their den, even feeding from my hands. Hunting and nesting peregrine falcons are shown in detail, as is all the comic-tragic sibling rivalry at buzzard nests. There are courting mergansers, ospreys, ravens, foxes and even a hunting wildcat. Through it all, I show the lives of the red deer herds.

AT HOME WITH EAGLES (£16)

A 102-minute VHS tape showing with incredibly intimate detail the story of three pairs of courting, hunting and nesting golden eagles – one pair exchanging incubation duties, a second pair trying against the odds to hatch infertile eggs, and the third pair who are successful in raising their chick from egg to flying stage. Never before have the secret lives of the king of birds been revealed in such fascinating detail. Two eminent naturalists have described it as *probably the greatest eagle film ever made.*

FOREST PHANTOMS (£12)

This 60-minute VHS tape takes six barn owls through a full year, from chicks to hunting adults. Also starred are the forest phantoms of the day – rare goshawks at the nest, as well as nesting buzzards, long-eared owls, foxes, and, yes, even *eagles* again.

MY BARN OWL FAMILY (£12)

A 52-minute VHS tape of my barn owls Blackie and Brownie, and how they finally raised four youngsters to flying stage. We see them incubating eggs, hunting the woods and pastures, perch hunting from my garden fence, and taking prey back up to the loft. Intimate glimpses of their complicated behaviour inside the loft and nest box; and all the growing stages of the chicks are recorded in loving detail. Also shown are the daytime 'invaders' of their world – a badger who was unusually tame, a fox who used my sheep walls to spy prey, a beautiful female kestrel who came for any food the owls left on the table – not to mention chaffinch hordes, bellicose siskins, cheeky jays and other entrancing characters.

RIVER DANCING YEAR (£15)

A 92-minute VHS tape celebrating the superb wildlife of Scottish rivers – from the raging upper waterfalls where salmon leap heroically to reach their spawning grounds; through serene reaches where swans, herons, moorhens, mallards, dippers, goosanders, gulls and kingfishers go about their lives and, finally, to where the river enters the sea and the estuary kingdom of the great sea eagles. We see foxes playing in a riverside garden, a vixen giving suck to her four cubs …a boisterous badger family, digging, playing hilarious judo games, and even taking food from my hands …a grooming, prowling and hunting wildcat …otters fishing and in their holt … peregrines guarding their chicks …herons catching fish and even swallowing a duckling, a young golden eagle preparing to leave its nest…ospreys catching and bringing fish to their grown young …and a host of other species. Above all, it is a long insight into the world of the rare white-tailed sea eagles, as a pair guard their flown youngster, exchange beak-to-beak greetings, and provide glorious flight sequences when they hunt for prey in their kingdom at the end of the river.

WILDEST SPAIN (£14)

A 77-minute VHS tape about Europe's finest wildlife. It tells of successful treks and adventures all over Spain in pursuit of wild bear, wolf, lynx, wild boar, ibex, black stork, very rare vultures and eagles, plus many other species in a magical European country not hitherto known for its often excellent wildlife conservation.

Books

GOLDEN EAGLE YEARS (£12)

The re-issue of the book long out of print, which contains more and better colour pictures than the first edition. It tells of my first five years studying Scotland's magnificent golden eagles. The treks, the pitfalls and defeats, the joys and triumphs, are fully described.

ON WING AND WILD WATER (£7)

Superior Cape paperback of my second eagle book.

MY WILDERNESS WILDCATS (£5)

This is the American version of my first wildcats' book, with black and white pictures only.

(*All above prices of books and videos include first class post and packing, and please indicate if and how you want them signed. Cheques payable to Mike Tomkies*)

Please send your remittance and delivery address to:

Mike Tomkies, c/o Royal Mail, St George's Lane, Hawick, Scotland, TD9 0BB

Dec. 2002